FROM DISMAL SWAMP TO SMILING FARMS

From Dismal Swamp to Smiling Farms

Food, Agriculture, and Change in the Holland Marsh

Michael Classens

Library and Archives Canada Cataloguing in Publication
Title: From dismal swamp to smiling farms : food, agriculture, and change in the Holland Marsh / Michael Classens.
Names: Classens, Michael, author.
Description: Includes bibliographical references and index.
Identifiers: Canadiana (print) 20210275898 | Canadiana (ebook) 20210276002 | ISBN 9780774865463 (softcover) | ISBN 9780774865470 (PDF) | ISBN 9780774865487 (EPUB)
Subjects: LCSH: Agriculture—Ontario—Holland Marsh—History. | LCSH: Land use, Rural—Ontario—Holland Marsh—History. | LCSH: Holland Marsh (Ont.)—History.
Classification: LCC S451.5.O6 C56 2021 | DDC 630.9713—dc23

Canadä

UBC Press gratefully acknowledges the financial support for our publishing program of the Government of Canada (through the Canada Book Fund), the Canada Council for the Arts, and the British Columbia Arts Council.

This book has been published with the help of a grant from the Canadian Federation for the Humanities and Social Sciences, through the Awards to Scholarly Publications Program, using funds provided by the Social Sciences and Humanities Research Council of Canada.

Printed and bound in Canada by Friesens
Set in Garamond Premier Pro by PageMajik
Proofreader: Alison Strobel
Indexer: Cheryl Lemmens
Cartographer: Eric Leinberger
Cover image: Frank Jonkman

UBC Press
The University of British Columbia
2029 West Mall
Vancouver, BC V6T 1Z2
www.ubcpress.ca

S | H
M | P

The Sustainable History Monograph Pilot

Opening Up the Past, Publishing for the Future

When you cite the book, please include the following URL for its Digital Object Identifier (DOI): https://doi.org/10.14288/1.0398733

For Serena, Emry, Maude, and Clement

CONTENTS

ILLUSTRATIONS

MAP

FIGURES

PREFACE

I started writing this book in the "before times," as we say now. The global disruption caused by COVID-19 has since been swift and staggering, and very likely it will be enduring. The global pandemic has exacerbated fundamental inequities of the industrialized food system while underscoring its profound unsustainability. More than this, the global capitalist food system is a key culprit in the emergence of COVID-19 in the first place. As agricultural capital seeks out ways to bring previously uncommodified natures into circulation, the frontiers of agriculture are expanding into ever more previously remote areas of the world. This self-expanding logic is "both the propulsion for and nexus through which pathogens of diverse origins migrate from the most remote reservoirs to the most international of population centers."[1] The rate at which these zoonotic diseases – those that originate in nonhuman animals and jump species into humans – are emerging seems to be accelerating. Indeed, in the past twenty years, there have been three significant pandemics – COVID-19 in 2020, H1N1 in 2009, and SARS in 2003.[2]

Though the evidence was already robust, this most recent pandemic has strengthened the argument that planetary survival may depend on more socially just, ecologically sound, and localized/regionalized food systems. And yet, amid the upswing of a second wave of COVID-19 infections in Ontario, the provincial government set to "hacking and slashing" legislation that protects landscapes in the province. Nested within Bill 229, a pandemic recovery measure, were provisions that dramatically reduced the power of conservation authorities and increased the use of ministerial zoning orders, enabling increased development of the countryside.[3] The government also fast-tracked approval of a development proposed within a fifty-four-acre wetland, all of which led seven members of the Greenbelt Council to resign in protest.[4] Not long after these resignations, the province announced plans to revive the Bradford Bypass, colloquially known as the Holland Marsh Highway, an east–west thoroughfare linking Highway 400 and Highway 404 that runs straight through the northern part of the Holland Marsh.

The socioecological politics of landscape change, the pathologies of the industrialized food system, and the challenges and promise of localized food systems are central themes within the following pages. The story of these themes is one ultimately refracted through my own limitations and capabilities as a researcher and writer. As the preeminent environmental historian William Cronon reminds us:

> When we describe human activities within an ecosystem, we seem always to tell *stories* about them. Like all historians, we configure the events of the past into causal sequences – stories – that order and simplify those events to give them new meanings. We do so because narrative is the chief literary form that tries to find meaning in an overwhelmingly crowded and disordered chronological reality. When we choose a plot to order our environmental histories, we give them a unity that neither nature nor the past possess so clearly.[5]

The data I draw on come from a variety of sources. I extensively scoured a number of archives for information relevant to the Holland Marsh, including the Archives of Ontario, Agriculture and Agri-Food Canada, Bradford West Gwillimbury Public Library, Ontario Workplace Tribunals Library, Simcoe County Archives, and a variety of online repositories. Additionally, the ProQuest Historical Database helped me find several hundred useful news accounts of the Holland Marsh published by some seventeen news outlets.

I also spent a good deal of time in and around the Holland Marsh over the course of nearly eighteen months. I made many trips to the area for interviews, which took place on farms, in barns or storage facilities, or on the front yard of a Marsh home (with a glass of lemonade in hand) – and on one occasion in the cab of a John Deere tractor during the onion harvest. Often I travelled there to attend specific events. Some of these were large annual community gatherings common to other rural areas themed around harvest time and featured crops, here including the Bradford West Gwillimbury Carrot Fest and the Holland Marsh Soupfest. I also attended meetings of the Holland Marsh Growers' Association and a screening of a film it had produced, *The Marsh Mucker's Tale* (2013). I also spent two days at the 63rd Annual Muck Vegetable Growers Conference, talking to farmers and researchers, listening to presentations, and walking the floor (an erstwhile hockey rink) of the farm-equipment and chemical trade show. On a handful of occasions, I simply wound up in the Marsh and wandered around, driving around the perimeter on the severely narrow Canal Road or cutting through the area on the idiosyncratic and potholed interior roads. With my dog, I hiked through Scanlon Creek Conservation Area, which is grazed by the Holland River as it heads toward Cook's Bay and Lake Simcoe. And out of sheer curiosity, I tracked down the point where the river – a marshy, slow-moving version of it at any rate – empties into Cook's Bay – roughly fifteen kilometres north of the fields. I also draw on existing works about the Marsh by local historians, including George Jackson, Dorothy Cilipka, Albert VanderMey, and the Bradford West Gwillimbury Local History Association. I am grateful for the stories these authors tell about the Marsh – they have no doubt shaped my own.

ACKNOWLEDGMENTS

I want to begin by thanking Dr. Gerda R. Wekerle, professor emerita, for her guidance throughout the original research for this book. At the centre of Gerda's mentorship style is an uncommon amalgam of support and discipline, idealism, and pragmatism. She was generous with her guidance and patience while consistently challenging me to look beyond where I was at any given moment. We had many inspiring and energizing discussions about this book, of both the brass-tacks and the blue-sky variety. She gave me the space to explore and the structure to succeed. I am very grateful for Gerda's ongoing mentorship and friendship.

Thanks also to Scott Prudham. Scott's capitalist-nature seminar at the University of Toronto was the first "geography" course I had taken since grade 11 in high school – it was a revelation and it changed the way I understand the world. Similarly, Stefan Kipfer exposed me to a rich diversity of theoretical, conceptual, and methodological approaches that are woven into the fabric of this book. I must also acknowledge Anders Sandberg, Sarah Wakefield, and Peter Vandergeest, each of whom read an early draft of the manuscript. That they would spend so much time and intellectual labour on my behalf is humbling.

My time in the Faculty of Environmental Studies at York University, where a good deal of the original research for this book was conducted, was generously supported by an Ontario Graduate Scholarship, a Social Sciences and Humanities Research Council of Canada Fellowship, and York University's Susan Mann Dissertation Scholarship. Funding from a Social Sciences and Humanities Research Council of Canada Postdoctoral Fellowship allowed me the time to conduct additional research and to begin writing. I am grateful to have been so lucky in matters of finance. Thanks also to the friends and colleagues in FES and beyond with whom I have shared many conversations, ideas, struggles, and drinks. I undertook substantive revisions of this book while working as assistant professor in the Sustainable Agriculture and Food Systems Program in the Trent School of the Environment. I am grateful to Trent University as well as colleagues and collaborators in Peterborough for their support and friendship.

For their generous, probing, and insightful feedback on an earlier draft of the manuscript, I thank the two anonymous reviewers for UBC Press and Graeme

Wynn. Thanks also to James MacNevin, senior editor at UBC Press. Publishing a book during a global pandemic is a weird, challenging experience – James made it as pleasurable as I can imagine it being.

My deep gratitude extends also to the people in and around the Holland Marsh who were so generous with their time, insight, knowledge, and stories. I learned so incredibly much from you.

Finally, my deepest gratitude to the humans and the nonhuman with whom I most often share space – Serena, Emry, Maude, Clement, and Sue.

Sue – You have been the best kind of distraction a dog can be.

Emry, Maude, and Clement – When each of you arrived in our lives, you instantly made everything far more hectic, busy, and chaotic. But you also made it far more meaningful and, somehow, more manageable.

Serena – Finally, I can stop talking about "the book." Until the next one, I guess.

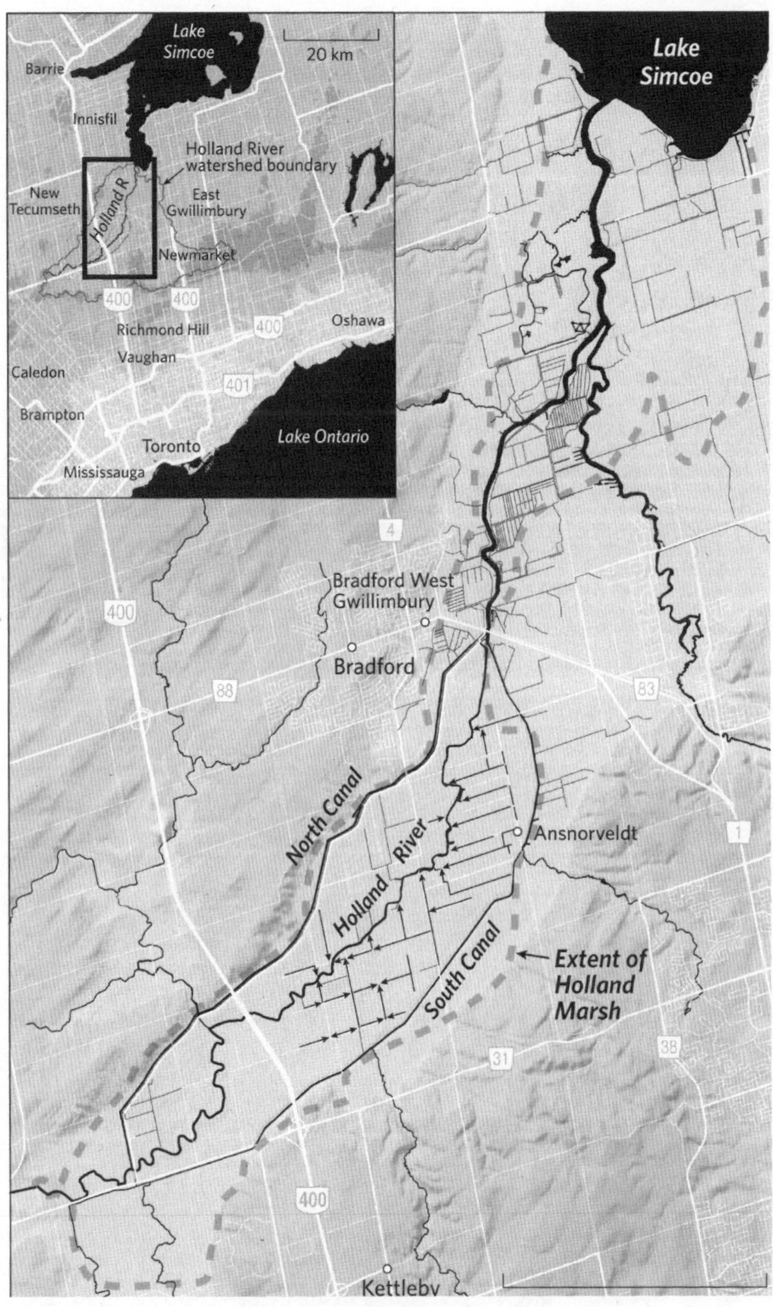

MAP 0.1. Parts of the greater Toronto area, central Ontario, and the extent of the Holland Marsh.

FIGURE 0.1. Orderly fields of the Holland Marsh. Courtesy of Holland Marsh Drainage System Joint Municipal Service Board.

FROM DISMAL SWAMP TO SMILING FARMS

INTRODUCTION

Culture's Marsh

LIKE MANY KIDS WHO grew up in southern Ontario, I sometimes went north in the summer for family vacations. As the family drove along Highway 400, leaving Toronto behind us, I always looked forward to passing Canada's Wonderland. The theme park – a sprawling spectacle of games, bright lights, and roller coasters in Vaughan, Ontario – seemed like an urban capstone. It was a carnivalesque punctuation to the urban agglomeration of Toronto and its ancillary suburbs. Beyond Canada's Wonderland was Canada's hinterland – a bucolic landscape of rolling hills, mighty forests, and pristine lakes.

From Canada's Wonderland to the south canal of the Holland Marsh – a three-thousand-hectare protected agricultural area – is about twenty kilometres, or roughly a ten-minute drive north on the highway. Despite the short distance, the two places could not be more different, or so I used to think. The low-lying, verdant fields of the Holland Marsh *are* a stunning aesthetic counterpoint to the towering infrastructure of the roller coasters, after all. The twenty kilometres between the two seemed like a transition zone – a liminal space between the city and *not* the city, between nature and society. The Holland Marsh was where society ended and nature started.

I have driven across the short stretch of Highway 400 that bisects the Holland Marsh dozens of times over the years, somehow always missing the obvious: The Marsh is not the natural place I imagined it to be. Crisscrossed with roads, teeming with tractors, and dotted with houses and barns, it is patently more *unnatural* than it initially seemed. While the fields in their bucolic splendour might belie the fact, even the land within the Marsh is far from natural, having been – quite literally – made in the mid-1920s, exhumed from the wetlands of the Holland River through an amalgam of human ingenuity, labour, and hubris. To borrow and adapt a phrase, in many ways this is culture's marsh.[1]

This, though, is only the most recent instantiation of the Marsh. Over the last 14,000 years or so, the material landscape has changed, how it has been interpreted has varied, and the ways it has been used have shifted profoundly.

As the Ice Age was drawing to a close, Paleoindian populations saw the area as temporary trapping grounds for arctic fox and arctic hare.[2] By about 6000 BC, Huron, and Algonquin peoples afterward, established more permanent camps near the Marsh, using it both for its nutritional bounty and for its convenient proximity to the Carrying Place Trail.[3] For some of the earliest European settlers to the area, the Marsh was understood as "a mere ditch" and a dangerous place to be avoided.[4] Soon after, colonial "foot soldiers in the manufacture of land," with a zeal for the "paramilitary regularization of the land into rectilinear parcels," largely understood the New World landscape as unruly, a commodity to be surveyed, inventoried, and brought under control.[5] By the early twentieth century, enterprising agriculturalists looked out over the Marsh and saw farmland, a "promised land with its broad acres of unbroken greatness."[6] Not long after this, a canal was dug around the wetland, the water was drained off, and a three-thousand-hectare polder assembled for the production of market garden vegetables, primarily carrots, onions, and celery.

By recounting the creation, use, and protection of the Holland Marsh, this book explores the complex, often overlooked, entanglements of nature and society, which are far less separate, or separable, than we assume. At the heart of this narrative is the notion that ideas about nature shape our concepts of agriculture, and that agriculture in turn shapes our ideas about nature. Nature is not the fixed thing we imagine it to be, but rather it is polysemous. Nature is social and nature is political. I explore these outwardly knotty ideas through an examination of the transformation of the Holland River lowlands and the agriculture this transformation enabled.

In the twenty-first century, we mostly think of wetlands as places to protect, not dredge, drain, and farm, yet in the 1920s, support for the conversion of the Holland Marsh was all but unanimous. Indeed, in 1920, *not* converting it to farmland would have been unthinkable. The irony, of course, is that since 2004, the Holland Marsh has been protected – not as wetland, but as farmland. Despite lingering around discursively in the moniker of the area, the antecedent landscape has been mostly expunged, though signs remain for the careful observer. As plans developed to drain the Holland River lowlands, the explicit intent was to reconstitute the wetland to produce orderly, productive, and profitable fields. Local media celebrated the fact that the "dismal swamp" in Bradford, Ontario, was finally being drained to make way for a much more agreeable contingent of "smiling farms."[7]

Fast-forward roughly a century, and in many ways, the resulting farmland is being similarly threatened, despite – perhaps because of – the farmland-protection measures pertaining to the area. While the idea of farmland protection is currently de rigueur among many scholars, activists, and government officials, the story of the Holland Marsh demonstrates that its dominant paradigm is insufficient to effectively preserve such areas. Widespread simplistic and ahistorical understandings of the very character of farmland and landscape change have resulted in the development of preservation policies and practices that may fall short of their intended outcome. Put simply, conventional farmland-preservation measures are typically designed to protect a particular kind of capital-intensive farming, not the land itself: *Farming* preservation must be seen as distinct from *farmland* preservation, yet this distinction is rarely, if ever, made in scholarship, public discourse, or policy debates. The case of the Holland Marsh demonstrates that farmland preservation is a product of normative ideas about landscapes and land use, ideas that are ever changing and based on historically contingent notions about "nature." The Marsh, protected as a Specialty Crop Area under Ontario's Greenbelt Plan, has become a poster landscape for farming protection under the guise of farmland protection. And yet, these protective policies may be hastening the demise of this iconic, multimillion-dollar agricultural juggernaut known widely as Ontario's salad bowl.

The stakes for how we think about "nature" and how we use our peri-urban landscapes could not be higher. It is becoming increasingly difficult to overstate the multiple, intersecting, and coproduced socioecological crisis of the contemporary period. From mass malnutrition and the arrival of a planetary fire age to global pandemics and an imminent climate reckoning, the socioecological limits of the earth are seemingly within sight.[8] Agriculture is at once a key culprit in these crises and essential to their resolution.

From as early as the mid-nineteenth century – when a thriving trade arose to replenish Europe's soil with guano from South America – agriculture has been enabled through a global metabolic rift.[9] The so-called externalities of global agricultural production were vastly intensified during the green revolution as a raft of chemical and technological innovations were hastily embraced, rationalized within complementary neo-Malthusian and productivist discourses. The consequences have been catastrophic.

More recently, examples abound of the ways in which agriculture can contribute to repairing the widening socioecological rift. Lessons from this work are worth underscoring. Agro-ecologists and allied academics and practitioners have demonstrated the promise in reexamining the socionatural relations inherent in agriculture. Rather than taming nature – the operative logic of contemporary industrial agriculture – agro-ecologists insist on a more humble approach that rejects the premise that "nature" is controllable in the ways proponents of industrial agriculture assume.[10] At the same time, a broad consensus is emerging suggesting that key crises related to the contemporary food system can be mitigated – and reversed – in place-based efforts focused on strengthening existing and forging new links between eaters and growers within discrete geographies.[11] This work reveals the social and ecological benefits of relocalized food systems and compels us to reexamine our reliance on long-haul industrial agriculture.

I focus specifically on the Holland Marsh for a variety of reasons – its productivity, its iconic status, and its proximity to Canada's most populace region and North America's third-largest city. On a clear day, the fields of the Holland Marsh are visible from the top of the CN Tower, the quintessential icon of downtown urban Toronto. That some of the most profitable and productive farmland in Canada is in such close proximity to, and increasingly threatened by, the nation's largest urban agglomeration itself makes this a noteworthy case within the catastrophe of the contemporary moment.

In this sense, the Holland Marsh is a proverbial canary in the coal mine – an example that can help us understand the history and complexity of the land at the centre of any putative efforts to relocalize food systems. The prized muck soil, as it is colloquially known, is a central character in the history of agriculture in the Marsh and receives herein an extensive explanation of its social and material significance.[12] Suffice it to say for now, muck soil is relatively rare and extremely fragile, much more so than mineral soil. As a result, from the moment the Marsh was drained nearly a century ago, this soil began to degrade. More than this, even if it were never farmed, the muck would inevitably disappear – agriculture is certainly hastening its demise. The Marsh, then, serves as a fascinating case study that reveals insight into human-environment relations, accentuates the contradictions and deficiencies of contemporary farmland-preservation paradigms, and highlights the challenges of forging more socioecological rational food systems.

Holland Marsh

Travelling northward from Toronto, the northern slopes of the Oak Ridges Moraine highlands give way to a gentle descent to the fields of the Holland Marsh. Within the span of the southern canal – roughly fifteen metres across – a variable landscape of cultivated fields of corn, pastureland, exposed glacial debris, and wooded hillsides cedes to uniform fields of lush, green vegetables. The farmed area of the Marsh – which vaguely resembles a banana if seen from a sufficient height – is separated into two sections. The main polder is known colloquially as the "Big Scheme," from which the much smaller "Little Scheme" is pinched off at its north end at Yonge Street. The Holland River runs through the middle of the Marsh, serving as both a natural and political-administrative boundary. The fields on the west side of the river are in Simcoe County, those on the east side lay in King Township. As the river continues its northerly flow toward Cook's Bay on Lake Simcoe, the orderly fields give way to a landscape that resembles more closely the scenery conjured by the image of a "marsh." Marsh grasses, reeds, and small conifer shrubs populate both land and water, blurring the boundary between the two as if in a Group of Seven painting. Just before the Holland River empties into Cook's Bay, destined for Lake Simcoe immediately beyond, it is once again dammed, canalized, pumped, and diverted around a final small agricultural area known as Keswick Marsh.

In all, the Holland Marsh is a mixed-use wetland of some 7,400 hectares (roughly 18,200 acres), 60 percent of which is drained agricultural land and 40 percent is preserved marshland.[13] The cultivated land (roughly 3,000 hectares [7,400 acres]) supports 125 farms, together producing many millions of dollars in annual revenue by growing a range of market garden vegetables.[14] According to the Holland Marsh Growers' Association (HMGA), the total annual economic impact of the Marsh – the farm-gate value of the vegetables in addition to packaging, processing, and transportation – is $1 billion. This includes $130 million in annual carrot production and $160 million in annual onion production.[15] A 2009 study found that gross farm receipts were $7,130 per hectare in the Marsh, 3.7 times higher than the provincial average.[16] This makes the farmland there some of the most profitable in all of North America.

While the soil can support a wide diversity of crops, the pressure to be pragmatic within an age of capitalist agriculture has resulted in a highly homogenous crop base. Combined, onion and carrot production account for 70.9 percent of the annual output in the Holland Marsh. Other crops, including celery (7.3 percent), mixed greens (7.3 percent), "Chinese vegetables" (2.7 percent), and potatoes (0.7 percent), are less commonly grown.[17]

Conceptual Framing and Scholarly Landmarks

Agriculture and the Dynamics of Change in the Holland Marsh

Food for human consumption has existed in the Holland Marsh since time immemorial, and by a sufficiently lenient definition, probably always will. But agricultural production per se arrived in the Marsh within a very specific social,

FIGURE I.1. A: An aerial view of the manicured landscape of the Holland Marsh. B: The stark difference between the orderly agricultural fields of the Marsh and the land beyond the canal. C: Highway 400 bisects the Marsh. Courtesy of Holland Marsh Drainage System Joint Municipal Service Board.

cultural, political, and historical configuration. Emphasizing that food and agriculture in the Holland Marsh are distinctly *capitalist* in character puts a fine point on one of the main themes of this book. The Marsh serves as an exemplar of, but importantly at times a foil to, much of the recent literature concerned with the state of the contemporary agro-food complex. For over a century, scholars have questioned the extent to which agriculture is capitalist.[18] While no clear consensus has emerged, they have convincingly demonstrated that agriculture is significantly shaped by the constraints and opportunities to capital in the ongoing process of attempting to fully rationalize food production.[19]

Food regime theory, developed by Harriet Friedmann and Philip McMichael, is helpful in tracing the implications of this insight within the case of the Holland Marsh.[20] Friedmann and McMichael argue that historically contingent configurations of modes of agricultural production, capitalism, and state power have resulted in discernable periods of stability and crisis in the global economy over the past 150 years or so.[21] As they put it, the food regime analytic brings together "international relations of food production and consumption to forms of accumulation broadly distinguishing periods of capitalist transformation since 1870."[22]

The first period of relative global stability demarcated by Friedmann and McMichael was from 1870 to 1914. This first food regime was characterized

FIGURE I.2. Percentage of area by crop type grown in the Holland Marsh, 2006.

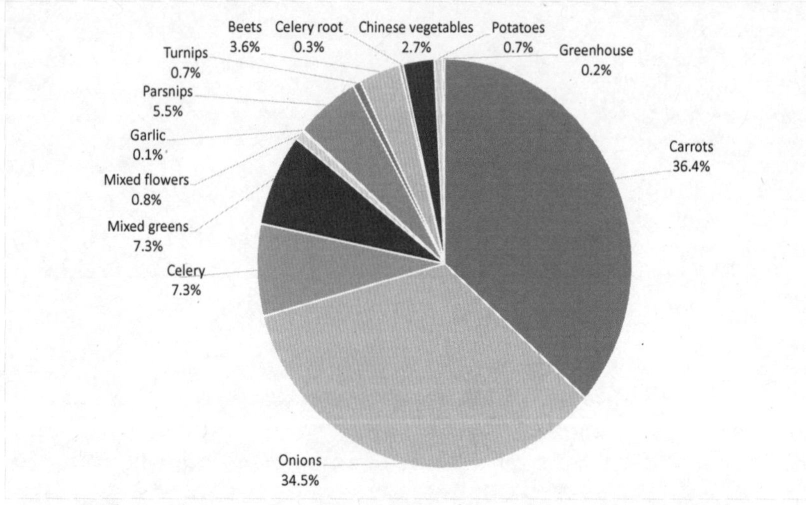

SOURCE: Planscape, "Holland Marsh Agricultural Impact Study," August 2009, p. ii, https://www.greenbelt.ca/holland_marsh_agricultural_study.

by monopoly trade relations between colonial (mainly the United Kingdom) and colonized states. Settler states in particular (such as Canada) were, during this era, important to maintaining British hegemony by providing the colonial market with a relatively cheap and abundant source of grain. The sociopolitical instability wrought by the two world wars also created economic uncertainty during which, according to Friedmann and McMichael, there was very little structured coherence to the global economy. As a result, there was no decisive food regime during the years 1914–47. But with the conclusion of the Second World War and the emergence of the United States as a postwar power, a second food regime emerged, lasting from roughly 1947 until 1973. This regime was characterized by the rise of the United States through the pretense of international development, primarily through the distribution of US grain surpluses. This was also an era characterized by the secular trends of intensive industrialization and commercialization of the agricultural sector. As national regulations – often through international agreements such as the General Agreement of Tariffs and Trade (GATT), which lasted from 1948 through 1994 – were altered to accommodate the influx of capital demanded by a rapidly industrializing global agriculture, state power began to erode vis-à-vis a burgeoning corporate globalization.

Owing in part to the intellectual force of the paragons behind the staples thesis, much of the social-scientific scholarship related to agriculture in Canada has tended to focus on macroeconomic trends, countrywide aggregate data, and commodity- or sector-specific analysis.[23] This rich body of work is invaluable, yet its shadow is long, and it has sculpted the trajectory of Canadian food and agriculture studies for decades.[24] Recently, however, the study of Canadian agriculture has benefited from a more particularistic, place-based approach.[25] Within this body of work, rather than forming the centre of analysis, macrotrends and global food regimes constitute the backdrop on which equally compelling and important histories of agriculture, food, and culture play out.[26] This study of the Holland Marsh is similarly positioned: It recognizes and attends to structural, global, and national trends in farming, biotechnology, and the like, but always in terms of how these trends affect and/or are affected by the goings-on within the Marsh. While the dynamics of capitalist nature play out there, they do so mediated through the specificity of place and time. As Shannon Stunden Bower observes in her seminal work on agriculture in the wet Manitoba prairie, this is "capitalism at a different scale."[27] My aspiration is not to gaze into the muck-soil fields of the Holland Marsh from the outside, but rather to stand in them, looking out at the world beyond.

Within this context, historians of agriculture have identified liberalism as a central modality through which agriculture and environmental change are mediated and modified in Canada. As James Murton puts it, understanding the environmental history of Canada requires moving beyond ideas about nature to recognizing "more general logics – such as liberalism – that implicitly encourage a particular form of engagement with nature."[28]

This perspective builds on Ian McKay's influential work asserting that Canada, as an ontological category, can be productively studied as a contradictory and complex project of liberal rule.[29] Countering the notion that it is simply a "vacant lot" and a "relatively minor" bounded geography where the dynamics of social and natural history play out, McKay insists that the country should denote within scholarship "a historically specific project of rule."[30] Initial waves of the violent colonial resettlement of what would become Canada were driven by political, economic, and social rationalities premised on aristocracy and deference to crown and clergy.[31] Throughout the course of the nineteenth century, this system would be replaced by one girded more firmly on the core elements of liberalism – liberty, equity, private property, and the primacy of the individual. As McKay argues, this emerging social ideology was "set down on the land," shaping both the landscape and its people.[32]

While there is a sociological distinction to be made between the Victorian liberalism that fuelled agricultural expansion across Canada from the mid-eighteenth century through the beginning of nineteenth century and the New Liberalism that emerged in the early 1800s, the functional role of nature (and, by extension, agriculture) was largely consistent.[33] And this remains true of the contemporary neoliberal era. A common thread stitching together the chameleonic and persistent liberal philosophy is an instrumentalist view of nature "in which the natural world is judged solely on its usefulness to human ends."[34] This manifests as a "a culture and society built on, and absolutely dependent on, a sharply alienating, intensely managerial relationship with nature."[35]

This managerialism requires rationalization. Unable to contend with the enormous complexity of the (socio)natural world, states have historically sought to make nature "legible" in ways conducive to facilitating control, regulation, and the extraction of profit. As Bruce Braun puts it, "far from constituting a field of readily intelligible objects, nature enters into history in part through its cultural legibility."[36] Nature emerges as legible to the state through the processes of inventorying, abstraction, and standardization of both landscapes and the discrete bits of biophysical nature that compose them. Land surveys, cartography, soil classification schemes – these are among the technologies that made the Holland River lowlands legible to the aspiring agriculturalists who transformed it. Braun extends James C. Scott's influential work by illustrating the "complex field of social practices" implicated in nature's rationalization.[37] While Scott conceptualizes the state as distinct from civil society, Braun demonstrates the ways in which knowledge about nature generated outside the state ultimately influences how it sees and acts on nature. In other words, the state is not a totalizing force, but rather more fluidly defines and acts on nature in strategic ways, informed by a wide array of social, political, and economic forces.

By exploring the ways in which capitalism and liberalism collided in the Holland Marsh, this book adds weight to the point. Refracting the global dynamics of capital through the lens of liberal-state rationality enables a more nuanced and place-specific analysis than allowed for by more economistic modes of analysis. The Marsh is a quintessentially idiosyncratic landscape – while capital and the state have certainly shaped it, so too has technology, civil-society institutions, biophysical properties, ecological crisis, and a range of other socionatural elements. Stunden Bower's work helps us understand how the internal logic of liberalism, in operation through the provincial government, propelled drainage on the Manitoba prairie. In contrast to this, the drainage of the Holland Marsh, while certainly supported by the state, was led by individuals (and supported further through the Ontario Agricultural College). Liberalism in Canada has shaped – and been shaped by – a range of actors, from voluntary associations to legal apparatus and academic institutions.[38] This book contributes to the small but important body of work revealing the ways in which capitalism and liberalism collided in place within the context of locally and regionally bounded areas of agriculture production in Canada.

Nature and Society

One of the foundational concepts of this book is that society and nature do not exist as separate entities, but rather they are constitutive elements of each other. Neil Smith was not the first to speculate on the conjoined character of nature and society, but his production-of-nature thesis remains among the most influential scholarship on the subject. "What jars us so much about the idea of the production of nature," Smith writes, "is that it defies the conventional, sacrosanct separation of nature and society."[39] He forwards the production-of-nature thesis, in part, through an analytic distinction between first and second nature. Previous to the spread of capitalism, Smith argues, first nature could be described as what is typically thought of when the word "nature" is invoked – a tree, a carrot, or a mountaintop. Second nature, on the other hand, is made from first nature – tables, carrot juice, or landscape paintings. As Smith puts it, "second nature is produced out of first nature."[40]

Under capitalism, however, the distinction between the two vanishes within the self-expanding logic of capitalist accumulation, for no first nature is left unaltered as "capital stalks the earth in search of material resources."[41] In other words, Smith argues that, either through direct manipulation (turning a tree into lumber) or indirect consequence (melting polar ice caps as a result of human-driven climate change), no area on earth has been left unchanged as a result of human activity. Within this context, the difference between first and second nature "ceases to have real meaning... [because] human beings have produced whatever nature became accessible to them."[42] He continues:

> Where nature does survive pristine, miles below the surface of the earth or light years beyond it, it does so only because as yet it is inaccessible. If we must, we can let this inaccessible nature support our notions of nature as Edenic, but this is always an ideal, abstract nature of the imagination, one that we will never know in reality.[43]

Critical geographers, in particular, have elaborated on ways to transcend dichotomous and rigid conceptions of nature and society "to grasp nature's social character ... to see how, in both thought and practice, the natural and the social melt into one another."[44] Noel Castree offers three specific ways to substantiate the conjoined character of nature and society. First, he points to the work critical geographers have done to demonstrate that knowledge of nature is always inflected with subjectivity. This both calls into question the possibility of an "objective" nature and hints at the ways in which nature can be thought of as irrevocably social. In an early and noteworthy essay, the preeminent critical geographer David Harvey takes on a neo-Malthusian establishment in arguing that global resource "shortages" were in fact nothing more than the uneven distribution of resources, the flow of which was largely determined by powerful Western nations. This critique calls into question assumptions about overpopulation and its relationship to starvation, resource degradation, and the like. In other words, Harvey exposes neo-Malthusian arguments to be fundamentally ideological and premised on a particular (and powerful) conception of nature.[45] Others have since moved the critique of "knowing" nature beyond its ideological implications, focusing instead on the discursive work mobilized toward privileged knowledge(s) of nature. These critiques demonstrate the ways in which power, articulated through ways of knowing about nature, is activated within gendered, racialized, and colonialized knowledges.[46]

Yet nature is clearly constituted by more than particular kinds of knowledge. To argue otherwise would be to deny the fundamental material aspect of biophysical nature. The second way nature can be seen as social is by understanding that its ever-present materiality is socially mediated and contingent. As an example, photosynthesis and its results are clearly not socially produced – that process initiated long before humans arrived. Yet photosynthesis can be harnessed and deployed in ways, such as through agriculture, that tend to reproduce conventional power structures and perpetuate inequalities.[47]

Taking this second argument one step further, Castree points to the third way critical geographers have challenged the supposed dichotomy between society and nature. Here, the claim is that material nature is not only engaged with in socially contingent and mediated ways but also physically reconstituted through those interactions.[48] As Erik Swyngedouw puts it, contemporary scholars recognize "that natural or ecological conditions and processes do not operate separately from social processes, and that the actually existing socionatural conditions are always the result of intricate transformations of preexisting configurations that are themselves inherently natural *and* social." Given the extent to which nature is imbricated with social processes, he argues that the social and natural are better reflected in the hybrid conception of "socionature."[49] Castree observes that employing this term "is not at all a denial of the material reality of those things we routinely call natural. . . . Rather it's an insistence that the physical opportunities and constraints nature presents societies with can only be defined *relative to* specific sets of economic, cultural and technical relations and capacities."[50]

Taking seriously the notion that the Holland Marsh is a socionatural landscape helps reveal important aspects of the dynamics that have gone into producing and reproducing the area. The Marsh was not created in a vacuum of endless possibilities – it was produced precisely because of the specific material and geomorphological character of the area. That it was once a wetland very much matters to the history and the development of agriculture there. It is important to underscore the materialist commitment of socionature – biophysical nature does not simply bend to every human whim but instead presents a variety of "obstacles, opportunities, and surprises."[51] To help clarify this admittedly tricky concept, scholars have delineated between the *formal* and the *real* subsumption of nature within industrial, capitalist production. In some industrial processes – mining, for instance – the characteristics of biophysical nature are such that it cannot be fully transformed, only exploited. Rocks can be mined, crushed for aggregate, and used in a variety of end-use products, but the biophysical character of the rock remains largely unchanged. In other industrial dynamics – agriculture, for example – the real subsumption of nature is able to occur through biological manipulation at the cellular scale. Seed germplasm is altered, soils are augmented, and plants are designed to be ever more efficient: "Nature, in short, is (re)made to work harder, faster, better."[52] This drive to control the landscape and the discrete bits of biophysical nature within it has been woven into the very fabric of the Holland Marsh. The "imaginary" of orderly, "smiling farms" has long been a seductive promise in the Marsh, and yet completing this project has remained always just out of reach due to the materiality and ongoing unpredictability of biophysical nature.

Yet the "social" contributions of socionatural production in the Holland Marsh have remained undeterred for nearly a century. Politics – the formal operations of governments in addition to social movements, civil society action, and the like – are fused into the fields and yields of the Marsh, enveloped in the process of nature's production. Limits to the production of socionatures, while partly material (as mentioned above), are also socially produced.[53] Within this context, environmental politics are seen to matter profoundly to the process of the production of socionature – an insight on display at various points in the history of the Marsh. The production of socionature is animated and negotiated through the environmental-political tensions between official state policy and the dissenting civil-society actors. Demonstrating that the government and politics matter to the production of nature (as I do below) reveals the process to be a highly contingent one. The Holland Marsh as a produced socionature was not inevitable, but rather produced (at least in part) through a confluence of contingent state power, institutions, and contentious politics unfolding over time.

And yet, while there are material and social elements that go into the production of the Holland Marsh landscape, there are equally important imaginaries that have contributed – and continue to contribute – to its production and ostensible protection. The story attached to the first vegetables to emerge from the Marsh is infused with technology, human ingenuity, assembly line precision, and a sterilized, cling-wrapped nature. In some of the earliest commercial advertising, potatoes from the Marsh are positioned by Eaton's as the equivalent of expensive hats and fur coats – items every modern woman should never be without.[54] Notions of progress, technological advancement, and even decadence were, in effect, inscribed onto the "nature" of the potato. In the contemporary period, conventional commercial ads as well as a variety of nonprofit organizations promoting Holland Marsh vegetables – Sustain Ontario, Local Food Plus, Friends of the Greenbelt, the HMGA, and others – privilege decidedly different notions of nature based on neopastoralism and rustic environmentalism. Contemporary boosters of the area have invoked a cultural and natural imagery of a romanticized past and the de rigueur language of "local food" to construct an imaginary that eschews the material reality and history of the area in important ways. Such efforts, ironically, attempt to recapture a bucolic character deliberately blanched from the area and its yields by Marsh boosters of a bygone era. So while agriculture in the area is rooted in a deep materiality mediated through politics and institutions, it also exists as a dematerialized spectacle of signs, referents, and symbols.[55]

Importantly, the development and deployment of various idyllic constructs is not merely a function of particularistic commercial interests. These ecological imaginaries are cast from within dominant structural systems, including capitalism, colonialism, patriarchy, and the like.[56] Put differently, imaginaries of nature are not fixed, nor are they politically benign. Smith underscores this point by noting that, "much as a tree in growth . . . the social conception of nature has accumulated innumerable layers of meaning in the course of history."[57] Nor are perceptions of nature formed ex nihilo, but rather imaginaries of nature – or ecological imaginaries – are ideologically and discursively mediated.[58] As Smith puts it, there is an *ideology* of nature, riven with the logic of capital, that influences how we think about and experience nature. As an example, the unrelenting exploitation of biophysical nature – trees, bituminous sands, rock quarries, soil – is enabled by the deeply engrained notion that nature is infinite, out there somewhere, and unlimited.[59] In recent Canadian history, the extent to which the state tends to protect this idea has been vigorously enforced, through, for example, the defunding of scientific research, the shuttering of libraries, and the labelling of environmental activists (particularly so called anti-petroleum ones) as "terrorists."[60] Similarly, privileged imaginaries of what nature in the Marsh "ought" to be is a key ingredient in how that area has been reproduced through the decades. And these normative commitments are reflective of the historical, social, cultural, and political configurations of the day.

In just a few generations, the Holland Marsh has undergone a profound socionatural transformation. The physical terrain of the area, once a swampy flood plain for the Holland River, exists now as a manicured landscape of fields, roads, houses, barns, irrigation canals, and culverts. At the same time, conceptions about what the Marsh "is" have also changed. Variously imagined as a mosquito-filled wasteland, an investment opportunity, a place for home and work, an agricultural site, and, more recently, a centre of high-end niche food production, its identity has been as unfixed and variable as its material referent.

It is important to highlight the socionatural dynamics at play in the Holland Marsh, partly because crops are not widgets and fields are not workshop floors. Farming is different from many industrial processes in that it is heavily influenced by weather conditions, pests, wind, and a litany of other factors that are not fully under human control – despite the best efforts of farmers, scientists, and agro-industry interests.[61] Biophysical and climatic elements introduce a sizable amount of unpredictability into agriculture, making it distinct from typical industrial formations. So while it is possible to think of agriculture as capitalist, it is also relevant to think of the components of agriculture as being shaped by capitalism. As some would have it, crops, seeds, and soil can all be considered bits of "capitalist nature."[62]

Emphasizing the notion that agricultural environments are fundamentally caught up in the broader processes of nature's production also brings to the foreground the unique character of stability and crisis associated with capitalism-in-place. Specifically, the ostensibly self-expanding character of capital is significantly restrained by the need for nonproduced (that is, "natural") inputs.[63] As capital uses biophysical inputs and creates outputs (pollution and such), it tends to draw down the resources available to its successful reproduction. In other words, biophysical properties are "underproduced" by capital, leading to the second contradiction of capital: In order to reproduce, capital needs ecological inputs (water, landscapes, plants, and so forth), but in the process of reproduction, it destroys (or renders unusable) these things. Within the Holland Marsh, this process can almost be demonstrated in centimetres of soil per year. The very moment the wetland was drained, exposing the rich composition of centuries' worth of decayed plant material to vastly increased levels of oxygen, was the instant this complex soil became more susceptible to oxidization, wind erosion, and water erosion through flooding. While there are mitigation techniques and technologies being employed by farmers to stabilize the soil, one of the defining features of the Marsh's local competitive advantage, its demise is inevitable.

Emphasizing the specificity of the kinds of biophysical nature transformed in the Holland Marsh reveals that accounts of the broad structural and historical trajectory of capitalist agriculture constitute perhaps an overly blunt approach to untangling agriculture's inherent dynamics.[64] Agriculture in the Marsh is in part a result of the postwar global industrial-food regime. At the same time, there are important lessons to be learned from exploring the specific processes by which the area became enlisted in global agriculture and by investigating points of disjuncture between global agriculture and agriculture in the Marsh. Looking at the specificity of nature in the area – or more accurately, the socionatural imbroglios that have resulted from the collision of global agro-industrial forces and local particularities – reveals insights into the complex interplay between agriculture, food, history, and capitalism.

Sociopolitical Aspects of Soil and Farmland Degradation and Loss

Its hydroponic variant aside, agriculture depends on the soil, and one of the central purposes of this book is to bring soil back in to view. Dirt, as the preeminent anthropologist Mary Douglas famously described it, is "matter out of place."[65] Douglas's anthropological and structuralist commitments led her to understand dirt (and its inverse, cleanliness, or the absence of dirt) as part of a broader sociocultural arrangement of meaning in which dirt was an ordering antagonist. "Where there is dirt there is system," she argues.[66] I largely agree with this assessment but take a slightly different tack, arguing that dirt, at least in part, is matter out of *view*. It is rare that we ever think about dirt unless – as Douglas observed – it is within the context of an absence of cleanliness. For most of us, dirt is something to be swept away from the kitchen floor, sprayed off the dog, or scrubbed out of our clothes.

Yet dirt is instrumental to our survival. We cannot live without food, almost all of which grows from the earth. Soil is also responsible for the cycling and purifying of fresh water, it is a condition of production for the growth of fibres the world depends on, and it supports untold numbers of flora and fauna. Ignoring the complexity and crisis of dirt is a luxury for only the most privileged – those who have access to consumable goods from around the world without ever having to confront the biophysical and ecological requirements of those items. As a normative commitment, then, this book is an attempt to bring attention to the "quieted disaster" of soil degradation and farmland destruction.[67]

While soil degradation and farmland loss are global scourges that threaten livelihoods, destabilize populations, and exacerbate climate change, conventional accounts of the problems typically miss the point by rendering soil and its uses apolitical. Indeed, this was largely the case up until Piers Blaikie and Harold Brookfield developed critical insights in the mid-1980s revealing the politics that adhere in all landscapes.[68] The critical subdiscipline their work inspired – political ecology – interrogates how landscapes and other things we deem to be natural (such as soil) are also always social, cultural, and political. In other words, landscapes are always produced by humans within particular historical and cultural contexts, though this is not always easy to see (recall my longstanding misreading of the Holland Marsh).

Some of the earliest policy and program interventions aimed at defining and remedying soil degradation focused on erosion in Africa in the 1930s. Employing questionable scientific methods, colonial agronomists ignited a moral panic that led to the imposition of compulsory antierosion practices, the prohibition of certain farming techniques, and the forced destocking and displacement of animal herds across the continent.[69] In assessing these early soil-conservation efforts, political-ecology scholars have demonstrated how concern for soil degradation in Africa in the 1930s incubated in the United States and spread throughout the so-called developed world as an expression of anxiety about the global implications of the American Dust Bowl. White occupiers demonized Indigenous farming methods as backward and destructive, and the colonial powers capitalized on this by expanding their land holdings under the facade of scientific management and ostensibly modern farming techniques.[70]

By the early 1990s, critical historians and others were deepening the critique of soil-degradation science and remediation efforts in 1930s Africa. The professed science of the colonialists was exposed as soil politics – unduly alarmist, dismissive of local biophysical conditions and knowledge, and ultimately deleterious to African agriculture.[71] This was a top-down colonial approach to both defining and providing solutions to the problem of soil degradation. A key insight of this body of work is that to deem a given soil as degraded is to implicitly place it within a normative context of ideal use. If the expectation is that a patch of land should produce a constant and prolific stream of fruit for export to the United States, then the slightest drop in phosphorus levels could be considered suboptimal, and thus the soil degraded. If the expectation is instead that the same patch should produce more moderately for the domestic market, then slight drops in various key chemicals may not constitute degradation.

The point, as Blaikie and Brookfield made thirty years ago, is that soil degradation, while not without a biophysical component, is really a social and political problem.[72] As Salvatore Engel-Di Mauro puts it: "Soil degradation implies a political position relative to how people relate to soils. This is why the matter of soil quality and hence degradation must encompass a study of social relations, not just soil properties."[73] Put differently, the extent to which a given ground is considered degraded is largely a function of its social, cultural, and political context.

The very fact that soil is primarily considered an agricultural input tells us a lot about the expectations we have of it. In Canada, as in most capitalist countries of the Global North, it has long been seen in instrumental terms – a natural resource to be exploited for profit through agriculture. Here, the first substantive efforts to survey and define soil (along biochemical, geochemical, and taxonomical lines) were initiatives of the Ontario Agricultural College.[74] The earliest surveys investigated how soil erosion affected farming and explored the feasibility of agriculture in previously unworked areas. The production of scientific knowledge about Canadian soil has been, since the first survey in 1914, largely a commercial enterprise defining soils only in relation to agriculture.[75] In the intervening century, the commercialization of soil science has intensified as publicly funded, nationally coordinated research has given way to privately funded, proprietary studies. These "specific-purpose surveys" are increasingly common for agricultural lands, but especially over the past decade or so, they are the purview of oil-and-gas companies looking to exploit bituminous soils and landscapes.

A key idea in this book is that farmland-preservation policies are based on normative, context-specific, and political ideas about soil and landscapes. If the normative assumption is that soil is really only useful in as much as it can be used for farming, then there is scarcely little opportunity to understand it separate from agriculture. Farmland-preservation policies, in a very real sense, "produce" soil as little more than a farming medium. And the preservation of farming is not necessarily compatible with the preservation of soil, particularity within the Holland Marsh, given the biophysically delicate character of its muck.

Within this context, the imposition of agriculture on the landscape can be framed as a normative expression of an idea about the "purpose" of nature. The original Marsh boosters were motivated by a variety of factors –moral, technical, financial, and others – but behind all these is the more basic notion that agriculture is a higher-order use of the landscape than is the preservation of a wetland.

To underscore this point, the Holland Marsh is now heavily protected as an agricultural area, the wetland having been expunged nearly a century ago. Yet, for reasons further elaborated below, the legislated protections leave the soil vulnerable. The degradation of farmland soil, as Blaikie and Brookfield point out, is a social problem, not only a biophysical one – this remains true within the context of farmland-protection policy. Nutrient leaching, wind and water erosion, and even soil subsidence can occur with or without human intervention, "but for these processes to be described as 'degradation' implies social criteria which relate land to its actual or possible uses."[76] Degradation is then, in many ways, a perceptual, relational problem. As an example, the terminal depletion of key soil nutrients on a piece of near-urban property would result in its devaluation as farmland and thus would be considered degraded by the farmer-owner, farm advocates, and others of a similar persuasion. But to a suburban land developer, devalued farmland may represent a promising opportunity to acquire premium development land on the cheap. Degradation, in other words, is somewhat in the eye of the beholder.

Suggesting that land degradation is partially perceptual in no way annuls the seriousness of the issue. The loss of farmland continues to exacerbate poverty, marginalization, ecological degradation, starvation, and other untold horrors throughout the world. But the biophysical phenomenon of degrading soil is not the proximate cause – rather the determining factor is the social context that enables and allows such devastation to result from changes in the biophysiology and biochemistry of soil. Farmers are, on the whole, compelled by the edicts of pragmatic production to pursue the maximization of short-term profit. Highly intensive agriculture depletes farmland in as much as it reduces its capacity to sustain similar levels of production (without the introduction of soil amendments in the form of fertilizers and the like). A given piece of land may be perfectly fine from a biophysical perspective but classified as depleted when the expectations of intensive cultivation and the demand for profits are placed on it.

So how do we move toward a perspective on farmland degradation that might prove to be more efficacious in terms of farmland preservation? At minimum, to better understand the character of the problem requires seeing farmland degradation as the product of irrevocably conjoined social and biophysical processes. Soil is only considered degraded in relation to the expectations placed on it; any perceived biophysical degradation is typically the result of human activity in one form or another.[77] The next step in understanding would ideally include knowing something about the history and context of both the biophysical properties of the soil as well as the social uses of it. Assembling an exhaustive historical record of a farmed area, its people, the soil, local culture, and so forth is obviously not always possible. Indeed, in the case of the Holland Marsh, there is scarce historical scientific and quantifiable data on the muck soil itself. Yet striving to assemble the clearest image possible of the socionatural conditions of the land through time, as this book attempts, is a promising methodological manoeuvre.[78] Next, moving toward a more thorough picture of farmland degradation (and its remedy) requires investigating the "chain of explanation."[79] This requires an analysis that takes into account the individual, social, and biophysical specificity of a given unit of agricultural production, then moving out to examine the concentric, interlocking spheres of relevant phenomena. This will vary case by case but can include the relations between producers within a given area, regional climatic conditions, and local political conditions through to national and suprastate actors and world economic trends.

The final step in developing a more nuanced understanding of farmland degradation is through adopting an inclusive definition of degradation itself. In conventional accounts, the assessment of whether a particular piece of farmland is degraded is premised on an analysis of some combination of the physical, chemical, and biological components of the soil. If certain thresholds of a given nutrient are absent, or the percentage of organic matter per unit is deemed insufficient relative to production demands, the soil is labelled degraded. At that point either the land is abandoned as farmland or efforts are made to remediate the soil. What technocratic definitions miss, however, is the broader social context of soil's degradation. I use Engel-Di Mauro's more ambitious definition of healthy farmland being that which "fulfill[s] everyone's needs in a community and contributes to developing or maintaining egalitarian relations."[80] This approach creates a much more complex picture of land degradation, its causes, consequences, and potential solutions, than conventional approaches have allowed. Ideally such an approach will lead to transcending the impasse that has seen the confusion about this issue continue unabated over the last few decades.

Before reviewing the conceptual development and deployment of farmland-preservation paradigms in Canada, it is useful to first briefly historicize two antecedent and related ideas, conservationism and environmentalism. This is only a cursory effort, though, as summarized below, with much more having been written about these shifting and historically contingent categories elsewhere.

A concerted conservation movement was part of the European zeitgeist from as early as 1880 and informed – along with US influences – the shape of early conservationism in Canada.[81] In the earlier part of the nineteenth century, conservationism in the colonies had little purchase, given the prevalence of the notion of an extensive, inexhaustible nature and related policies to support resettlement and natural-resource extraction.[82] There was a "myth of superabundance," of a land "rich in soils, and minerals, and forests, and wildlife."[83] But this was not a monolithic perspective – in the early decades of the nineteenth century, the Hudson's Bay Company developed and implemented a wildlife conservation program in response to rapidly declining beaver populations. This included harvest quotas, resulted in the shuttering of some trading posts, and led to the development of some of the first fur sanctuaries in North America.[84]

The conservationism of early twentieth-century Canada reflected Enlightenment-era conceptualizations of nature and liberal ideals with respect to human-environment relations. Nature was to be inventoried, categorized, and managed in ways that supported economic development and territorial expansion. A practical, instrumental desire to protect the environment thus fused with a perspective that nature could be managed and improved on through science and human ingenuity.

Perhaps no institution embodied this perspective better than the Commission of Conservation (CoC), a federal nonpartisan conservation-advisory body composed of academics and business leaders, ex-officio members from the federal departments of the interior and agriculture, and representatives from the provincial governments. The CoC was initiated in 1909, following a commitment by the Canadian delegation at an international conference on the conservation of natural resources, hosted by the so-called conservationist president, Theodore Roosevelt.[85] Its named committees hint at the tactical character of conservation at the time – mines, waters and hydropower, lands, forests, fish, game and fur-bearing animals, public health, and public relations. The CoC produced an impressive body of work – over two hundred reports from its founding through its disbandment in 1921.

The Committee on Land, chaired by Dr. James Robertson, is particularly salient here. Robertson was among one of the most forward-looking members of the CoC, rejecting chemical fertilizers in favour of compost and manure and advocating for a conservation-research agenda "by far the most advanced" among the academics involved with the commission.[86] For him, farmers were the foot soldiers of conservation, and the best farmers convened with divine and earthly elements to nurture productivity from nature. As he wrote in 1912,

> Farming is the marriage of the strength of old Father Sun to the inherent strength of old Mother Earth. The plant is the child and the farmer manages the business. That is his place in the economy of nature. So this is a noble calling at its best ... [The farmer is] ... a partner of the Almighty to make a new earth wherein dwelleth righteous farming and righteous living.[87]

In his remarks in the commission's first annual report, Robertson spoke evocatively and reverently about Canada's agricultural resources as "the chief asset in the landed estate of the people of the Dominion" and the CoC's role in managing those resources to extend "their enjoyment through the wise use of what we have."[88] He also warned of the "tremendous temptation for first settlers to become surface miners instead of real farmers who use and husband the treasures of the soil."[89]

The productivist, instrumental character of early-twentieth-century conservation was underscored most poignantly by US president William Taft, who Robertson quotes extensively in his opening remarks. At this time in history, draining wetlands for agricultural production was sound land stewardship. As Taft put it:

> In considering the conservation of the natural resources of the country, the feature that transcends all others, including woods, waters, [and] minerals, is the soil of the country.... To this end the conservation of the soils of the country should be cared for with all means at the government's disposal. Their productive powers should have the attention of our scientists that we may conserve the new soils, improve the old soils, drain wet soils, ditch swamp soils, [and] levee river overflow soils ... [so] that the soils from which they come may be enriched.[90]

The CoC was disbanded in 1921, representing waning support for the conservation agenda within the federal government.[91] Though by the 1930s, and in part spurred on by civil-society initiatives, an evolving form of conservationism was emerging across Canada. The National Parks Act was passed into law in 1930, the Federation of Ontario Naturalists was formed in 1931, Ducks Unlimited opened a Canadian chapter in 1938 to facilitate wetland restoration, and the Canadian Quetico-Superior Committee was founded in 1949 (an offshoot of its sister organization, the Quetico-Superior Council, based in the United States and founded in 1928).[92] There was a qualitative shift in this emerging conservationism that nudged the instrumental and productivist impulses of earlier iterations toward preservation.

This was a less anthropogenic effort, one that began to subtly recast the human-nature relationship. While certainly more radical than many of his contemporaries, Aldo Leopold's ecological philosophy is indicative of this shift. In the middle of the twentieth century, Leopold insisted that nature was still largely understood as something to be owned and used for human benefit. He famously called for a new ethic to inform human-nature relations: "There is as yet no ethic dealing with man's relation to land and to the animals and plants which grow upon it. Land, like Odysseus' slave-girls, is still property. The land relation is still strictly economic, entailing privileges but no obligations."[93]

Despite this critical posture, Leopold was optimistic that the nascent conservationism in North America at that time was indicative of a deepening respect for the so-called natural environment. For him, the land ethic was about extending to nature the same considerations community members show each other. As he put it, "The land ethic simply enlarges the boundaries of the community to include soils, waters, plants, and animals, or collectively: the land."[94] The leaky ontological categories of nature and society can be seen to be dissolving within Leopold's ecological philosophy – humans and nature were irrevocably intertwined in much more profound ways than earlier instrumental versions of conservation implied.

Rachel Carson's *Silent Spring* put a fine point on this and contributed to the emergence of an environmental movement that began to grapple with ecological contamination and collapse. In Ontario, a number of environmental organizations emerged in the 1960s and 1970s that rejected the liberal conservation ideal of instrumental use and instead developed a deep ecological rationale for nature's protection. The Algonquin Wildlands League, formed in 1968, agitated for – and won – extensions of protected wilderness areas in Algonquin, Lake Superior, and Killarney Parks and was instrumental in realizing a ban on logging in Quetico Park.[95] The first Earth Day was observed in 1970; Greenpeace launched in Victoria, British Columbia, in 1971; and DDT was banned in the United States, although more slowly phased out in Canada, beginning in the early 1970s. This was an emerging environmentalism that would inform the contemporary movement focused on public health and well-being, toxic landscapes, climate change, and the intersectional ways in which environmental (in)justice cleaves along gendered, racial, class, and spatial lines.

While concern for land quality had percolated as early as the late nineteenth century, deep concern for farmland degradation and preservation began to emerge in Ontario in a broader sense during the 1950s. Unlike the earlier anxiety circulating in the global context, which pinned farmland precarity on issues of soil erosion and poor farm management in the developing world, the threats in Ontario in the 1950s were tied to rapid postwar (sub)urbanization.[96] These earliest concerns were sparked by threats to high-value agricultural land, particularly the fruit-growing area on the Niagara Peninsula. In 1959, Ralph Krueger captured the latent anxiety:

> In recent years there has been much concern in Canada over the spread of urban land uses onto the choice Niagara fruit land. Commentators and editors of all the news media, as well as industrialists, fruit growers, planners, and government spokesmen, have been debating how much urban expansion has been affecting the fruit industry, and whether anything should be done to direct urban growth away form the best fruit land.[97]

Subsequent research in the area confirmed fears of farmland loss and eventually contributed to the creation of the Food Land Development Branch – later renamed the Food Land Preservation Branch – of the Ministry of Agriculture of the Ontario government in 1973.[98] By the late 1970s, Ontario had developed its first explicit strategies and guidelines for farmland protection, demonstrating that the issue had begun to have traction at the highest levels in provincial government.

Concern at the federal level had already coalesced in response to a national conference titled Resources for Tomorrow, which resulted in the creation of the Canada Land Inventory (CLI) in 1961. The CLI's mandate was an ambitious yet simple one – to inventory the nation's land and assess its "productive" capabilities.[99] The body found that only 15 percent of Canadian territory had any potential as farmland, quantifying – for the first time – Canada's agricultural potential. Far-smaller pockets in the Montreal Plain, southern Ontario, and the Lower Mainland in British Columbia were the only areas with land deemed to be Class 1 and Class 2 – the most productive, highest-quality farmland. Not surprisingly, subsequent to CLI's work, these three areas in Quebec, Ontario, and British Columbia became the main focus of farmland preservation work in Canada.[100]

Given that Canada's prime agricultural land was shown to be clustered around its most populated areas, the impetus behind what might be considered the first wave of protection policies and initiatives in Ontario came in response to anxieties over the loss of farmland in the face of urbanization. In the postwar boom, agriculture was losing out to suburban expansion in the zero-sum game of land use. Yet, over time, the actual loss of farmland proved to be fairly modest, estimated at around 3 million hectares country-wide between 1941 and the early twenty-first century.[101] And while farmland loss can have significant local and regional consequences, the rationalization and industrialization of agriculture meant that farming output increased at the national aggregate level despite a shrinking farmland base.[102] The productivist/scarcity rationale thus lost steam in the face of this empirical reality. Any worry that agricultural production would be stunted in Canada due to a shrinking land base waned in the face of a growing faith in agro-technologies to perpetually increase per-hectare yields.

In part as a reaction to this perspective and beginning in the late 1960s and early 1970s, a second wave of farmland preservation grew out of the nascent Canadian environmental movement. This was a shift in focus from the *quantity* to the *quality* of land.[103] Invoking Leopold's notion of land ethic, Mary Rawson was one of the first Canadians to write about farmland protection from an ecological perspective. Addressing the BC context, she noted that "the critical task of preserving food-producing lands" was, in part, a way to "nurture the growth of a new understanding of man's relationship to land, a new land ethic."[104] In Ontario, the Ontario Coalition to Preserve Foodland was formed in the early 1980s as an alliance of sorts between environmental groups and those interested in farmland protection. At the same time, larger mainstream environmental groups, such as the Sierra Club and Friends of the Earth, began taking on the issue of farmland preservation as a matter of key business. Within this perspective, protecting farmland was seen as a way of preserving the natural environment. Proponents of this perspective point to the environmental services of farmland – as a sink for carbon, a habitat for wildlife, preservation of the countryside, and the like.

While the environmental-protection perspective is still prevalent, a stronger influence in contemporary farmland preservation has more recently emerged – amenity protection. As Canada has become an increasingly (sub)urban country, the countryside is seen as a place to escape to for weekend getaways, summer holidays, afternoon drives, or permanent relocation. This "rural migration," as it is known, is characterized by "the movement of largely affluent urban or suburban populations to rural areas for specific lifestyle amenities, such as natural scenery, proximity to outdoor recreation, cultural richness, or a sense of rurality."[105] The influx of amenity migrants to the countryside has led to an exurban gentrification, whereby farmland protection is framed as part of a broader community-preservation paradigm by local governments in attempts to lure new residents.[106] Farmland-preservation policies are in this case bound up – perhaps subsumed by – those to accommodate the exurbanite imaginary of the pastoral rural.

This leads to the final theme under which the impetus for farmland preservation can be grouped – the agrarian ideal. Some argue that, in the Canadian context, the notion that agriculture has both cultural and economic significance – that there is an inherent rural virtue – can be traced back to the country's earliest history as a producer for colonial-export markets. Indeed, early farming in Canada was intimately tied to the creation of a national identity. Michael Bunce points out that there is both an economic and cultural aspect here. In an economic register, "physiocratic agrarianism – the belief that the true wealth of the nation is drawn from the land," imbues agriculture with a productivist authority – farming contributes economically, provides jobs, supports families, and builds sturdy societies. Farmers, too, are elevated – in the famous words of Thomas Jefferson – to "the chosen people of God."[107] The normative corollary of this leads to what some call the romantic iteration of agrarianism.[108] From this perspective, farmers come to be (unwittingly, perhaps) celebrated as land stewards, not (merely) farmers. Here, Henry David Thoreau is the patron saint, and both the urbanization and the industrialization of agriculture are seen to be the true threats to farmland. These pressures, from this perspective, can only be neutralized through a "back to the earth" movement emphasizing a culture of "traditional" farming from an idealized, bygone era. The rise of so-called agro-tainment and pick-your-own models illustrate the extent to which farmers are now cast as curators of the countryside – stewards of both the land and an idealized rural community.[109]

This is all to say that the impetus driving farmland preservation is not easily parsed. The truth is, there are multiple and at times competing perspectives driving these efforts. Yet, to reiterate, conventional farmland-preservation measures are typically designed to protect a particular kind of capital-intensive farming, not the land itself. *Farming*-preservation polices need to be understood as distinct from *farmland*-preservation policies, yet this distinction is rarely, if ever, made. The focus of this book – unearthing the socionatural history of the Holland Marsh and exploring the conditions and processes through which that farmland was made and maintained – reveals the specificity of the Marsh land base and sheds light on the limits of contemporary farmland-protection policies.

The following chapters draw on and develop these three conceptual touchstones – agriculture and capitalism, nature and society, and the sociopolitics of soil and farmland degradation and loss – through an empirical examination of agriculture in the Holland Marsh. It is important to understand these not as discrete categories, but rather as overlapping analytics with which to parse the ever-shifting configuration of change within the Marsh. The driver of a distinctly capitalist form of agriculture propelled the area's initial draining – a capitalism always refracted through the liberal project of the Canadian state. We see in the story of the Holland Marsh a kind of double movement – a to and fro of capital penetration followed by periods of liberal regulation to address the (ecological) externalities of production, as described by Karl Polanyi. The latest iteration of this – the Specialty Crop Area designation – ostensibly finds a resolution between ecological and economic sustainability. Yet the apparent resolution of this contradiction of capitalist agriculture is incomplete and temporary. Importantly, this approach as used in the Marsh is reflective of broader patterns of the regulation of biophysical nature within the Canadian liberal state. We cannot understand the history of agriculture without also understanding something about the history of "nature" in Canada.

What we witness in the Holland Marsh is not a wholesale and unregulated expression of global industrial agriculture because the geologic history and biophysical composition of the area resists being so neatly integrated into industrial models of production. Yet this is not to suggest that the productivist impulses of capitalist agriculture were nonexistent in the Marsh. Indeed, they were, and continue to be, but they are continually refracted through, modified by, and complicated within the biophysical specificity of the area. More than this, as socionatural theory demonstrates, are the discursive elements and imaginaries of nature that (re)produce agriculture in the Marsh. The ideas that various actors – farmers, boosters, marketers, policymakers – have about the biophysical nature of the Marsh are a key driver in shaping the material landscape.

The most important expression of this dynamic is with respect to the soil – the raison d'être for draining the area in the first place. Shifting understandings of conservationism and environmentalism have modified the (re)production of the soil over time. The original drainage of the Holland River lowlands was enabled through a matrix of regulation and justified through a rhetoric of improvement as fundamentally conservationist. Fast-forward nearly a century, and the landscape is protected as a Specialty Crop Area, cased within a logic of environmentalism and farmland protection. Yet despite decades of regulation, justified within shifting discourses of conservationism, environmentalism, and farmland protection, the soil's steady subsidence has continued.

Chapter Overview

In the following chapter, I take up a discussion of the very earliest history of the Holland Marsh area, from roughly 14,000 years ago up until roughly 1925, and explore how various aspects of the past have enabled and shaped the current-day Marsh. I focus explicitly on how relevant social and natural elements collided and eventuated in the production of the material agricultural landscape of the Marsh – in other words, how the physical land came to be produced out a "dismal swamp." Within this context, the geology of the area stands as a sturdy foundation, serving as the biophysical canvas on which the socionatural activity of muck farming would eventually emerge. Before the farms, however, was the wetland, a complicated, vernacular landscape accommodating to various uses before it was transformed into fields. I discuss how a wider regional reclamation geography, enabled by a shared Great Lakes basin geology, provided the early Marsh boosters – in particular Professor William Day – with examples of drainage projects to study in southern Ontario, Michigan, and Ohio. While Day and the Holland Marsh Syndicate would draw on other similar projects throughout the region, ultimately they would create their own social and political configurations in order to mobilize the resources (not only financial but also political) necessary to drain the Holland River valley.

In Chapter 2 I attend to the period of time between roughly 1925, when the excavation of the canal system began, through to 1935, by which point meagre commercial agricultural production had begun. This is the period during which the material landscape of the Marsh was thoroughly transformed from an abstract idea of land into actual, farmable fields through a confluence of policy, technology, labour, and capital. I discuss the Herculean efforts required to dredge a twenty-seven-kilometre-long canal out of the peaty bog and argue that the spectacle of it all whetted the appetite of would-be farmers and hungry consumers alike. The transformation of the landscape was also predicated on a host of institutional and legislative supports that preceded the draining, establishing important legal and discursive precursors to the agricultural activity to come. As the fields emerged out of the swampy water, they were thrust into abstract exchange relations, assigned (inflated) value, and propelled into a complex and multispatial political economy of food and agriculture.

For the farmers in the Marsh, the timing of the land's emergence could hardly have been worse. I begin Chapter 3 (1935–54) by exploring the hardships those early families had to endure as a result of the effects of the Great Depression. The socionatural confluence of low consumer demand, on the one hand, and prodigious supply crowding the newly minted fields, on the other, made for a disastrous start to commercial agricultural production. As I detail in this chapter, the crops emerge as a stability strategy for the farmers, while agriculture in the Holland Marsh truly flourishes during the immediate postwar years.

Farmers there (and elsewhere) leveraged their newfound clout, as producers of calories to feed the war effort at home and abroad, to engage in unprecedented social organizing. The Marsh emerged during this era as part of the "modern countryside." Liberal notions of an ordered, productive, and profitable rurality animated state-making projects, making farms and farmers an important part of the postwar transition. At the same time, advances in chemical synthesizing, cooling technologies, and transportation infrastructure began to change farming in the Marsh and elsewhere. For the farmers, who had typically only ever shipped to the Toronto area, improvements in produce durability and transportation and storage technologies suddenly made markets accessible around the country, the continent, and even overseas in Europe. This empirical reality resulted in a period of profitability and stability in the Marsh, though this was not to last.

The enthusiasm with which farmers embraced the tenets of an emerging mechanized, productivist, and chemical-dependent global agriculture continued well into the post–Second World War period. In Chapter 4 (1954–80) I explore how these tendencies and related socioecological contradictions led to crises of farming in the Holland Marsh. The period is bookended, on the one hand, by Hurricane Hazel (1954), a devastating and deadly storm that exposed the hubris of modernist notions of human domination over nature. Hazel demonstrated that the Marsh boosters had not in fact conquered nature along the Holland River. This lesson would inspire farmers, with ample state support, to redouble their efforts to expunge the area of nature and its inherent contingencies and unpredictability. By 1980, on the other hand, this cavalier attitude toward the biophysical environment had resulted in the emergence of ecological and public-health disasters that would put the production of nature in the Marsh under intense external scrutiny.

In Chapter 5 (1980–present) I pick up on the theme of crisis in the Holland Marsh by exploring the details of two prominent crises that surfaced in the early 1980s – elevated birth anomalies in and around the area, and algal-bloom outbreaks on Lake Simcoe. The "smiling farm" narrative was severely undercut by revelations that Marsh agriculture was implicated in both of these quiet disasters. This, in turn, catapulted the area into a constellation of emerging regional environmental politics. As a result, farmers have been made to adjust to prevailing environmental sentiment through various regulatory and legislative measures. At the same time, (sub)urban expansion has accelerated in recent years, bringing suburban yards in almost direct contact with the fields and resulting in increased tensions on both terrains. As the social and political conditions within which nature is produced in the Marsh change, farmers have sought to enlist biophysical nature in ever-more efficient ways to search for ways to control their fields and crops with (ostensibly) increasing precision in order to get as much out of the biophysical nature as possible. Ultimately, however, uncertainty and contradiction persist in the fields of the Holland Marsh.

CHAPTER 1

The Production of Land, 14,000 BC–1925

Cultivating an appreciation for the complexity of the transformation of the Holland Marsh begins with understanding the socionatural origins of the land. There was nothing inevitable about the arrival of intensive cultivation to the area, but neither could the same kind of agricultural land there be produced just anywhere. The Marsh is the result of a confluence of biophysical, topographical, ecological, sociocultural, and political conditions, yet these all rest – at times uneasily – atop a sturdy geological foundation. These elements collided and eventually produced the material agricultural landscape of the Marsh.

The material foundation for the farmland was established over 14,000 years ago, assembled within a millennia-long, prehuman history of grand geological processes. The resultant wetland was used by various waves of human inhabitants – first Indigenous populations, then later colonial settlers – in very different ways. Initially, Indigenous people used the area as a hunting and fishing ground and as a node along the Carrying Place Trail.[1] Later, white-settler sensibilities initially rendered the landscape a wasteland – a mere ditch, as John Galt put it. Yet over time, perceptions shifted as the result of changing material conditions, including less available, less accessible farmland and the flow of information and knowledge about marsh farming throughout the shared geology of the Great Lakes basin. The pursuit of profit was part of the motivation for transforming the wetlands into fields – importantly, this transformation did not occur until after capitalist farming was commonplace throughout Ontario – but the driving impulse was more than simply money. Deeper-seated cultural desires to harness, manipulate, and control "nature" with human ingenuity and technology were equally integral animating factors.

Despite all this, the transformation from wetland to farmland could not have occurred without an enabling political milieu. A range of regulatory, legislative, and quasi-judicial infrastructure buttressed the initial drainage plan. The state, not just the market, put its full weight behind the production of a particular form of landscape in the Holland Marsh. Consistent with conservationist sentiment of the day, canalizing and draining the wetland was understood as land improvement and as part of the broader agricultural tradition of the fledgling country. The opportunity, within this context, to renovate a wasted landscape into useful fields was far too attractive to pass up.

The Material Origins of Muck Farming

The story of the Holland Marsh starts before the Holland River lowlands were drained and transformed into farms, before Paleoindian populations were hunting and gathering in the wetland, and even before there was any wetland in the area to speak of. The natural history of the Marsh, a precursor to its socionatural history, starts roughly 14,000 years ago at the end of the last Ice Age. During the Quaternary glacial period, the Laurentide Ice Sheet, an expanse covering a good deal of what would become Canada and the United States, advanced and retreated in response to temperature fluctuations over many millennia.[2] The hard crystalline rock of the Precambrian Shield, beginning just north of Lake Simcoe, was largely impervious to the erosive weight of the ice. But as the sheet advanced and retreated over the softer limestone and shale rock abutting the Precambrian Shield to the south, it scoured out depressions that would become the Lake Simcoe watershed. As the ice of the Wisconsinan glaciation period made its terminal retreat northward, it left behind a mix of crushed limestone and shale debris in the form of gravel, sand, silt, and clay.[3] These depressions and deposits accumulated into four physiographic regions within the West Holland subwatershed: the Oak Ridges Moraine, the Schomberg Clay Plain, the Peterborough Drumlin Field, and the Simcoe Lowlands.[4] The latter is a broad valley extending south from Cook's Bay, hemmed in by the higher-relief moraine, plain, and drumlin features.[5] What is now the Holland Marsh sits at the top of a finger of the Simcoe Lowlands that slopes gently toward Cook's Bay and Lake Simcoe beyond.

While this landscape resembled "an old gravel pit or quarry" in the immediate postglacial period, vegetative life soon began to blanket the barren landscape.[6] Paleovegetation reconstruction paints a picture of a shifting vegetative profile of the Lake Simcoe watershed over time – from a forest-tundra mix, to a boreal parkland/forest mix, through to a mixed-forest landscape.[7] As water drained slowly through the Simcoe Lowlands into Cook's Bay and Lake Simcoe, what would become the Holland Marsh slowly began to form. And as climatic conditions shifted over time, so too did the vegetative composition of the wetland, ranging from arboreal swampland to herbaceous marsh.[8] Today, the Marsh shares its portion of the Simcoe Lowlands with a variety of wetland types, including deciduous and mixed swampland in the south end, north end, and in patches along the east side along with shallow marsh and rare open and shrub fen in the north where the Simcoe Lowlands empty into Cook's Bay.[9]

For centuries, the flora grew, died off, then grew and died off again. Over time, the decaying plant material – what would become peat – spread out across the section of the Simcoe Lowlands now occupied by the Holland Marsh.[10] Over millennia, an expanse of accumulated plant material filled the shallow water of the valley, creating the marshy wetland. Technically, the Marsh, before being drained, would have likely been classified – according to the Canadian Wetland Classification System – as an organic peatland marsh, a central characteristic of which is the accumulation of peat.[11] By definition, organic peatlands contain greater than forty centimetres of peat accumulation. Although the peat has already vanished in some spots on the edge of the Marsh, in the middle, where the muck and peat are deepest, there is still up to around two metres left.[12] Prior to draining, the peat would have been significantly deeper than this.[13]

Long before the landscape was resettled through colonial agricultural expansion, the wetland provided for Indigenous populations. Indeed, archeologists have identified Early Paleoindian, or Clovis, sites in and around the Holland Marsh dating back nearly 14,000 years. No fewer than ten sites scattered along the Holland River from Cook's Bay up through to the southwestern tip of present-day Holland Marsh indicate that the area was intermittently populated throughout the Early and Late Paleoindian periods as well as into the Archaic period.[14] These earliest inhabitants gathered on what was at the time the shores of a receding Lake Algonquin, a landscape of spruce-parkland, and adjacent areas interspersed with various grasses and sedges.[15] While migratory caribou were the game of choice, evidence indicates that the Clovis people would have had access to a prehistoric array of culinary choices within the broader Great Lakes basin, including

> mastodons and mammoths up to ten feet tall at the shoulder; woodland muskox; shrub fox; fugitive deer and stag moose; flat-headed and long-nosed peccary pigs the size of small deer; the short-faced bear, a superb predator twice the size of [the] modern grizzly; the tapir; the wild horse; giant beaver the size of a bear; the dire wolf; and ground sloths the size of cattle.[16]

While there is some debate with respect to the cause, there is consensus on the conclusion that many of these charismatic megafauna did not persist through the Younger Dryas, or the Big Freeze, which lasted about a millennia, from between 12,900 to 11,700 years ago. The Indigenous hunter and gatherers in the area would have continued to hunt caribou, in addition to deer and moose, as the climate warmed after the Big Freeze. As early as 5,000 years ago, Indigenous populations installed permanent fishing weirs between Lake Couchiching and Lake Simcoe. From 4,000 to 1,000 years ago, agriculture began to supplement hunting, fishing, and gathering. By about AD 1100, the "Three Sisters" – the sacred triumvirate of corn, beans, and squash – were being cultivated throughout the Great Lakes basin.[17]

By about AD 1350, the Holland Marsh area was under the stewardship of the Wendat, whose territory included a large swath of land from the north shore of Lake Ontario to Georgian Bay. As a result of disease and warfare inflicted on the area by incoming colonialists, the Wendat population was decimated and eventually dispersed. By the mid-seventeenth century, the Haudenosaunee controlled the territory. They were soon after displaced by the Anishinaabeg, who later entered into three treaties within which the Marsh still exists. The Toronto Purchase (or Treaty 13) was signed in 1805 and covers the southwestern tip of the Marsh. In 1818, the Nottawasaga Purchase (Treaty 18) was negotiated for a tract of land that includes the western part of the Marsh. Finally, in 1923, the Williams Treaty was signed for a tract that includes the eastern side of the Marsh.

A Swampy Imaginary: Revealing Agriculture in the Holland Marsh

John Galt, a surveyor for the Canada Company, famously remarked of the Holland Marsh in 1825 that it was a "mere ditch swarming with mosquitoes, flies, bullfrogs and water snakes."[18] The place of which he spoke had been named in 1791 by Canada's first ever surveyor general, Major Samuel Holland, who likewise failed to see any agricultural potential in the wetland.[19] In part, the swampy landscape was a toss-away to the early surveyors – unimportant, inconsequential, empty, and perhaps seen as little more than a nuisance. Holland Landing, just east of the Marsh, was the prized location of the area. Long used by Indigenous people as an important trading post, Holland Landing was even considered briefly in the 1820s as a possible capital of Upper Canada. The botanist John Goldie extolled the site for its natural and unique beauty, noting in 1819: "Since I came here I have seen a number of rare plants.... There are a species of *Asclepias* with orange flowers very handsome, a species of *Euphorbium* with white flowers, a *Ranunculus*, together with some others which were not in flower, that I had never seen before."[20]

In contrast to this was the Holland Marsh to the west. Settlers in the mid-nineteenth century saw this area as a useless swamp.[21] This echoed the sentiment of the influential British journalist and social reformer George Godwin, who devoted a good deal of his 1859 book, *Town Swamps and Social Bridges,* to expanding on the notion that marshes are "dark and dangerous" places of "degradation and filth."[22] Similarly, the nascent Canadian state did not recognize the area in any official capacity other than as an agglomeration of physical features to be catalogued and accounted.

The early colonialists had little interest in draining wetlands initially, preoccupied as they were with "inventory science," the "mapping and cataloguing of resources and other natural phenomena."[23] This was no politically benign activity, though, tied up as it was with Baconianism (the belief that accumulating facts led to new scientific theories) and Newtonianism (the idea that nature is orderly, mechanical, and subject to universal precepts). Instead, these early scientific forays cataloguing the nation's "resources" were instrumental in the forging of a national identity and the expansion (materially and ideologically) of the liberal Canadian state. Agriculture was not only an incipient economic driver of the economy but also crucial to the *idea* of Canada as a thriving – and worthy – colonial partner. Agriculture, in other words, was a central tenet of successfully making the Canadian state. As Suzanne Zeller puts it, "Canadians realized that their very future depended upon Canada's image abroad as an agriculturally promising country."[24] There was an additional normative, ethical element to these attempts to rationalize the landscapes of the new world – taming the wild frontiers was, for the colonial settlers, part of the process of developing a "proper" civil society.[25]

On the one hand, then, it is curious that Holland and others did not understand the reclamation potential of the Marsh, especially given that wetland farming has been an important agricultural practice for millennia. This method can be traced back to the very cradle of civilization in Mesopotamia, where people congregated along river valleys and flood plains for the fertility offered by the mucky soil. While there is no accurate appraisal for the total quantity of global freshwater wetlands, there have been estimates that in some regions – including Australia, Europe, and North America – up to 50 percent of marshlands have been transformed to agricultural use, suggesting that wetland conversion has been a widespread historical phenomenon.[26] In Ontario, up to 80 percent of wetland areas have been transformed, lost, drained, or converted to other uses.[27]

On the other hand, given the preponderance of much more accessible and easily reclaimed land well into the mid-nineteenth century, it is not surprising at all that the early surveyors failed to seize the agricultural potential of the area. Compared to converting a wetland into farmland, the investment required to transform far drier and very abundant land in what is now southwestern and central Ontario into productive farmland paled in price and effort. Besides this, the specific configuration of state regulations and supports were designed to enable the conversion of woodlands, not wetlands, throughout the eighteenth and nineteenth centuries. The first and far more significant wave of agricultural transformation in the province was aimed at the vast tracts of woodland throughout southwestern and central Ontario. Indeed, as David Wood puts it, "The domain of southern Ontario was transformed from one ecologic category to another – from woodland to farmland – in less than a hundred years by an army of axe-wielding settlers and woodsmen."[28] The rush to clear woodland for farmland in the late eighteenth and early nineteenth centuries was so fevered that Robert Leslie Jones referred to the would-be farmers as "land-butchers."[29] No doubt perilous and exhausting work, however backed as it was by state support, woodland farming was far preferable to wetland farming.

Yet there was something more going on here to dissuade the colonial agriculturalists from pursuing wetland farming. The ecological imaginary of the wetland – the cultural significance it held at the time – prevented such areas from being drained and transformed into fields earlier than they were. Holland Marsh was projected on, its materiality discursively transformed, by generations of settlers who were fearful and wary of swampland. Beset with Puritanical undertones and moral panic, the Holland River wetland of the nineteenth and early twentieth centuries was perceived as fit only for Indigenous populations, bootleggers, and desperate settlers. But the social context that ensured it remained undeveloped for so many years also contributed as a precipitant for its eventual reclamation. The fear and mistrust the first generations of settlers had for wetland ecologies eventually inspired efforts by subsequent generations to tame the Marsh through agriculture. That the landscape became legible as productive farmland when it did was a result of the shifting socionatural context within which the Marsh was understood, a double-headed process through the demonization of wetlands and the lionization of marshland farming.

Of Morality and Muck

John Thorpe had passed on long before the first crop was harvested from the fields of the Holland Marsh. A Bradford resident, mill owner, and a demonstrably pious man, Thorpe wrote a series of circulars in the latter stages of his life vilifying intemperance.[30] The fact that a robust bootlegging industry was thriving in the Marsh, just down the hill from his house, no doubt provided plenty of inspiration. His papers are moralizing expositions, ample evidence that he would not have been a supporter of the bootleggers toiling away in the swamp below his perch atop the Bradford highlands. Would-be whisky makers were likely drawn to the area for a number of reasons. The Holland River wetlands offered ample protective cover against the prying eyes of the authorities (moral and otherwise) in the stands of coniferous trees and shrubs. Also, the abundant supply of water provided a key ingredient for the "swamp water" spirits, while the ready supply of peat provided plenty of fuel for the fires needed to roast the malted barley, an essential step in the process.[31]

The peat, of course, had less controversial uses, most notably as fuel for home heating. As a matter of routine – and initially a noncommercial activity – residents of the Marsh area would cut large bricks of peat out of the wetland for home use. Perhaps not coincidentally, discussions at York County Council to ramp up commercialization of such peat harvesting emerged around the same time as talks to convert the area into farmland began.[32] To a man with the temperance zeal of Thorpe, however, one can imagine that peat harvesting was a suspect activity. And although his derision was not directed primarily at it per se, the peat likely would not have fully escaped his scorn, given its role in the making of whisky. To be fair, neither Thorpe nor Galt were alone in their derision of the landscape – well into the early twentieth century, the area was regularly referred to as "a "useless marsh" and a "desolate waste."[33]

In the Toronto area in the late nineteenth and early twentieth centuries, mistrust of wetlands was not simply due to the general attitude toward the landscape. Instead, in the early 1890s, a more specific threat loomed, as warnings of a potential cholera outbreak in downtown Toronto escalated. Ashbridge's Bay, a wetland in very close proximity to the city centre, was fingered as the culprit, putting a fine point on the perceived dangers of marshes. Kivas Tully, a city councillor and engineer, began writing about the public-health and economic benefits of transforming that wetland into a working harbour in the mid-nineteenth century. In 1892, just one year before a cholera outbreak was predicted for Toronto, he wrote that if the development was allowed to commence, "the source of these endemic diseases (e.g. cholera) which afflict the citizens, would be thus destroyed, and what is now a positive evil would be converted into a benefit – and a profit to the city."[34]

The spectre of cholera created panic among the public and policymakers alike.[35] At the time, the world was in the midst of a fifth international cholera epidemic, and fear of the disease was rampant. Within this context, wetlands of all descriptions took on a nefarious reputation and were assumed to be certain breeding grounds for cholera and other diseases. Along with other landscapes unfamiliar to European settlers such as tropical rainforests, they were considered sickly places.[36] The fear was such that one need not even come in direct contact with the materiality of a particular marsh – simply smelling the noxious stink of a fecund wetland was assumed to be enough to contaminate one's health. Despite the miasma theory of disease transmission being widely discredited by the 1880s, notions that a fog or vapour wafting from a wetland might cause disease persisted for much of the nineteenth century.[37]

Even before this, there was already a pervasive and deeper-seated suspicion of wetlands in the settler populations of North America, as suggested with John Winthrop's famous utopian call, in the 1630s, for the New World to comprise cities "upon a hill."[38] In an era of tense confrontation between Indigenous and colonial populations, Winthrop's pronouncement amounted to a proverbial line in the sand – the hills were for the Europeans, and the lowland swamps for everyone else. This Puritanical prescription, already pervasive in Europe, "othered" swamps and wetlands and established them as dirty and godless places. Certainly, they were no place for respectable, productive, or pious people.

Within this cultural perspective, however, is a liberal, productivist corollary. Informed by the impulses of modernity and the liberal logics of improvement and profit, wetlands became revealed as ideal landscapes through which to manifest order, cleanliness, and productivity. By the mid-nineteenth century, most of the available agricultural land in Ontario was taken, compelling enterprising farmers to turn their attention away from the woodlands.[39] In the process, a normative politics emerged within which the act of draining became valorized as an antidote to what the wetlands represented. This was more than simply a way of making productive farmland: It was a way of purging the landscape of the evils of disease and waste, a way of improving the land and bringing its resources to bear on the material and spiritual well-being of the fledgling nation.

On the Canadian frontier, the impetus behind landscape transformation was an important part in the colonial attempt to bring "social order to an apparently disordered world."[40] As James Giblett puts it, "Wetlands were like heathen savages to be converted by the gospel of discipline and drain[ed] in order to live clean and useful lives."[41] Within this context, "taming nature" through agricultural drainage was more than simply a matter of landscape change, it was a way of introducing civilizing values to the Canadian colony. By the late nineteenth century, a culture of "aquaterracide," backed by a range of policy and scientific innovations, had arrived to the North American colonies, with farming becoming a viable, even celebrated, antidote to the wetland condition.[42] And, of course, all this fit very squarely within the logic and ethic of colonial agricultural expansion.

Reclamation Geographies and the Genealogy of Drainage

Once the agricultural potential in the landscape became legible, marshes, bogs, and other wetlands were understood as opportunities for investment and development through the imposition of agriculture. In the late nineteenth and early twentieth centuries, they became important sites within which biophysical nature and capital were brought together within the context of agriculture. As Holland Marsh–area technicians, scientists, politicians, and residents began to take seriously the prospect of reclamation farming, the wetland was transformed in their imaginations into a veritable techno-scape of ordered and efficient agricultural production. The emergence of particular, privileged landscape "legibility" is shaped by ongoing human interpretations about the *value* of a landscape. Thus, as word of the success of other reclamation projects travelled to the Bradford area – within a milieu of shifting wetland perceptions and imaginaries – farming as a viable land use for the Marsh slowly became legitimated.[43]

This opened up many opportunities for the penetration of capital and power into the Holland River lowlands. While the area had supported meagre underground distilling and marsh-grass-harvesting operations, as well as larger-scale commercial mattress manufacturing, the economic activity resulting from the introduction of agriculture immediately dwarfed these preceding industries.[44] After the initial wave of agricultural colonization that saw the transformation of the Ontario woodlands, word of the economic success of muck-crop farming filtered in from towns within the shared Great Lakes basin – specifically from parts of Michigan and Ohio.

Crucially, as the landscape was revealed as potentially productive and profitable, novel private-property relations were formalized and enacted in the Holland Marsh.[45] While the vast majority of the Marsh had been privately owned for decades previous to being drained, the land was more or less valueless in financial terms. Indeed, at the time of one of the first surveys of the area, in 1819, the land was considered so valueless that no effort was made by the original surveyor to continue the concession and lot lines through the Marsh to the actual Holland River. In a paper delivered to the Association of Ontario Land Surveyors over a century later, in 1934, Edward J. Cavell remarked that the original surveyor

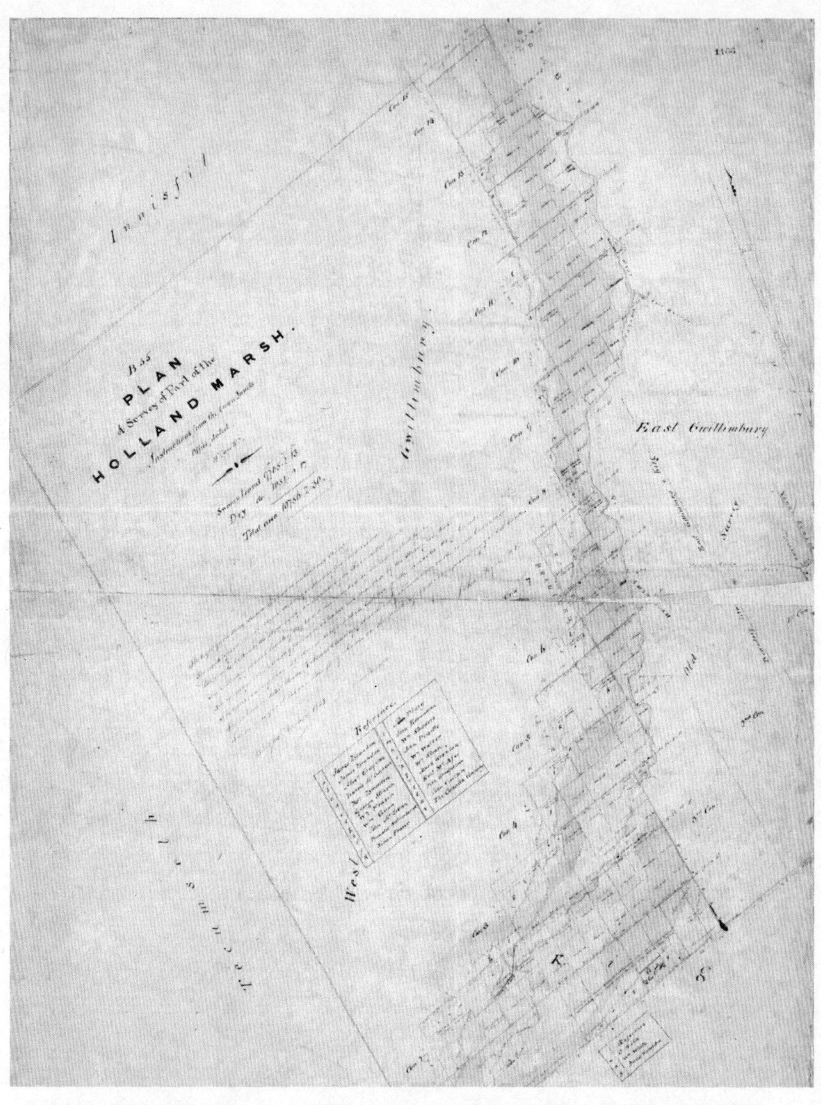

FIGURE 1.1. Ryan's survey. The lot lines on this 1852 map can be seen to be extending through to the Holland River. Areas north of the Concession 3 lines on the east side of the river are not complete in this survey. Courtesy of Archives of Ontario, ARDA – Holland Marsh, RG 16-1, B388426.

"posted the lots on the high land, carrying his concession lines only to the edge of the marsh and on his plan shewed a large tract of waste land."[46] Another survey of the area, conducted in 1852 by John Ryan, a provincial land surveyor, included work to extend the previous lines through to the river on both sides (see Figure 1.1).

This extension of the lot lines is indicative of a subtle recasting of the character of available land after 1850. Wetlands were still largely considered valueless, but given rapid population growth and a dwindling land base, settlers began looking for arable land beyond what was most easily accessible. The best parcels were snapped up by eager settlers in the early nineteenth century, largely from Britain and Ireland – often via the United States – who were drawn to Upper Canada with the promise of cheap land. Between 1840 and 1850, the population north of the Great Lakes more than doubled, from 450,000 to 1 million residents. Eighty-three percent of these people settled in rural areas and initiated a "rising tide of land clearing, burning, and turning."[47] For those with land adjacent to the Holland River, the marshy section was likely an inconvenience. As local historian George Jackson has observed, "By 1852 most of the highlands had been taken up and the marsh lots were an extension of the highland lot and not considered to be of much value."[48] In other words, the farmland on the higher ground surrounding the Marsh – and throughout many other areas of what would become Ontario – was the coveted commodity.

While at least part of the Marsh landscape can be considered a commodity from 1805 onward, in as much as it was exchanged within the context of a treaty between the British and Anishinaabeg, it remained essentially worthless. The marshland had very little exchange value in that it was simply tacked onto existing parcels of land and was largely ignored. It also had very little use value – being unfarmable, in the conventional sense, in its current state – within an emerging settler state in which agriculture was a centrepiece.

Despite the increasing importance of agriculture to the social and economic development of the colony by the 1850s, it would be inaccurate to label the settler agriculture of Upper Canada or Lower Canada as distinctly capitalist during the first half of the nineteenth century. In Lower Canada (Quebec), agriculture was typically a mix of subsistence and market farming "more committed to family-centered well-being than to profit."[49] France created a propertied class – seigneurs – through a system of land grants and associated political rights. The farmers in Lower Canada were allowed to work sections within a particular fiefdom, though they did not own the land. In exchange for use of the land, the seigneur would take "feudal appropriations" from the farmers in the form of surplus wheat, labour, or cash.

In Upper Canada, the early agricultural system was quite different. Settler farmers were granted land – free or at a nominal rate – by the government as part of the colonization process into the mid-nineteenth century. This served the colonial officials in a few ways: On the one hand, over 1 million settlers arrived to the region in the first half of the nineteenth century.[50] The promise of free and cheap land drove the newcomers to settle and "improve" ever more of the landscape. Often, stipulations were attached to the grant – settlers were expected to build a small house, clear fields, and make the land productive. Land was the cost the colonial government was willing to pay the settlers for the heavy work of clearing it, building transportation networks, and simply occupying territory farther westward. On the other hand, as the settlers cleared fields and began growing wheat for export to the homeland, the British government was fortifying access to a steady supply of grain. This was a settler-colonial, mercantilist system of exchange – subsistence farming still being very much a part – more so than it was a fully developed iteration of capitalist farming. At the same time, these early Upper Canadian farmers were girding their households and local economies. While wheat production constituted the largest source of revenue for most (composing 20–50 percent of farm income), in the early to middle nineteenth century, many operations were quite diversified. Farmers produced potatoes, peas, pork, butter, horticultural vegetables, fruit, and poultry to feed their families. Small surpluses – usually no larger than what might support one other family – were sold and traded locally.[51]

The precise moment in which farming became capitalist (whether in Ontario or simply within farming generally) is the subject of much debate and beyond the scope of this book.[52] But it is worth emphasizing that the social and cultural dynamics affecting the Holland Marsh were fundamentally altered as it was brought under production through agriculture. While the Marsh remained a valueless castoff landscape through the nineteenth century, this changed fairly suddenly with the prospect of drainage.[53]

The moment of drainage is crucial to the production of nature in the Holland Marsh. Not only was new physical material land "made" through the drainage of the marsh, but the process also necessitated new social formations and relations. Exchange relations, policies, legislation, novel scientific and technological innovations, and a land-ownership syndicate all became folded into the process of the Marsh's production. As others have demonstrated, making landscapes legible – and making biophysical nature legible to capital – always involves social and political decisions that inevitably reflect various relations of power. In the case of the Marsh, a new privileged legibility was instituted, one that continued to dismiss the value of the wetland, though it began to see the profit potential inherent in transforming the landscape into orderly fields.

Indeed, in 1911, a councillor for King Township speculated that, if properly drained, an acre in the Holland Marsh would escalate in price from one dollar to between forty and fifty dollars.[54] By the mid-1920s, news stories about the possibility of draining the Holland River lowlands calculated the financial windfall by highlighting the per-acre returns (in the range of three hundred to five hundred dollars) of similar reclamation projects in the geologically cognate areas of southern Ontario and northern Michigan. Newspaper editorialists emphasized specifically that the Marsh, when drained, would yield vast wealth, not just carrots and onions.[55] At the same time, local drainage boosters speculated that the new land would support "a thousand families of workers growing fresh vegetables" while countless others worked in various "factories springing up from year to year as the area develops."[56]

One of the most evocative expressions of fervour came from the Bradford grocer W.D. Watson, who, in 1911, wrote to Professor Day, the eventual patriarch of agriculture in the Holland Marsh. Watson reported, "As I stood tonight at sunset and looked over our promised land with its broad acres of unbroken greatness with the wooded hills of King [Township] in the background I felt a glance of pride at the immense possibilities which lies [*sic*] in the scheme."[57] This was a bold imaginary for someone standing at the edge of what had been known for decades as a dangerous, undesirable wasteland. Similarly, the anticipatory, even celebratory, tone of local news columns reporting on the expected profits and economic benefits of farming in the Marsh belied the physical materiality of the wetland. Where did this optimism come from? Why did Watson see "immense possibilities" in the landscape, while generations of settlers before him had dismissed it? These shifting attitudes and the growing faith in the landscape as a potential ally, not foe, can be understood as part of the broader process of nature's production and connected to a wider reclamation geography.[58]

This shift, of course, was unequal, and not everyone was convinced of the efficacy of marsh-drainage projects, particularly ones the magnitude of Holland Marsh. The Bradford West Gwillimbury town council began seriously discussing the possibility of draining the Marsh as early as 1910, committing twenty-five dollars to "help defray the expenses of an engineer toward the lowering of the water in the Holland River and marsh lands adjacent thereto in connection with the Township of King."[59] Alexander Baird, a civil engineer and Ontario land surveyor, was retained to draw up a preliminary drainage plan, which he filed with King Township in July 1910.[60] But due to lack of interest from "the owners of the marshland in the Gwillimbury side of the Holland River," the plans were shelved, if only temporarily.[61]

Draining the Holland Marsh was not seriously discussed again until 1924, when a West Gwillimbury bylaw was introduced and passed appointing Baird once again as the engineer to undertake an "examination and to prepare a report, plans and specifications" for a drainage project.[62] In his context, Baird was a key conduit through which this regional reclamation was spread. He was a well-respected, experienced drainage engineer, having worked on projects throughout southern Ontario – indeed, he references some of these smaller undertakings in Essex and Kent Counties and Point Pelee in his Holland Marsh report. In the introduction to his official report, Baird speculates on how profitable the Marsh will become, comparing it very favourably to other existing projects: "These lands when reclaimed and placed in a condition to permit of their cultivation and usefulness will become one of, if not the greatest producing sections of your part of the country and its most valuable lands and will enhance and enrich the township treasury."[63]

Meanwhile, farther south in northern Michigan and Ohio, marsh farming was already well established and attractively profitable. As momentum for the Marsh drainage project began to build by the mid-1920s, rumours about the success of wetland farming in the United States began circulating in local media. *The Globe* reported on an interview with Professor Day: "Mr. Day is very much interested in the survey which has just been made. . . . He claims that the soil, latitude and climate are identical with those at Kalamazoo, Mich[igan], which is famous the continent over for the quantity and quality of the celery produced on the marshes of that vicinity."[64] Early in the 1900s, the Kalamazoo-area celery industry was yielding between 4 and 5 million dollars' worth of celery every year.[65] In addition to prodigious crops, the area was also publishing trade material promoting muck-crop farming. Kalamazoo in the late nineteenth century was akin to the Wild West – except celery, carrots, and onions were the prized commodities, not gold. Operations like the Kalamazoo Celery Company were key exponents of the increasing enthusiasm for muck-crop farming during the era. In 1896, the company – leveraging a moment of alleged exasperation in the face of an overwhelming clamor for information – sponsored the publication of *How to Grow Celery Anywhere.*[66] The introduction sets the book's overall tone:

> Kalamazoo has no successful competitor in Celery Culture, either for quality or quantity produced. The celebrity of Kalamazoo celery has awakened so great an interest and desire to imitate, that inquiries received (from

> almost every section of the country) by principal shippers at this point regarding its cultivation, are becoming a serious burden if any attention whatsoever is paid to them. At best these inquiries could be answered only to a very limited extent. To meet the EMERGENCY we have published this book "How to Grow Celery," being a complete exposition of the methods of successful celery growing in this "famous Kalamazoo Celery" district.[67]

There is no doubt that Kalamazoo's success served as inspiration for Day and the other Holland Marsh boosters. Indeed, in 1910, Day noted that the soil samples he took from the Marsh were "almost identical in composition to the famous onion lands of Point Pelee, the strong sugar beet area of Wallaceburg, the wonderful celery lands of Thedford in our province, and the world renowned celery sold of Kalamazoo, Michigan."[68] Ever the savvy salesman, he organized a scouting trip in 1924 for councillors from the towns of West Gwillimbury and Bradford, and King Township to tour several drainage schemes in Kent and Essex Counties. Day recounted a few years later, "Everyone in the party was fully convinced that the reclamation of the Holland Marsh was entirely feasible, and easier than some of those inspected."[69] Even now, contemporary farmers in the Marsh reminisce about reconnaissance trips to Kalamazoo and parts of New York and Ohio in the 1960s and 1970s. In any event, the muck-crop farming in Essex and Kent Counties of southern Ontario, as well as the Kalamazoo site, were undoubtedly inspirational and instructional to Day and the other early boosters.

A striking element common to drainage reports like Baird's and the quasi-commercial communication/propaganda materials like *How to Grow Celery Anywhere* is the emphasis on the tools and technologies of the drainage trade. Clearly, there were profits to be made from the development of wetlands – even today, the Holland Marsh remains one of the most profitable per-hectare agricultural landscapes in North America. And as discussed above, there was an ethical undercurrent operating below the surface contributing to the compulsion to drain the wetland. But to reduce the impetus driving the reclamation of the Holland River valley to either profits or a moral imperative to tame the land would be a mistake. For the boosters of the reclamation economy, taming the wild landscape also provided an opportunity to showcase audacious technologies and cutting-edge scientific research.

Indeed, before moving to the Holland Marsh to try his hand at drainage and farming, Day was a physicist with the Ontario Agricultural College (OAC).[70] Under his direction, and with ongoing research support from the school, the bold plan to drain the wetland was developed. For him and the other boosters of the original drainage scheme, the feat was as much about creating new farmland through reclamation as it was about transforming the landscape with technology. Day authored a number of technical scientific booklets, published by the influential OAC, on everything from how to handle on-farm sewage disposal to tillage and crop rotation and, of course, tiling and drainage.[71]

Day's central academic work on drainage is essentially a report-cum-how-to-manual, very much in the style of other work published by the OAC. Day was clearly a believer in the technologies of drainage and water management to transform landscapes, writing, "many farms and various districts once wet and useless have been transformed by underdrainage into the most productive in the land."[72] As a long-time scholar of drainage theory and practice, he puzzled over why more farmers had not undertaken drainage work: "Contact with the people tells us why ... the critical operations of drainage are even less understood than its benefits – farmers, generally, have no way of telling whether they have fall enough for underdrainage, what the grade of a proposed drain should be, nor any method of digging to a grade, or planning a general drainage system."[73]

Drainage constituted a body of knowledge to which the average landowner or farmer had very little access. Day undertook the study to impart the highly technical, specialized knowledge to others – in effect, to proselytize on behalf of the liberal state in order to make converts of those who failed to see the latent productivity and profit of the wetland. In an effort to advertise the benefits of drainage and educate landowners and potential farmers on the practical techniques, Day and the OAC held workshops across the province. He was holding such sessions in the Holland Marsh area as early as 1910 and advertising through local media. One such announcement read: "This meeting should be of special interest as some difficulty to drain is involved. Besides the discussion of the particular problem there will be a demonstration of methods of finding the fall over a ditch, determining the grade, defining true to grade, etc. Those of our readers interested in drainage should not miss this meeting."[74]

There is, then, an element of technological fetishism to the early impulse driving the drainage of the Holland Marsh. One can imagine the farmers in attendance at one of Day's seminars learning the tools and techniques of drainage and having their perceptions of what farming consisted of fundamentally transformed. His message was that farming was not a dirty, tiresome drudgery but, instead, a refined pursuit for thinking men and scientists. The people of the Marsh would not simply work existing land with plough horses and hand tools, they would use modern techniques and cutting-edge technologies to *build* and *master* a landscape. Day was not alone in convincing would-be farmers of this techno-dream, however. Instead, he was only one, albeit a central figure, in a larger network of individuals and institutions involved in the production of nature in the early days of Marsh agriculture.

The Holland Marsh Syndicate and the Emerging Social Formations of Nature's Production

The Holland Marsh Syndicate was born shortly after the Bradford grocer Watson first invited Professor Day to visit and assess the Marsh in 1909. In addition to a noted and experienced technician, Day proved to be an adept businessperson, forming the syndicate in 1911. The group consisted of five members – Watson and Day, who each held five of the fifteen existing shares; R.L. McKinnon and David Baird (the son of Alex Baird, the chief engineer on the drainage project), who each held two shares; and W.G. Lumbers, a produce wholesaler in Toronto, who held one share.

The syndicate's initial concern was to seek out private capital to pay for the technology, materials, and labour it would take to drain the Holland Marsh. Day took on the brunt of this work, seeking financial support from businessmen in Toronto. While he was busy attempting to raise capital, Watson remained in the Bradford area, leveraging his local connections to sign options with local landowners within the Marsh for the right to purchase the land at a later date. In all, he negotiated options with over seventy individual landowners in the area for 970 hectares (2,395 acres) of the wetland on the West Gwillimbury side and 1,310 hectares (3,236 acres) on the King side, or 80 percent of the entire area proposed for draining. To be clear, this meant that, in effect, within about a year of forming, the Holland Marsh Syndicate effectively owned 80 percent of the land intended to be reclaimed. Watson, however, abruptly left the syndicate in 1912. On his departure, he signed his shares and the land options over to Day, making him the majority landowner within the proposed drainage area.[75]

Meanwhile, Day's efforts to secure funding from venture capitalists had stalled. Prior to the start of the First World War and the end of the first food regime, markets for grain were as close to a sure bet as exists in farming, given the grain-hungry British markets, the recent arrival of publicly financed grain elevators, and favourable state policies for grain production in general.[76] At the same time, a significant financial downturn in Canada in 1912–13 meant that investment capital was scarce. Within this context, investing in a scheme to drain a wetland to grow market garden vegetables likely seemed unduly risky. The global austerity pressures of the Great War meant that investors were in no hurry to dedicate scarce resources to a massive construction project to create what was essentially an experimental farm (success with marsh farming in other places, notwithstanding). Indeed, from roughly 1913 onwards, all activities to drain the Holland Marsh were more or less suspended until the conclusion of the war.

In the years immediately following the Armistice, however, public spending was emerging as a way of boosting home economies and to develop job markets for the returning veterans. Perhaps sensing opportunity (while also conceding that private investment funds were likely not forthcoming), Day and the Holland Marsh Syndicate leveraged public tools. As stipulated within the Ontario Municipal Drainage Aid Act of 1916, financing for such a project could be provided by money borrowed from the implicated municipalities, with the province providing a grant for up to 20 percent of the gross costs of the endeavour.

Day and the syndicate worked with a supportive council in West Gwillimbury and filed a petition under the Drainage Aid Act in 1924. Given the geography of the wetland – and that the Holland River is both a natural and legal border between King and West Gwillimbury – the drainage plan could not be completed unless King Township council also signed on to it. But that body was reluctant to participate, unconvinced that the project would be successful. Exercising its right under the Drainage Aid Act, King Township filed an appeal to the petition with the drainage referee. Its primary argument in the appeal filling was "that the scheme of the drainage work as it affects the Township of King, should be abandoned as same will not be successful."[77]

Drainage law in Ontario has a complicated, almost two-hundred-year history.[78] It began with the 1835 Act to Regulate Line Fences and Watercourses, which, for the first time, codified in legislation an authorization process for manipulating the flow of water through farming landscapes. The 1835 law also enshrined a funding principle establishing that the cost of drainage construction would be shared among the individuals and bodies concerned in proportion to their interests. Given that more of the land proposed to be drained from the Holland Marsh was on the King side of the river than on the West Gwillimbury side, King Council would be responsible for more of the cost. The Drainage Act also enabled the appointment of a drainage referee, whose role it is to interpret the legislation, hear submissions and appeals, and generally sort out the inevitable and frequent concerns over the burden to pay construction costs.

Ultimately, King Township's appeal was denied, and the Holland Marsh drainage petition was approved. The drainage referee at the time was K.C. Henderson (whose long tenure ran from 1906 to 1934). Henderson was an experienced drainage lawyer from Ottawa who had little time for those seeking to use appeals to block the progress constituted by drainage projects. His cavalier attitude toward drainage roughly matched that of the Kalamazoo Celery Company. At the 1915 annual meeting of the Association of Ontario Land Surveyors, Henderson, a regular attendee, reportedly gave a memorable speech, at one point opining, "Of course the danger, as we know, is mainly in the Court of Appeal, because I have never hesitated to say this from the bench and I say it now, that I try to work the Drainage Act out in such a way as to dig drains and not print appeal books."[79]

In hindsight, given Henderson's perspectives on drainage projects as well as those of the state, King Township's appeal had virtually no chance of resulting in a cessation of the project. Yet it is notable that in his ruling, Henderson emphasized – twice – that while he ultimately dismissed the appeal, he empathized with the filling of it. "This is one of those peculiar cases where I do not at all criticize the section of the township council in bringing this matter before the court."[80] Even with nearly two decades of experience at this point in his career, he recognized the near-singular ambition of the Holland Marsh project. "This is not an ordinary drainage scheme. . . . I have seen several cases where streams have been dammed, although I must frankly say I have had none where as large a portion of [a] stream has been dammed as this."[81]

Once forwarded on to the provincial government, approval was largely a regulatory formality.[82] That the Holland Marsh Syndicate secured additional funding for the drainage project through the Drainage Aid Act underscores the liberal-state imperatives of instrumental land use and improvement. The cost for the project would be shared by each municipality in proportion to the amount of drained land each would have in its jurisdiction. The reluctant King Township would be on the hook for the greatest part, totaling $76,663.80; West Gwillimbury's bill would be $52,281.00; and the village of Bradford would owe $1,825.20. Culture's marsh, already present in the imaginations of Day, Baird, and the other Marsh boosters, was about to become a material reality.

Conclusion

While the instrumental pursuit of profit played a part in driving the imposition of agriculture, as conventional political economists would point out, there were other, equally important dynamics propelling the process. The liberal desires to tame the landscape, to advance the colonial project through cataloguing the territory, and to improve the land through cultivation were each crucial to the development of agriculture in the Holland Marsh. The culture of "aquaterracide," backed by a range of scientific and policy interventions, was part of a broader thrust of "taming nature," a social ideology being "set down on the land," as Ian McKay puts it, and in this respect part of normalizing nation building through landscape change.

Notwithstanding the bootleggers and marsh-grass harvesters, up until 1925, human-driven physical changes in the Holland Marsh landscape had not been systematic: That is, there had been no widespread agricultural-related changes there. Yet the production of nature in the Marsh required a good deal of discursive and material work well before a single crop was ever grown. The land became subject to different ownership and regulatory regimes; it was bought, sold, and traded for; and it was projected on by a generation of eager farmers – again, all before a single seed had been sown.

Yet while the Holland Marsh boosters had, to some extent, mastered the imaginary of nature through excited news headlines and tales of abundant yields in Michigan and Ohio, they had yet to confront the messy materiality of the landscape. As the dredging machine was about to make its first cut of the twenty-seven-kilometre canal that would eventually encircle the Marsh, one can imagine that the mood among the boosters and onlookers was generally optimistic. Their mastery over nature was about to be realized, as the smiling farms were chopped out of the dismal swamp.

CHAPTER 2

The Production of Fields, 1925–35

Nature's form (the geological history and marshy materiality of the wetland) and imaginary (created through the general dismal-swamp, smiling-farms rhetoric) contributed to producing the land, laying the groundwork for the future development of agriculture in the Holland Marsh. The state encouraged the drainage through enabling legislation, the support of pro-improvement bureaucrats, and capital in the form of funds to pay for the project. For their part, Marsh boosters and a supportive media deployed a range of imaginaries heralding a Promethean dream of tamed landscapes, corralled water, rich muck soil, and profit. All of this, however, occurred before a single metre of the canal had been dug, before a single excavator had been started, and well before a single vegetable had been grown in the Marsh.

From 1925, when excavation of the canal finally began, into 1935, by which point regular, however unprofitable, crop production had been established, was a seminal decade for the Holland Marsh.[1] Its material landscape was thoroughly transformed from an abstract idea of reclaimed wetland into actual, farmable fields through a confluence of policy, technology, labour, and capital. This was the period during which the liberal ideals of an orderly, productive, and profitable nature – shepherded within a paradigm of private-property relations – were carved into the land, and capital began circulating through the landscape like never before.

But while the land was commoditized and taken under private ownership in ways not previously seen there, a contradictory dynamic resulted from canalizing the wetland. As the dredger cut a twenty-seven kilometre canal, ostensibly severing the Holland Marsh from its immediately adjacent landscapes, it simultaneously bound together the farmers, Bradford, West Gwillimbury, and King Township in a shared administrative geography. Though the implications may not have been fully appreciated initially, such an extensive and complex canal and hydrological system would require intensive management, persistent maintenance, and ongoing monitoring. This eventually bore novel administrative arrangements designed to facilitate nature's (re)production.

During this period in the history of the Holland Marsh, fields emerged from the wetland – created, portioned off, bought, traded for, and sold. The land of the Marsh was commodified – as fields – in ways that departed dramatically from anything that had occurred previously in the area. The discursive and material transformation of the landscape also had an attendant conceptual element. As the dredging machine cut its way through the peat and clay, and as arterial drainage ditches appeared and tile laid, fields emerged. Yet the visceral materiality of the process of making this farmland belies the attendant conceptual abstraction that was taking place. Just as the fields were emerging, the land was being thrust into abstract exchange relations, assigned (inflated) value, and propelled into a complex political economy of food and agriculture. This transformation, then, was no simple material process, rather it was a defining moment in the history of the Marsh.

At the same time, the materiality of the *process* of drainage cannot be ignored. Up until work on the canal began, draining the Holland Marsh remained purely theoretical. William Day and Alex Baird did have some experience with other drainage projects in southern Ontario and were familiar with the details of still others in northern Michigan and Ohio, yet neither had been at the helm of one so large – indeed, a drainage project the size of the Holland Marsh scheme was without precedent in Ontario. Meanwhile, the dredge workers, local residents, and would-be farmers who had all heard so much about the promise of a *drained* Marsh were confronted with the inconvenient reality of the *draining* itself, a process that ended up taking three years longer than expected. The form of biophysical nature is not always so easy to change. Throughout the transformation, the physical materiality of nature presented itself, stubbornly resisting the tidy image Marsh boosters had in mind. Heat, cold, frozen ground, broken machinery, and exhausted workers all exposed the fact that, if agriculture was to come to the Holland Marsh, it was going to take more than a few headlines about smiling farms.

The Science and Politics of Underdrainage

Controlling water, as it continues to be in the contemporary period, was a central preoccupation of agriculture in the early part of the twentieth century. Indeed, as Ross Irwin put it, "Profitable returns from farmlands depend first of all on effective drainage."[2] This was particularly true within the Great Lakes basin, with its shared geological history, but also applied to other parts of Canada.[3] The challenge of controlling water in the fields with the latest techniques and technologies seemed to be the main preoccupation of boosters at times, with crop production an ancillary benefit.[4] Within the Holland Marsh, Day was the chief prognosticator of drainage, and he brought with him the gravitas of the Physics Department at the University of Guelph and the Ontario Agricultural College (OAC).

From the mid-1920s until the postwar recovery, Ontario's economy, partly based on agriculture, struggled, as did most other agriculture-dependent economies. Day understood that large drainage projects required public investment, but he also knew that there was precious little funding to go around during the lean years of war. Yet for him, the preponderance of potential (that is, undrained) farmland in Ontario was seen as an attractive investment opportunity. Day's own estimates, in 1909, put the number of hectares of current farmland simply in need of *improved* drainage in Ontario at over 1,906,000 hectares (4,710,000 acres). He added to this another 2,023,000 hectares (5,000,000 acres) of untouched landscape comprising "slash land ... swamp, marsh and wasteland" for a total of nearly 4,050,000 hectares (10,000,000 acres) simply in need of drainage.[5] Day argued further that those 1,906,000 hectares only requiring improvement would see an average production increase of $50 per hectare, a total growth in annual yield of $94,200,000 – this before factoring in the economic stimulus of draining the untouched land or of the labour required for such an ambitious project. In the articles he published on the subject, Day does not provide much in the way of details about his assumptions and estimates. This is likely due, in part at least, to the fact that the OAC Bulletins were more a tool of popular education and communication (or perhaps popular imagination) than they were an academic forum. As a result, it is difficult to confirm the veracity of the estimates. But it is clear that invoking the potential of a $94,200,000 increase in provincial farm profit would have piqued a broad interest (and surely at least some skepticism) during a period of acute economic depression.

To facilitate realizing the promise of a thoroughly drained province, the OAC sent a small army of drainage advisers to traverse Ontario, convening with willing farmers and landowners free of charge – part of the liberal state's efforts to support agriculture and increase the total amount of land under active production. The majority of the costs involved – the advisers' salaries – were paid for by the government, with the farmer or landowner covering the other marginal costs. Day described the details of the OAC's expectations in a 1909 publication: "There is no charge for the services of our drainage advisors ... but their travelling expense, consisting of railway fare at a cent a mile each way for this work, meals on the way, if any, and cartage of instruments, if any, must be paid by the parties for whom the surveys are made."[6]

The work of the OAC under Day's direction further underscores the state's land-use preference – agriculture over almost anything. Within the context of an entrenched drainage interest, wetlands were seen as little more than inputs into the production of profitable agricultural landscapes. At the same time, however, Day's drainage work with the college was not *only* about the pursuit of profit. In addition, it afforded him the opportunity to flex his intellectual muscle – to solve problems with emerging technologies, something that surely would have appealed to the professor. Day's passion for drainage in general, and for draining the Holland Marsh in particular, was certainly fuelled by the desire to see a profit, but it was at least equally motivated by his desire to solve the landscape by managing and controlling it. A two-part Bulletin publication authored by Day in 1909 articulates the penchant he (and by extension, the OAC and Ontario) had for drainage and shows the extent to which drainage was a priority for the provincial government in particular. The first part explains the benefits of drainage and tiling, extolling the advantages of better soil, earlier seeding times, control of water through damming, and the like, while the second describes the process of building the infrastructure. Day describes the tricky process of surveying the land – an essential step in corralling it for use as farmland – while pointing out the indispensability of the college:

> When it comes to planning of a general system for 50 or 100 acres, a system composed of several miles of drains, every part of which must fit in with every other part, the grades of which must be sufficient for effectively draining all low spots, and yet not require too deep digging in knolls, the depths of which must, nevertheless, be great enough in flats to protect the tile from frost, the outlets for which must be ample and free – when it comes to the planning of such a system, many of which are imperative in almost every county if proper drainage is to be secured, few, if any, have been or are now in a position to undertake such work intelligently, and for obvious reasons: Firstly, because some knowledge of surveying and mapping is needed, and secondly because a surveyor's level is essential, neither of which the farmer has. Nor until recently has he been able to obtain assistance in the matter.[7]

Although somewhat condescending in tone, Day is right in his assumption that very few farmers would have had any formal training in conducting land surveys and likely would not have had the resources to purchase surveying equipment – thus the need for provincial support to train a generation of farmers to transform wasted wetlands into productive fields. Even if some immigrant farmers brought with them specific skills, expertise, or knowledge about drainage from their home countries, Day and the OAC would likely have not been interested, preferring instead to institute a routinized, scientific set of protocols. These newcomers were conscripted into the mammoth project of laying a meshwork of drainage tile clear across the province, one field at a time, and were expected to heed the direction of authorities like Day. Elaborating the strategy in part, he continues:

> In the autumn of 1905, however, the department of Physics, which had for some years been teaching the subject of drainage, was authorized to go out through the Province, when farmers applied for assistance, and make a general survey of the land, locate the outlets and the drains, determine the grades and size of tile, and finally send the farmer when ready a map of his farm showing the complete system of drains, the grades, the sizes of tiles, etc. It is the writer's intention to give here a brief description of the method of surveying the land and laying out the system, and a detailed description and interpretation of a map, not in the hope of enabling farmers to undertake these general surveys, for we know the work is too involved and the instruments needed too delicate and expensive for that, but in order that when we have made a survey for a man and sent him his map, a copy of this bulletin will enable him the better to understand the map and construct his drains according to it.[8]

The OAC's extension work, led by key prognosticators like Day, can be seen as a device by which the state promoted and reinforced privileged ways of living in and interacting with particular landscapes. Providing farmers with maps of their land – lain over with technical measurements and drainage infrastructure – was also a way of cultivating a particular legibility. Farmers, the implication was, needed to see their fields not for what they were, but for what they might become if properly drained. There is a clear instrumentality in the perspective of the early Holland Marsh boosters, backed by the Ontario government, which positions the landscape as useful only in as much it is acceptably ordered, controlled, and profitable. Certainly, the Marsh had use value to many people previous to the introduction of agriculture – Indigenous populations, bootleggers, and draft-dodgers-cum-naturalists made use of the area previous to its transformation. By the early part of the twentieth century, the promoted use, in keeping with the agriculture-driven economic-development policies of Canadian settler-state politics, was to transform the wetland into fields. Various appendages of the state apparatus – including the Drainage Aid Act, the OAC, and its bulletins – built up a cultural, discursive, and legal scaffold to support the material transformation of wetland landscapes and the production of nature in the Holland Marsh.

In this respect, the efforts of Day, the OAC extension program, and the provincial government to cultivate a prodrainage milieu cannot be ignored. Appeals to science and technology, emphasizing the technical difficulty of the work, were ways of imbuing this perspective with authority. Underdrainage within this context was not simply about turning swampland into fields, but rather it reflected a higher purpose animated by the mobilization of cutting-edge science, technology, and techniques. Unprecedented in ambition and scope within 1920s Ontario, drainage of the Holland Marsh clearly fits within the sentiment of the day while extending and amplifying that logic. To onlookers, the Marsh project was an exemplar of the prodrainage perspective, a showy project backed by academic experts, the OAC, and the provincial government. The scientific dazzle captured the imagination of local residents and the media in a profound collision of culture and science. As the *Globe* reverentially reported in the autumn of 1926, the drainage of the Marsh was the showcasing of scientific advancement – a shared cultural moment and the expression of a dream:

> Seeing this great change, those watching this great reclamation project begin to understand in a concrete way that it is not an experiment, that the dream of a generation of advanced agriculturalists is about to be realized and the Holland Marsh will be converted into a garden that will blossom as the rose and support a thousand families of workers growing fresh vegetables for Toronto and other cities of the dominion.[9]

Dredging began on September 25, 1925, following the design set out in Baird's engineer's report. The plan was an audacious one – to cut a twenty-seven-kilometre-long ditch, up to twenty metres wide and two metres deep, around the Holland River Marsh; dam the northern end of the Holland River near Yonge Street; and install two pumps nearby capable of moving over seventy-five thousand litres of water each per minute.

Dredging the canal was as much a public spectacle as it was an engineering construction project. When the scow – a large platform built in the Marsh on which the dredger would float – was complete, it was celebrated with a community dance. "A very large crowd attended the dance on the new scow on Saturday night. Mr WG McLellan was the floor manager, with the Schomberg Orchestra, led by Bill George, playing for them."[10]

On the first day of dredging, "The crowd on the riverbank raised a cheer as the dredge nosed into the bank and lifted the first buckets of muck, soil and water;

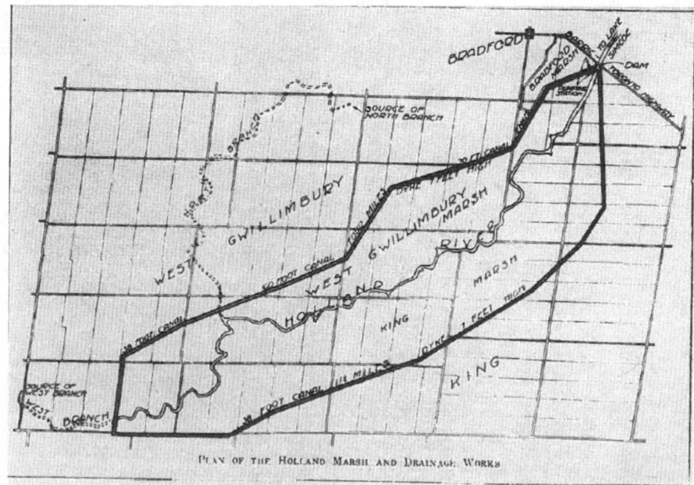

FIGURE 2.1. Drainage plan from 1924. An earlier version of this map was included in Baird's original drainage proposal in 1911. Courtesy of Archives of Ontario, ARDA – Holland Marsh, B388426.

the first cuts in carving out the 27-kilometre canal around the perimeter of the Holland Marsh."[11] This machine was brought to the Bradford area by rail in four pieces and assembled onsite. It was almost twenty-five metres long and nine metres wide, with a twenty-metre boom. There was a shorter eleven-metre "dipper stick" mounted to the main boom, on which a large shovelling device, capable of excavating about one-and-a-half cubic metres of material at a time, was mounted. The dipper stick swung on the boom through a system of cables and pulleys, propelled by a steam-powered engine. As the dredger worked, it would cut through the plant material and moss to a layer of clay below. This material was pulled up and deposited on the outside of the canal to create an embankment as the work proceeded.[12]

The dredger itself, which required five people to operate, was more or less amphibious. It was designed to be able not only to drag itself through the hybrid landscape with its boom arm but also to float in the canal as it was dug. The engines were powered by coal, wood, or a combination thereof. Two houseboats followed the dredger: One provided sleeping and eating accommodations for the crew, while the other carried fuel. Two much-smaller dredgers were simultaneously in operation, one digging the "Little Scheme," the other working on the eastern part of the main canal. The main dredger would typically work twenty-four hours a day, from the time the marsh had thawed in the spring until it had frozen in the winter.

FIGURE 2.2. People on the dredger. Front row (left to right), Margaret Campbell, Margaret MacDonald Saint, and Katherine Wilma Saint. Back row (left to right), Gordon Davey and Bill Davey. Courtesy of Bradford West Gwillimbury Public Library, Joe Saint Fonds.

The work to build the main canal lasted from the fall of 1925 until the spring of 1929 – roughly three years longer than originally intended. Cold, long winters; regular and unexpected maintenance of the dredger; layovers in quicksand; crew exhaustion; and tight finances all served to delay the project. Nevertheless, by 1930, when the initial canalization was complete, Day had become emboldened by the relative success of the scheme:

> At every stage of this project from its inception to the present time there has always been some wise one to rise in his wisdom and solemnly warn us "it can't be done." But all difficulties to date have been safely negotiated ... It appears, therefore, that the Holland marsh reclamation is one of the biggest events that have happened in Ontario in recent years.[13]

Eager to show off the new land, Day planted a thirty-seven-acre (fifteen hectare) test plot that year, from which he grossed twenty-six thousand dollars. He boasted that wholesalers in Toronto had never seen Canadian-grown head lettuce throughout the entire growing season until he provided them with it from July through October. And, according to Day, this was no fluke. The modern fields he had created were disentangled from the perennial concerns of weather, able to respond equally well in wet and dry seasons: "Our pumps protect us in wet seasons. But now, besides having pumps for the wet ones, we have irrigation for the dry ones, hence we fear neither wet or dry."[14] For him, the test plot was proof of concept that the emergent technologized landscape of the Holland Marsh had transcended the material constraints of farming elsewhere. Even seasonality could be transcended with adequate planning and investment in technology: "We'll have diversified crops, and canning and soup factories and then see how easy it is. In the summer, we'll sell everything we can and what we can't we'll can, and then in the winter we'll sell all we can, and by spring be ready to start all over again."[15]

As the *Globe* pointed out, Day was a convincing visionary sort. If a wetland could be transformed into such prodigiously profitable farmland, nothing seemed impossible: "A few years ago this portion of the Bradford district was not even thought of agriculturally, but a few facts submitted by Professor Day tend to disillusion even the most skeptical."[16]

At the heart of this transformation was the soil – virginal muck soil, millennia in the making, and exposed for the very first time. The muck took on an almost magical quality, and indeed Day opined in one public presentation that wheat farmers in the highlands (the areas directly adjacent to and surrounding the Holland Marsh) would have to raise a preposterous one thousand bushels of wheat per acre (about 67,000 kilograms per hectare) to equal the revenue enabled by the muck soil.[17] This was not a simple financial appeal: Day, having been embedded in agriculture for as long as he had been, would have known that even one hundred bushels per acre (roughly 6,700 kilograms per hectare) would have been a stretch for the vast majority of wheat farmers anywhere. Instead, his exaggerated claim is a reflection of the mysticism attached to the muck soil, something he certainly worked to cultivate through salesmanship.

Similarly, the amount of time and effort it had taken to drain the Holland Marsh added to the almost supernatural character of the muck soil. While lesser dirt could be had by simply removing a few shrubs, muck soil required the painstaking work of dozens of men and women over many years, highly advanced machinery, and significant public investment. For almost five years, a rapt public watched workers, dredgers, engineers, and scientists plod away on the drainage project. Readers of the the *Globe* were assured that "samples of the soil in the swamp [were] taken and sent to Ottawa for analysis," where tests confirmed that "the soil is of the very highest quality."[18] The Homemaker, a weekly women's column in the *Globe,* gushed over "the level verdure of the Holland Marsh."[19]

FIGURE 2.3. A: The dredging machine. B: Men stand in front of a tile machine with a row of tile. C and D: The drained marshland is broken. From Bradford West Gwillimbury Local History Association, *Governor Simcoe Slept Here* (2006), and courtesy of Bradford West Gwillimbury Public Library.

By the early 1930s, headlines in both the *Globe* and the *Toronto Daily Star* raved about Day's test-plot harvest.[20] In 1933, an editorialist waxed about the "'black muck' soil, enriched by yearly decay of lush vegetation," assuring readers that when it was under full cultivation, "the Holland Marsh, so long a desolate waste, will be the scene of intensive cultivation on a scale hitherto unknown in Canada."[21] So central was the yield of the drainage – the muck soil – to the identity of the area that farmers in the Marsh would come to be known colloquially (and somewhat disparagingly at times) as "Marsh Muckers."[22] By the early 1930s, the Marsh was well on its way to becoming as famous as Celeryville or Kalamazoo – Canada's own salad bowl. And similar to those places, the muck soil was the featured star.

Socionatural Soil: Pedology and the Anatomy of Muck Soil

All the years of work, planning, public and private investments to carve the canal through the Holland River lowlands were all done for one reason – to access the muck soil. The near-legendary status of such earth throughout the Great Lakes basin had engrossed Day and others in the Bradford area for decades. And for decades, it had lain tantalizingly close, yet frustratingly so far away, covered by millions of litres of swampy water. And while the ultimate intention was to grow vegetables, controlling the water to expose the muck soil was a massive victory on its own.

This is all to suggest that the muck soil in the Holland Marsh has both a social and natural basis – a product of popular imaginary and human intervention as much as the biochemical and biophysical properties of a millennia's worth of rotting vegetation. The dynamics that created (and subsequently continually re-create) the muck soil are essential to the making of food, farmland, culture, and farmland protection in the Marsh.

Soil of any type is a very complicated thing. Its basic unit is known as a "pedon," defined as "the smallest, three-dimensional body at the surface of the earth that is considered to be a soil. Its lateral dimensions are 1–3.5 mm and its depth is 1–2 mm."[23] Pedons accumulate into dozens of different kinds of soils, defined through a complicated taxonomic system consisting of orders, great groups, subgroups, families, and series. This taxonomy has developed iteratively over the course of roughly one hundred years in Canada through the work of regional soil surveys.[24]

The earliest versions of soil surveys were largely an exercise in Newtonian inventory science, mostly tailored to the burgeoning Canadian resource economy.

Pedology (the study of soil) grew rapidly in the early 1900s in Canada, and by the mid-1930s, most provinces had some modest survey infrastructure in place. Typically, university departments of agriculture, soil, or chemistry work with provincial and federal departments of agriculture to conduct soil surveys on areas of commercial interest. Given the economic importance of soil to the regional agricultural-dependent economies of Ontario, Saskatchewan, and Alberta, it is not surprising that these areas were the most heavily surveyed in Canada by the mid-1930s.

Yet soil surveying remained largely fragmented across the country until a shared technical language emerged through the National Soil Survey Committee of Canada, formed in 1940. The Soils Section of the aptly named Canadian Society of Technical Agriculturalists held the original organizing meeting. Later changed to the Canada Soil Survey Committee, and currently known as the Canadian Soil Information Service (CanSIS), the variously named body has always been housed within the federal department responsible for agriculture (a title that also changes periodically). In addition to establishing and enforcing a shared technical language and taxonomy of soil for all provincial and territorial counterparts, the early version of the national organization also provided standardized definitions for key terms and the taxonomic structure, lending an air of authority to the burgeoning science of soil. In its modern form, CanSIS acts as an authority and clearinghouse for information on soil designations while also functioning as a "coordinating body among the soil survey organizations in Canada supported by the Canada Department of Agriculture, provincial departments of agriculture, and departments of soil science at universities."[25]

The rise of pedology in Canada and the attendant emphasis on soil classification in the early to middle 1930s is crucial to understanding how the muck soil was understood by the earliest Holland Marsh farmers and how this has continued. As John R. McNeill and Verena Winiwarter point out, soil's history has too often been ignored in accounts of agricultural and economic history. As remedy to this oversight, they argue that soils need to be understood as "entities with histories" that are both affected, and in turn affect the so-called human world. They argue further: "What people believe about soils influences (although it does not necessarily determine) what they do with them, whether they conserve and nurture them, whether they abuse and abandon them. What people understand – and misunderstand – about soils is thus a necessary part of any history of the nexus between soil and society."[26]

For Day and the original Holland Marsh boosters, there seemed to be a central misunderstanding, willful or otherwise, about a fundamental characteristic of the soil. The organic order of soil – which includes the Marsh's muck soil – is defined by the Soil Classification Working Group as being composed of 30 percent "organic" material (as distinct from clay, rock particles, crushed minerals, and so forth) per volume. These organics making up the soil are always at different stages of decomposition: For example, leaves worked into a garden in the fall will, by midsummer the following year, likely be fully decomposed and unrecognizable as leaves. Similarly, bogs, swamps, wetlands, fenlands, and the like all have organic materials at different stages of decomposition, ranging from a fibrous, peaty texture through to a fully decomposed silt-like material.[27] This makes for a dynamic situation because the humification (the degree to which an organic is decomposed) of the plant material is constantly changing, a complex process sensitive to oxygen levels, temperature, soil microbes, and the like.

The earliest Holland Marsh farmers and boosters either did not understood this complex dynamic of the muck soil or were not particularly concerned with such details. The central contradiction of the organic order of soil, when brought into the context of capitalist agriculture, is that the moment the water that created it is removed, the muck becomes far more unstable and ultimately will vanish completely. This is an illustration par excellence of a key contradiction of capitalist agriculture – elements essential to production are destroyed through the process of production.

Swamp and marsh water are hypoxic, or low-oxygen, ecologies due to the fact that they contain so much dead organic material. As plants grow, mature, and die off, they fall into the water that supports them, creating layer on layer of dead material. Since the process of decomposition is significantly inhibited by the absence of oxygen and marsh water is hypoxic, this material decomposes at an extremely slow rate. This also means that the peat/muck mix accumulates at a very slow pace. According to a report jointly published by the Ontario Ministry of Agriculture, Food and Rural Affairs, and the Muck Crops Research Station, it takes roughly five hundred years of plants growing, dying off, and slowly decomposing to result in just thirty centimetres of muck soil.[28] In other words, muck soil is not a renewable resource on a commercial, capitalist time scale.

The relatively stable dead material, once uncovered, becomes very unstable and oxidizes, thus decomposing, at a rapid rate – the technical term for this process is "subsidence." According to the same report, this constitutes a "major chronic problem" of organic soils (within the context of capitalist agriculture, though not stated as such).[29] Cameran Mirza and Ross W. Irwin conducted what appears to be the earliest study to measure the rate of subsidence in the Holland Marsh.[30] They found that the organic soil subsides at a rate of about thirty centimetres (one foot) every ten years, constituting a "substantial and serious loss."[31] Thirty-five years later, Mary Ruth McDonald and Jim Chaput repeated Mirza and Irwin's 1963 calculation and arrived at a similar conclusion, the "muck soil, *intensively cropped*, subsides at a rate of 30 cm of soil every 10 years."[32] They continue:

> This process can be slowed by the application of copper, a well-designed water-control program, a wind abatement and cover crop program and minimum cultivation. These steps are essential for long-term continued use of organic soils for agriculture. With good water table control and soil management practices, the rate of subsidence can be reduced to 4.7 cm every 10 years.[33]

When optimal subsidence-mitigating conditions are implemented, according to McDonald and Chaput, just under five centimetres of soil will be lost every decade. To put this in different terms, thirty centimetres of soil (which, as pointed out above, would take roughly five hundred years to form) could vanish in sixty years *under optimal conditions*. In the worst-case scenario, that same thirty centimetres of soil would decompose and erode away in as few as ten years if Mirza and Irwin's original 1963 calculation holds true.

The issue of subsidence, however, seemingly was not identified by the early Marsh boosters as much of a concern. Day did invoke "settling" of the soil in a 1927 article in the *Canadian Engineer*, but he refracts the inconvenient reality of subsidence through his optimistic salesmanship, suggesting that that the settled soil is all the better for irrigation.

> All round the area the water in the canals is on the same level as Lake Simcoe. Once the muck is drained, it settles a great deal, so that the land surface, originally nearly on a level with the lake surface will in a few years be from 1 to 2ft below it. Consequently, in dry seasons the water from the canal may be led by pipes to irrigate the reclaimed land.[34]

It is not until Mirza and Irwin's 1963 study that subsidence seems to be identified as a significant problem, and not until the 1970s did any concern over it begin to get traction.[35] In the decades that followed, a number of subsidence-mitigation measures were implemented, from a more careful monitoring of water levels (to ensure the soil stays relatively moist and does not dry out and blow away) to the application of copper (to reduce the soil enzymes responsible for converting organic carbon to carbon dioxide, thus slowing the oxidization process).[36] But, of course, there is no intervention, or combination of interventions, that will entirely halt subsidence. Farmers in the Holland Marsh now understand that this process is happening and do what they can to mitigate it, but they are generally resigned to the fact that there is nothing that can stop it. In some areas on the edge of the Marsh in 2020, the muck soil is already completely gone. Farmers in these areas have either transitioned to other crops, built greenhouses, or have simply abandoned the land, at least for now.

In any case, employing mitigation techniques to slow soil subsidence does not fit within the logic of industrial, commercialized, intensive farming. The political economy of capitalist agriculture demands a formula of minimizing input costs and maximizing profit. It is a prescription that does not permit for long-term ecological planning, but rather demands immediate-term pursuit of profits. There is a fundamental disconnect between the time horizons of muck soil and capitalist agricultural production. Within the context of scrambling to secure an income for another year, farmers are largely unable to take on the task of mitigating subsidence to any great extent. The fact that agriculture within the Holland Marsh is conducted so intensively (with farmers tending to relatively small concerns, ranging from roughly twenty to one hundred hectares) means that they cannot afford to let land lay fallow as often as conservationists might recommend. The contradictions of muck-crop farming, touched off as the water drained from the land and perhaps underappreciated at the time, shaped and will continue to shape the future of farming and land use in the Holland Marsh for decades to come.

The Socionatural Contradictions of Canals and Dykes

As the dredger slashed its way through the perimeter of the Holland Marsh, it was exposing yet another set of contradictions. The emerging canal became the delineation for a novel administrative geography composed of farmers and the three adjacent governments of Bradford, West Gwillimbury, and King. At the same time, the canal itself became a novel socionatural feature that required intensive monitoring and maintenance. Also in the wake of the dredger were the contradictions of nature's production. All of these have rippled across the landscape, and beyond it, for the past ninety years.

Before the drainage project was complete, landowners recognized their emerging shared fate and formed the Marsh Landowners Association in early 1929, appointing Day as its president. They were initially displeased with the pace of development and sought to develop a collective platform through which to articulate their claims within the complex administrative context.

One of their first orders of business was to agitate for a commission with powers to manage the vast, emerging drainage infrastructure. They wanted to focus on breaking the new land, digging miles of ditches to further facilitate drainage, and generally get on with the work of farming. While the canal did facilitate a certain amount of draining, a complicated network of ditches and drainage tiling was needed as well. Landowners had to carve up their newly formed fields with ditches running either inward toward the Holland River, away from the river toward the canal, or both. These ditches facilitated further drainage and control over water in the fields. Whereas digging the canal was largely a public infrastructure project, in as much as Simcoe County, King Township, and Bradford each paid for it in proportion to the amount of drained land in their respective jurisdiction, fine-tuning the drainage with ditches and tiling was the responsibility of individual landowners. As a result, this interior network emerged slowly and unequally, with some land not being ready for crops until well after the end of the Second World War.

In the meantime, however, the Drainage Aid Act furnished provisions to establish a commission to manage such projects. At the urging of Day and the Marsh Landowners Association, the Holland Marsh Drainage Commission was established in 1930.[37] The commission's membership comprised the reeves of the three jurisdictions within which the Marsh lay – the village of Bradford and the townships of West Gwillimbury and King. Its name and composition has changed over the decades, but the commission's function as an administrative and political vehicle to manage matters in the Marsh has remained largely consistent. This has, at times, been an uneasy partnership, and most recently there have been calls by those on the Bradford West Gwillimbury side to have the legal boundary redrawn such that the entire Marsh falls under its administrative jurisdiction.[38] Not surprisingly, politicians in King Township do not agree.[39]

From as early as 1933, even before the entire area was under production, the commission was concerned with the state of the canals and their associated banks and dykes, which in some cases doubled as roads. The banks – mounded muck soil dumped beside the canal as the dredger did its work – were settling, subsiding, and being pounded down by increased traffic, ultimately becoming unsafe for travel and at risk of failing.[40] By the 1940s, the canals and river were filling with silt, washing away the precious muck soil and compounding the problem by filling the watercourses back in. This made the area more susceptible to flooding and increased wear and tear on the pumping infrastructure. This issue persisted into the 1950s as yet others were introduced, namely, the building of Highway 400, which essentially served as a large dyke and severed the Holland Marsh east to west into two parts, each of which required additional pumping infrastructure. In the 1960s, drag lines were used to clean the main drain (the erstwhile Holland River) at a cost of nearly sixty-thousand dollars annually.[41] By the 1960s, the river and canals were also being overrun with plant growth, fed by the fertilizer runoff from the fields. In the late 1970s and early 1980s, two barges were purpose built, one for each side of Highway 400, to remove weeds from the main drain. On top of all this, there remained continual maintenance to the pumps, pipes, tiles, roads, and bridges.

The administrative burden of managing the persistent maintenance work and finding the necessary budget falls to the commission, now known as the Holland Marsh Drainage System Joint Municipal Service Board. Working in coordination with the drainage superintendent, the board sets the annual levy assessed to farmers in the Marsh and coordinates budgetary priorities with the governments of Bradford West Gwillimbury and King Township. Fiduciary pressures, in part a result of the complex administrative arrangement, effectively means that the commission (or board) has operated on a shoestring budget since its inception ninety years ago. While the work of managing the complex drainage system is essential, no one wants to pay for it.

The maintenance crisis came to a head in the 1990s. While upkeep of the canals, main drain, dykes, and pumps has been ongoing since the original drainage of the Holland Marsh in the late 1920s, with the exception of more substantive work done immediately after Hurricane Hazel in 1954, it was never more than the minimum necessary for continued operation. By the 1990s, up to 65 percent of the south canal was full of sediment, including portions that were virtually fully filled in, to the extent that surveyors could walk across the south canal without getting wet. Additionally, lower water levels in the canals resulted in higher water temperatures. When combined with the high level of runoff nutrients available, this created ideal conditions for weed growth, which exacerbated the problem, further restricted water flow, and increased the risk of flooding.[42] Significant – and costly – repair work was needed immediately.

Initially, King Township balked at this project. The drainage superintendent at the time, Art Janse – in the position for three decades – sent a tersely worded letter to the King Council threatening to disband the commission if the township refused to support the effort. As Janse pointed out, disrepair of the drainage scheme now became a legal and insurance liability. If a flood did occur, and the commission, Bradford West Gwillimbury, or King Township were found to be negligent in their responsibilities for the drainage scheme, they could be found liable. And, indeed, there was plenty on the line. In a 1999 assessment of the Holland Marsh, its land, 501 houses, 350 barns, 125 garages, 256 greenhouses, two halls, one church, one library, three pumping stations, and one experimental station were valued at $110,000,000. This estimate did not take into account the abundant farm equipment and any crop loss that might result from a one-hundred-year storm event.[43] Janse's ultimatum was no idle threat – he, perhaps better than anyone, understood the risks of not addressing the crisis of the canals.

While these old tensions continued to broil, new ones were emerging. The administrative boundary of the Holland Marsh, always firmly established by the perimeter of the canal system, was always just that – administrative. What Day, Baird, and the original Marsh boosters neglected to recognize was that, despite fundamentally altering the hydrological system of the area, the Marsh remained firmly embedded within a larger watershed. By the mid-2000s, both in response to a need for an expanded ratepayer base to pay for the extensive required canal work and in recognition of the upstream sources of sediment clogging up the canals, the administrative boundary and watershed boundary were united.

This, of course, was a contentious process – indeed, the resulting legal case found its way to the Ontario Superior Court of Justice. At the heart of the matter was the issue of assessments. From the very beginning, the costs related to the drainage system had been shared between Bradford, West Gwillimbury, and King in proportion to the amount of reclaimed land in each jurisdiction. These costs were often passed on to the farmers in a similar fashion, with each farmer given an assessment each year for their share. By the late 1990s, Bradford West Gwillimbury was proposing that assessments be made also for landowners in East Gwillimbury, Caledon, Newmarket, and New Tecumseth – the towns within the broader watershed (King was also a respondent in the case, still reluctant to pay for the canal and dyke work). Its claim hung on Section 76 of the Drainage Act, which states:

> The council of any local municipality liable for contribution to a drainage works in connection with which conditions have changed or circumstances have arisen such as to justify a variation of the assessment for maintenance and repair of the drainage works may make an application to the Tribunal ... for permission to procure a report of an engineer to vary the assessment.[44]

The original assessment schedule from Baird's report in 1924 (updated in 1949 and again in 1990) was the one used through the early twenty-first century. In 1931, Caledon, New Tecumseth, and King paid a one-time fee of $1,200 to Bradford in acknowledgment of the 23,000 acres (9,300 hectares) in their jurisdictions that empty into the Holland Marsh Drainage System. Beyond this, however, the communities within the watershed had not contributed financially to the maintenance of the system. For Bradford, it was clear that in the intervening ninety years, "conditions had changed and circumstances had arisen." Ken Smart, an engineer with extensive experience in the Holland Marsh, noted two significant changes in the tribunal proceedings. First, he argued that, in the 1920s, most of the highland agriculture above the Marsh consisted of relatively small-scale cattle operations. By 2002, the same land was being intensively farmed with cash crops, which dramatically increased the amount of eroded soil and fertilizer runoff that ended up in the Holland Marsh canals. Second, Smart underscored that the vast (sub)urban, residential, and commercial development in the area put multiple and intensifying pfressures on the drainage system.[45] In other words, the upstream conditions – incorporating some 65,000 acres (26,000 hectares) of land – had changed fundamentally since the 1920s, contributing significantly to the deterioration of the drainage scheme.

In his ruling, drainage referee Delbert A. O'Brien noted the "rather unorthodox circumstances" of including thousands more landowners, for the first time ever, in assessments for the Holland Marsh drainage system.[46] Yet he agreed that the threshold of Section 76 had been met – conditions had changed enough and sufficient circumstances had arisen to justify a reassessment. Interestingly, he noted that the case involved a public-policy component. The Holland Marsh – as a drainage system – was of such significance that it needed to be looked at through the broader lens of public benefit and safety.

> The host Municipality [Bradford] was legally obliged to commence report to a Drainage System which is much more than a conventional drainage system and which embraces the interests of not only thousands of residents, but of Government Authorities at all levels. The public safety factors are foremost and involve potential serious flooding, a risk of highway accidents resulting from faulty barriers on the dyke roads, as well as inadequate bridge structures. Progress is stalled until the assessment puzzle is resolved.[47]

In the end, O'Brien ruled that 75 percent of the total cost of developing a comprehensive reassessment – some $1.1 million – would be paid for by Bradford and the residents within the interior of the canal system. The remaining 25 percent would come from the respondents in the case. This effectively increased the drainage landscape of the Holland Marsh from 7,000 acres (2,800 hectares) to 65,000 acres (26,000 hectares) and from a few hundred people to several thousand. Interestingly, the new de facto members of the Holland Marsh drainage assessment base would only be on the hook for the maintenance of the canals and dykes. The other components of the drainage system – the main drain and the pumping infrastructure – would continue to be assessed to the interior landowners only.

After a lengthy environmental assessment process, lasting from 2004 until 2008, and the preparation of a nearly seven-hundred-page engineer's report, completed in 2009, work on the Holland Marsh Drainage System Canal Improvement Project began in 2010, with completion in 2016. The plan was nearly as ambitious as the original drainage scheme and included full relocation of some sections of the canals and widening and deepening others elsewhere.[48] The total cost of the project was over $26 million, with landowners within the Marsh in Bradford and King Township on the hook for roughly 90 percent of the cost. For the first time ever, however, landowners in those districts outside of the Marsh, as well as those in Caledon, East Gwillimbury, New Tecumseth, and Newmarket, were also charged for this maintenance, expanding slightly, though importantly, the administrative geography of the Marsh.

The Syndicate Affair: Power and the Politics of Drainage

While the legal troubles of the canal and dyke system have played out over decades, another important legal issue related to the original drainage scheme emerged before all of the fields had even been broken. In the winter of 1932, Clifford Case, a Conservative member of the provincial parliament for York North (which overlapped with the King side of the Holland Marsh) accused the drainage project of being "fraudulent and iniquitous."[49] Case had essentially two main claims. The first, after an extensive investigation, was allegations that the original drainage petition prepared by the Holland Marsh Syndicate and sent to the province was filled with forged signatures of "stenographers, brothers, sisters, and farmers' sons," most of whom did not own land in the wetland and many of whom lived 125 kilometres away in Guelph (where Day had lived previously).[50] He argued that the petition had been padded with names of people who did not own land in the area as a way of skirting the residency requirement of the drainage-petition procedures. If this were true, it would have been a clear violation of the Drainage Aid Act, which requires that signatories own land in the area pursuant to the petition.

Case's second charge against the syndicate was that it had failed to pay the taxes on the drained land and schemed to have King, Bradford, and West Gwillimbury landowners (in addition to the province through the Drainage Aid Act of 1921) pay for the entire drainage through their property tax. He claimed that the syndicate was refusing to pay $30,000 in back taxes and was selling parcels of farmland without disclosing that the taxes on each were in arrears. Case had harsh words for the syndicate, claiming: "They put you [landowners, King and York townships] through the wringer . . . [T]hey hung you up on the line and they didn't even come back to see if you had dried up." In short, his complaint was that the syndicate "was in for a big real estate speculation which would net it millions of dollars."[51]

Day defended himself and his fellow members vehemently in the media, arguing that all the signatures on the drainage petition were legitimate, attached to actual local residents, and that the financial dealings of the Holland Marsh Syndicate had always been conducted in good faith. He pointed out that West Gwillimbury, as the primary signatory of the petition under the Drainage Aid Act, had breached its contract with the group by not upholding its terms stipulating that the drainage work would be completed by 1926. So, while it was true that the syndicate had not paid taxes on the land between 1926 and when the drainage was completed in 1929, Day argued that its members were not responsible for the payments because the entire drainage project had not been completed. In short, the township was not living up to its end of the bargain, and thus, Day claimed, the syndicate did not owe taxes on the land for the intervening years.

More interestingly, Day argued further that the land was valueless until drained, the syndicate having held the land in good faith throughout the period of the First World War until enough capital and labour could be marshalled for the project.[52] Its members had paid taxes on the land (even though it was undrained) up until they were obligated to (1926), at which point the municipal authority, having *not* met their own responsibility, became the taxpayer.

The situation evolved from a local matter to a provincial one when Thomas Kennedy, minister of agriculture for Ontario, got involved:

> I feel the townships should investigate. . . . I have asked King Township Council, and I shall ask the Council of West Gwillimbury Township to meet me immediately to clean up this situation in the interests of the taxpayers of the two townships. There is a petition in the hands of the Clerk of West Gwillimbury with names purporting to be signed by W. H. Day and R. L. McKinnon, by power of Attorney, when some of these people have admitted to me they do not, and never have, owned land in this area, and have never, to their knowledge, given Day permission to sign their names by power of attorney.[53]

Under pressure from the minister, the reeve of King Township, E. Milton Legge, requested an inquiry into the matter in mid-February 1932. Legge met with Attorney General W.H. Price, who requested that the councils of King and West Gwillimbury investigate under Section 257 of the Municipal Act. County Judge Charles H. Widdifield was appointed to the case after the first judge approached, J. Herbert Denton, oddly said he was too busy.

On reviewing the case, Judge Widdifield, after initially adjourning the inquiry on the grounds that the original drainage petition could not be found, released an interim report in early March 1932. He found, first of all, that there had been no wrongdoing whatsoever, writing, "If I am right in my construction of the statutes, it seems to me there is nothing left to investigate, and it will be a waste of time and money to proceed."[54] At the same time, Widdifield went on to argue that he did not actually have proper jurisdiction to make a ruling because the initial signatory of the original drainage petition had been signed by West Gwillimbury (the Simcoe County side), not by King Township. A special joint meeting of the West Gwillimbury and King Township Councils and the Holland Marsh Drainage Commission was held on March 9, 1932, to review the findings and determine if a Simcoe judge should be appointed to investigate the case.

A few days later, on March 14, and with springtime farming activity ramping up, reports stated that the inquiry was going to be dropped altogether. The special joint meeting had determined that there was not enough evidence to pursue the matter any further. As Reeve Edgar Evans of West Gwillimbury put it, "we have nothing to probe, unless we have further evidence."[55]

The details of this episode are somewhat obscured by the passage of time and the lack of documentation, so it is likely impossible to ever fully understand the veracity of Case's accusations and what the Holland Marsh Syndicate actually did. What is apparent, however, is the extent to which the state (and its appendages) had cause to put an end to any controversy as soon as possible. The drainage project, which had initially been approved as early as 1912, had already been stalled by the First World War, a lack of capital and labour, and various construction delays. Case's accusations risked furthering delaying farming in the Marsh by having the project tied up in litigation for months, possibly years. By 1932, the land was drained, though not yet all ploughed, and small test plots were already producing impressive yields. In other words, the Marsh was tantalizingly close to becoming the agricultural juggernaut Day and the other boosters had dreamed for decades it would become. At the same time, a provincial government looking to boost employment and economic activity during an era of acute economic depression had very little incentive to further delay the development of the Marsh.

This is not to suggest that the strong incentive to drain the wetland resulted in a cover-up – indeed, there may well have been nothing to cover up. Case's accusations may have been baseless. His angry reaction in the media may have simply been political grandstanding. Regardless, what is made clear through this episode is the extent to which culture and politics were enmeshed in the process of landscape change and the production of nature. The *social* perceptions of the Marsh had changed dramatically in a relatively short period of time. It had once been reviled, feared, and simply ignored as a castoff. Yet by the 1930s, public battles were being waged between high-ranking politicians and businessmen over the very same landscape. As the political and cultural context outside the Marsh shifted, the landscape within morphed as well. By the early 1920s, Canada was facing some of the highest-recorded unemployment rates in the country's history due to declines in manufacturing and an agricultural sector struggling through drought and the effects of the Great Depression. The potential of the Holland Marsh – the cultivated imaginary of smiling, profitable farms that would employ thousands of workers – stood as too alluring a prospect to local and regional government leaders to be disrupted.

Conclusion

In the decade from 1925 to 1935, the Holland Marsh was transformed materially and administratively. As the water drained from the land, new socionatural hybrids emerged, which required novel political configurations to conduct the messy work of ensuring nature's satisfactory reproduction. As the canal severed 7,000 acres (2,800 hectares) from its adjacent landscape, it simultaneously bound together Bradford, West Gwillimbury, and King. The uncooperative character of nature strained this administrative-political apparatus from the very beginning. Subsiding soil, silt, failing dykes, sagging canals, and settling roads all created tensions and tested the resolve of this uneasy partnership. Realizing the liberal-state ideal of an orderly, productive nature – at least within the Marsh – proved a messy process.

CHAPTER 3

Crops, Markets, and the Production of Stability, 1935–54

By the mid-1930s, the canal system was complete, much of the ancillary drainage infrastructure had been put into place, and regular agricultural production had arrived to the Holland Marsh. While the Marsh boosters had been busy with the production of land and fields for the previous few decades, from the mid-1930s onward, the focus shifted to the production of agricultural crops. As this occurred, a changing constellation of actors, institutions, and biophysical characteristics were folded into the production of nature in the Marsh.

The central focus of the farmers during the tumultuous two-decade period between 1935 and 1954 was to control the crops in order to produce some stability – a condition they had largely achieved by the fall of 1954. At the macrolevel, this was partly due to the consolidating US global economic hegemony – a trend in postwar capitalism that ushered in a sustained period of American geopolitical and economic dominance – and the stability it temporarily produced in world agriculture.

In the Holland Marsh, farmers attempted to extend and deepen this stability by corralling the biophysical characteristics of the crops in as profitable a way possible. They did this through three primary mechanisms: by drawing on emerging technologies; by organizing for the development of physical infrastructure, especially storage and packaging facilities and transportation networks; and by agitating for and organizing important social infrastructure. The social and physical infrastructure that emerged during this period signalled the beginning of the process of fine-tuning the landscape and farming practices to the biophysical requirements of the crops. The carrots, onions, lettuce, and celery grown in the Marsh required a different supportive infrastructure than the corn and wheat grown immediately outside the perimeter of the canal, with the landscape beginning to reflect this during the 1935–54 period. For farmers in the Marsh, the crops became a route to salvation, a way to manufacture socioeconomic stability. These socionatural interventions were co-implicated in the production of Marsh crops, which, in turn, aided in the production of temporary stability.

FIGURE 3.1. Monthly farm labourer wage in Ontario, 1920–50 (unadjusted canadian dollars).

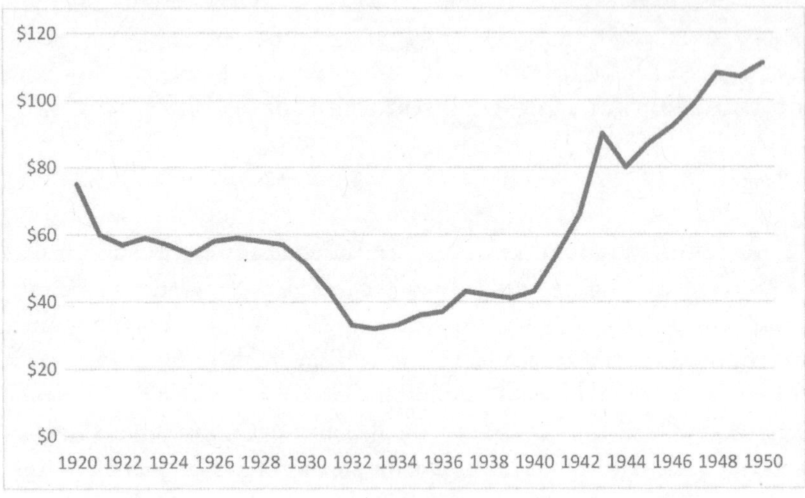

SOURCE: Statistics Canada. "Historical statistics of Canada, Section M: Agriculture. Monthly wages without board for male farm labour, Canada and by region and province, 1909–1974." 2014. Series M78-88. https://www150.statcan.gc.ca/n1/pub/11-516-x/sectionm/4057754-eng.htm.

In some ways, the emergence of regular farm production in the Holland Marsh could not have come at a worse time. In the mid-1930s, the Canadian economy was mired in a deep economic depression, the product of a complex amalgam of continental drought, labour surplus, and stock market collapse that compounded negative effects on both the supply and the demand sides of the agricultural sector.

Many agricultural workers – and labourers in other sectors – were left reeling in the face of this and struggled to find jobs. The work that was available often paid less than it once did. In California's Salinas Valley, for example, throngs of "Dust Bowl refugees" were considered lucky if they were able to keep a job at half of what they were making a decade earlier.[1] In Ontario, meanwhile, average monthly wages for farm workers fell from $75 in 1920 to a low of $32 by 1933 (see Figure 3.1). Making matters worse, scarcity kept commodity prices persistently high, meaning food was unaffordable for many. But higher commodity prices did not translate into higher profits for farmers. In Ontario, annual total net income for farms fell from roughly $133 million in 1926 to a low of $40 million in 1932 and 1933 before recovering fully, though this did not happen until 1941.[2]

FIGURE 3.2. Total net farm income (×1,000) in Ontario, 1926–50 (constant 2000 dollars).

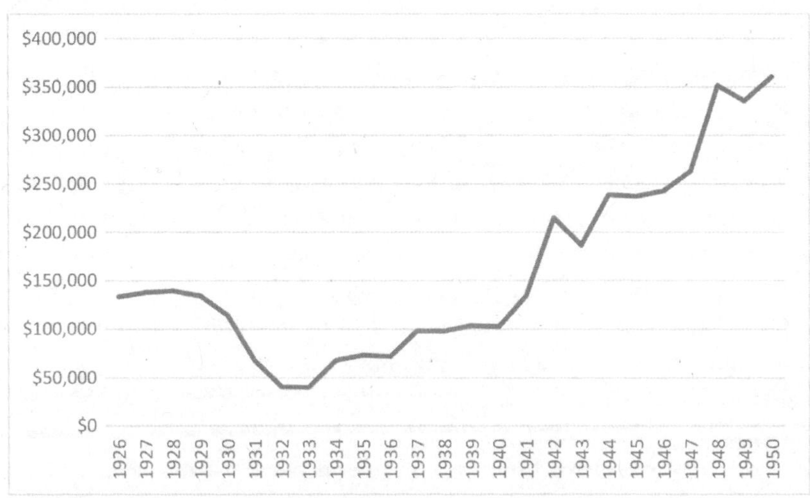

SOURCE: Statistics Canada. "Net farm income (×1,000)." Table 32-10-0052-01. https://www150.statcan.gc.ca/t1/tbl1/en/tv.action?pid=3210005201.

In contrast to this trying interwar period, the Second World War and the years beyond – roughly 1939–50s – can be considered the twentieth-century apex of Friedrich Engels's much earlier speculation that the "peasant [farmer] is a very essential factor in the population, production and political power."[3] As the rains came, wartime consumption increased demand, technology improved, and nascent welfare-state agricultural policies began to emerge, farmers' fortunes changed dramatically. They would emerge from the turbulent interwar period of global instability as a powerful political economic bloc and a key player in the consolidation of welfare-state power throughout the mid-1940s and 1950s.[4]

Perhaps sensing their growing leverage and wanting to insulate against lean years like those they had just experienced, a new agrarian politics emerged in Canada as farmers redoubled efforts to organize, network, and strategize as a distinct political bloc.[5] While Canadian farmers have a long history of progressive organizing, including deep ties with the Co-operative Commonwealth Federation, the more radical forebear of the New Democratic Party, the level and sophistication of their organizations increased dramatically during the 1940s and 1950s.[6] During this era, farmers in the Holland Marsh rallied their political and cultural clout through their crops. For example, anger over lettuce prices, which led to extreme violence in California during the late 1930s and 1940s, manifested itself more peacefully, yet still stunningly, in and around Toronto. To protest prices, Marsh farmers were known to drive truckloads of lettuce into town, set up in the parking lot of major-chain grocery store, and hand out their produce for free. This illustrates not only the activist political tenor many of them adopted throughout the 1930s and 1940s but also the extent to which the produced natures of the Marsh were at the centre of this emerging politics. The National Farm Radio Forum, the Canadian Federation of Agriculture, the Ontario Federation of Agriculture, and the passage of the Farm Marketing Act all served to strengthen the agricultural sector as it struggled to adjust to the postwar global economy.[7]

This was also a period of rapid population growth in the Holland Marsh, a process that fundamentally transformed the social and natural fabric of the area. The virginal fields of the newly drained Marsh lie in stark contrast to the desiccated fields farther west, a fact that drew domestic farmers eastward from the prairies. At the same time, many European farmers moved westward to North America in search of peace and stability after decades of war and upheaval in their home countries. For a time, this migration satiated the growing demand for stoop labour in the Marsh while also addressing the wider problem of unemployment across Canada. Indeed, programs run by the federal government furnished unemployed men with five acres (two hectares) of land and a modest shack, all at no charge. One program represented a partnership between the governments of Canada and the Netherlands, which bore the cost equally, for settling Dutch farmers in the Marsh during the immediate postwar period.[8]

Programs like these and others meant that the total land under tillage in the Holland Marsh increased from about twenty-five hectares (roughly sixty acres) in 1932 to over four hundred hectares (one thousand acres) by 1934.[9] Transplanting so many families into the Marsh meant that not everyone would be successful.[10] Yet given the hyperfertility of the newly broken soil, the rapid increase in hectares under production, and the access to underdeveloped markets, farmers were more likely to fail due to overproduction than to underproduction.

The Confounding Cornucopia

It had always been assumed that the many mouths in Toronto would consume the food produced in the Holland Marsh – indeed the city's growing population was built into the original drainage proposal as a justification for the project. Until the farmers in the Marsh had their first significant yields, however, that prospect remained largely an abstraction. Professor Day's test plots were certainly encouraging, but they did not necessarily suffice, on their own, as a proof of concept for the broader ambitions of having the Marsh become Toronto's market garden. While they demonstrated that the land could yield an abundance of carrots, onions, lettuce, and celery, this was only part of the equation.

After over a decade preparing the landscape and navigating the political and cultural apparatus required of that transformation, Holland Marsh farmers were for the first time forced to confront the biophysical nature of crops. Initially, however, they had little success in building the social infrastructure necessary to realize the profit potential of the productive windfall the muck soil represented. The bioavailability of key nutrients in the fresh muck – potassium, phosphorus, nitrogen, and others – along with a string of fair-weather growing seasons made for bumper crops throughout the 1930s.[11] But this did not translate, at least initially, into bumper profits.

Farmers lured to the Holland Marsh by tales of cheap – sometimes free – land and abundant yields had to confront the complex reality of high yields and perishability. Those from western Canada, fleeing the misery and poverty of a prolonged drought on the prairies, moved eastward and, on the whole, fared no better in the Marsh than where they had out west.[12] They would have spent years struggling to get anything to grow in the dried, desiccated fields of the prairies only to find the opposite problem in the Marsh – overproduction. As reported by the *Globe and Mail* in 1937, one such family "was driven from Western Canada by the drought only to be again faced with threatened poverty because [their] crops are too abundant."[13]

Conditions that year were so bad that an untold amount of produce was abandoned to rot in orderly rows, to be ploughed back into the fields, or to even be hauled off to garbage dumps. Selling the produce in the midst of such overproduction become almost unthinkable. The Toronto market was glutted, and there was no way to ship the produce much farther afield, given the lack of suitable technology and infrastructure. These dire circumstances drove prices through the floor and many farmers to distraction. The *Globe and Mail* reported on how absurd the situation eventually became for at least one Marsh farmer:

> He showed the reporter his little pink slip from the market. The bushel of cauliflower was dumped into the garbage when it spoiled before a buyer could be found. The turnips met the same fate. For the rest of the shipment he received \$6.70. From this amount the market deducted \$1.41 for commission and handling fees. His baskets cost him \$2.62 and the charge for hauling the vegetables to the market was \$2.66. Added together and

subtracted from the total return these figures indicated that Mr. Ferguson went into debt exactly 19 cents on his shipment of produce.[14]

The overabundance of crops was in itself only a challenge due to the particular biophysical characteristics of the crops. The true problem was one of both quantity and quality. Carrots, onions, celery, and especially lettuce all had an extremely short shelf life in the 1930s. People in the twenty-first century take for granted the genetic manipulations and storage and transportation technologies that extend the life of vegetables and hasten their delivery to modern supermarkets, but farmers in the 1930s did not have these luxuries. They had to work quickly in the fields while seeking out emerging markets and technologies to profitably corral the biophysical characteristics of their crops.

The farmers' struggles were clearly not merely a "natural" problem, one born only of the fertility of the fields and the copiousness of the crops. Instead, the institutions, rules, and practices mediating the production and exchange of produce were equally implicated. Local grocery stores and markets in Toronto – such as the Stop & Shop –invoked the farmers' hardships to convince customers to buy more: "Plan vegetable menus and lend a helping hand."[15] This, and similar ads, were on the one hand commercial appeals meant to increase the Stop & Shop's sales figures. Yet, on the other, they also revealed one of the fundamental challenges Marsh farmers faced in the middle to late 1930s. The problem was not so much an abundance of crops, per se, but rather an abundance of a particular kind. Had every farmer in the Marsh been growing a different type of vegetable, local markets would have likely been able to absorb the supply. As it stood, though, capitalist farming in the Marsh sought to exploit specific characteristics of the soil, meaning that production consisted of a highly specialized crop base entailing primarily onions, carrots, celery, and lettuce. Growing lower-value crops, such as wheat or soybeans, did not make much sense within the logic of intensive, small-plot, capitalist agriculture. Growing wheat in the muck would be seen as a waste of good soil. Aside from this, the economies of scale required for its production in the Marsh were absent – wheat farmers, even in the 1930s, required far more than the three or seven hectares most Marsh farmers had in order to turn a profit. Crop specialization in the area, at least in the 1930s, had a distorting effect and revealed a contradiction in the compulsion to grow profitable produce: The more conventional muck crops the farmers grew, the lower the prices went and the less profitable their agricultural endeavours became.

Marsh farmers could have diversified their crop base as a way of reducing the supply of carrots, onions, lettuce, and celery. Increasing the variety of items grown in the Holland Marsh while reducing the hectares dedicated to conventional muck crops would likely have meant higher prices all around. Farmers could have worked in concert to grow a variety of table vegetables, from tomatoes and asparagus to zucchini and spinach. Yet they likely would have seen this as too risky – and certainly outside the script of Celeryville and Kalamazoo. Rather than attempting to increase their profits and livelihood security by shifting away from growing a narrow group of table vegetables, Marsh farmers consolidated their focus on the conventional muck crops. From their perspective, the problem was not about too many carrots and onions, but instead a lack of demand for them. The answer seemed simple: band together, organize, and develop markets – and the necessary transportation technology – for the crops they were already growing.

Market Madness in the Holland Marsh

As the fields of the Holland Marsh continued to churn out a seemingly endless supply of fresh vegetables, the contradiction may not have been readily apparent: what was heralded as the strength of the area was also its vulnerability. The original vision Day and the other Marsh boosters had of a socionatural conveyor belt churning out fresh market vegetables – after a lengthy and turbulent start – had largely come to fruition. Yet the volume in with which the produce was emerging from the fields by the late 1930s, and the fact that it had to be sold fresh, were at odds with the social and technological infrastructure available at the time. In other words, the volume and freshness of the crops – in the absence of marketing infrastructure, refrigeration, and efficient transportation – were clear vulnerabilities. Time, then, was not on the Marsh farmers' side. Unlike producers of more storable crops (corn, wheat, and soybeans, for example), Marsh farmers had to sell their vegetables within days of harvest. Wheat producers could ration their harvests out over months in order to avoid glutting the market and thereby maintain some control over price. Marsh farmers, however, did not have this luxury in the 1930s.

Exacerbating the absence of supporting technologies to ship, store, and preserve their produce was the fact that there was very little social infrastructure for farmers to voice their displeasure or agitate for an improvement in the conditions of their livelihood. As it stood in the early 1930s, Holland Marsh growers were at the mercy of the middlemen – brokers who sold the produce to buyers in Toronto. Recall the unfortunate farmer who owed the buyer nineteen cents after shipping a load of produce to Toronto. The result was that farmers had very little control over their crops once they left the fields and thus had very little control over their incomes. They were price takers, not price makers, as the saying goes. This uneasy realization had begun to set in by the late 1930s.

Holland Marsh farmers' frustration was part of a broader discontent sweeping across the province during the era. The agricultural-extension work of the provincial government and the OAC related to issues like drainage – the very kind Day was instrumental in delivering to the Marsh – was increasingly seen by farmers to be the function of an out-of-touch, top-heavy bureaucracy. As Ruth Sandwell points out:

> By the mid-1930s, many rural dwellers across the country had largely given up what limited faith they might have possessed in provincial efforts to improve farming and farm life by providing university-educated experts to teach farmers scientific methods through farm instruction. The Great Depression had made it clear that these initiatives were largely beside the point.[16]

To the struggling Marsh farmers – many recent immigrants hardened by their experience overseas and the endemic discrimination they faced in their new country – the top-down advice from the OAC was nearly offensive. Farming techniques and drainage, vastly improved by the influx of immigrant Dutch farmers, who brought with them an abundance of marsh-farming experience from their homeland, were not the issue. These people did not need further education from a paternalistic extension program. They clearly did not need help growing vegetables, given that high yields was the central problem in the first place. Farmers were clearly tired of so-called experts telling them what the answers were. Within this context, a host of farmer-led organizations emerged, giving growers a platform from which to collectively voice their frustrations. The chorus from around the province by the mid-1930s articulated that the most pressing issues they faced were related to "marketing, distribution, farm incomes and social organization."[17]

Of course, farm organizations played a role in Ontario previous to the 1930s, but they became more active, important, and robust late in that decade and on into the 1950s. The earliest ones included the Patrons of Husbandry and the Patrons of Industry, both of which emerged in the 1880s in response to what is considered the first "cheap food policy" in Canada, initiated by the government of Sir John A. Macdonald in 1879. Further along, in 1919, the United Farmers of Ontario wielded considerable power in the operation of formal politics and are credited with playing a key role in the defeat of the Conservative government in the 1919 provincial election.[18]

While these earliest organizations did not survive into the 1930s, others emerged to take their place. Nationally, the farmers' movement of the 1930s was led by an upstart Canadian Chamber of Agriculture (forebear to the Canadian Federation of Agriculture), at times a combative organization and vociferous advocate for farmers' rights. At the provincial level, the era also saw the birth of the Ontario Federation of Agriculture (OFA) and the National Farmers Union, Ontario Branch.[19] In 1936, the founding conference of the OFA, then referred to as the Ontario Branch of the Canadian Chamber of Agriculture, brought delegates together to outline priorities for the new organization. The parent Canadian Chamber had, just two years before, established its own priorities, including uniting and coordinating the interests of farmers across the country through provincial chapters and promoting the social and economic well-being of all farmers.[20] When delegates met to establish the Ontario branch in January 1936, they ratified support for the national priorities while establishing key regional priorities of support for marketing boards and for producer and seller collectives for key crops.

In an address to the gathered delegates of the 1939 annual meeting of the OFA, President H.H. Hannam forcefully restated these priorities. In his reportedly rousing speech, Hannam openly critiqued the Canadian government for standing by while a generation of farmers was driven to poverty for lack of markets. He emphasized that a familiar culprit – low prices – had caused the trouble: "This factor, which is the most important of all, means continuing hard times for primary producers the world over . . . [T]he problem of basic commodity prices, to give the producer an adequate living, is one which the leading nations have failed to solve."[21]

A main concern for Holland Marsh farmers in this respect was the inordinate power of the commission agents to draw off their already meagre profits. While direct-to-market selling was still a common practice in the 1930s, the role of commission agents was strengthened as growers became increasingly desperate to find markets for their produce. This dynamic put farmers at the mercy of the agents, who could provide a network through which to access markets. They could facilitate the selling and distribution of produce to markets in Toronto at a time when such access was at an exceedingly high premium. Standard practice dictated that agents took in excess of 12.5 percent commission on transactions plus a set fee based on the size of shipment.

To farmers, the commission agents were selling access to markets in Toronto, a precious commodity given the extent to which supply was outstripping demand. To the grocers and market owners in the city, they were selling a predictable, reliable source of produce. And in mediating between the two, commission agents emerged as de facto graders of produce. In the 1930s, Holland Marsh vegetables were not subject to standardized grading schemes like some other commodity groups in the province, an absence forming part of the impetus behind the initial attempt to launch a growers' co-op. This position gave the agents an inordinate ability to manipulate both the farmers and the grocers. When buying from the former, the temptation for unscrupulous agents was to convince them that their produce was of a lesser grade and offer a correspondingly lower price. When selling to the grocers, they would reverse the claim and insist on the high quality of the produce and demand a higher selling price. The agent would therefore be left with their 12.5 percent commission, a set fee based on the size of the shipment, plus the difference in price between what they bought the shipment for and what they sold it for.[22] The difficulties this created for the farmers, of course, were only exacerbated by the prolific yields rolling off the fields.

Farmers were not alone in their frustration with commission agents. Federal legislation enabling the formation of marketing boards passed in 1934, though it was ruled unconstitutional by the Privy Council of the United Kingdom (still the court of final appeal at the time) in 1937, in part because it was seen to infringe on provincial jurisdiction. In order to fill the void left in the absence of federal legislation, the provincial government passed the Farm Products Control Act, 1937, which enabled the development of collective marketing boards. In theory, these boards provided new opportunities for farmers to market their produce as part of a larger collective, within which consistent grading schemes could be agreed on and routinized marketing protocols established, thereby closing off opportunities for the middlemen to manipulate prices and giving farmers more control over their carrots, onions, celery, and lettuce.

In practice, however, many farmers remained skeptical that marketing boards would bring them any benefit. The government's overture seemingly was not enough – indeed, even Deputy Minister of Agriculture J.B. Fairbairn, himself a farmer, was publicly critical of the government's inaction and began calling for the creation of a centralized food terminal. Ideally, the terminal would provide a meeting place where farmers and marketers could interact, eliminating the need for middlemen altogether. It would "permit control of supply and demand, and would yield better prices to the producers as well as bring substantial advantages to the consumers and retailers."[23] Yet despite these early calls for a food terminal by Deputy Minister Fairbairn and others, funding and materials were difficult to acquire during the war years. As a result, construction on the Ontario Food Terminal would not begin until 1952.[24]

In the absence of a central food terminal, farmers in the Holland Marsh, bolstered by the rhetoric and increased activity of the Ontario Branch of the Chamber and leveraging the new legislation, banded together to form the Holland Marsh Growers' Co-operative Exchange in 1937. The goal of the Growers' Co-operative was essentially to collectivize aspects of production, distribution, and sales. In a draft of its founding document, the group declared its intention to "co-operatively produce, grade, buy, sell, manufacture and deal in fruits and vegetables and their by-products and all other products of the farm; to buy, sell, manufacture and deal in containers, feed, fertilizer, machinery and all other farm supplies and to do all things incidental or conducive to the attainment of the aforesaid objects or any of them."[25]

Typically, marketing boards and producer co-ops comprise discrete commodity groups – for example, potatoes, hogs, or wheat. Indeed, by the late 1930s, a number of commodity-specific boards were already well established, including the Tender Fruit Producers' Marketing Plan, the Ontario Asparagus Growers' Marketing Plan, and a marketing board for cheddar cheese (later consolidated within the Ontario Milk Marketing Plan). In contrast to this, the first Holland Marsh marketing board and co-op were based on regional origin rather than a specific kind of crop. As marketing-board historian John McMurchy points out, however, the newly enabled boards and co-ops were designed to succeed through uniformity, not heterogeneity.

> Regardless of all of the other programs that marketing boards may develop, the need to enforce a common position among their own producers is paramount . . . It is normal and expected that there will always be differences in opinion between producers on various points. It is vital for marketing boards that they maintain sufficient credibility among producers to persuade those producers who do not agree with the majority's decisions to abide by such decisions nonetheless. This credibility is attained by establishing the boards as producer organizations elected by producers.[26]

Despite the promise of the enabling legislation the Farm Products Control Act ended up being of little value in the Marsh farmers' attempts to gain control of their vegetables. On the one hand, they suffered from producing a crop base that was too homogenous, too focused on carrots, onions, celery, and lettuce. There simply was not enough demand in the immediate vicinity of the Holland Marsh to absorb the abundant volume of such a relatively narrow range of produce. On the other hand, farmers suffered as a result of their crop base being too heterogeneous to be contained within a single marketing board. The biophysical distinctions of carrots, onions, celery, and lettuce, and the resulting divergences in marketability, growing imperatives, transportation requirements, storage needs, and the like, were differences not easily distilled into a common position and wrangled into one marketing board or co-op. In other words, lettuce growers in the Marsh had very little in common – as farmers – with onion growers. While a lettuce grower in the late 1930s might want to prioritize mobile refrigeration and road and rail construction, an onion grower might be more interested in stationary cold-storage technologies. The biophysical characteristics of each crop can tend to result in divergent political priorities.

Perhaps a function of the challenging times, latent intercultural tensions emerged to reveal some rather xenophobic perspectives within the Holland Marsh during this period. Notably, in 1937, existing Marsh farmers balked at the idea of bringing immigrants – specifically Dutch immigrants – into the area. In 1937, they protested to T.A. Crerar, federal minister of mines and resources, claiming that bringing more farmers into the fields would lead to more produce and further saturate an already glutted market.[27] They also claimed – as recounted in a letter from Crerar to the premier of Ontario – that they were already only getting five cents for a dozen bunches of celery and that any further downward pressure on prices would put many of them out of business.[28]

The cultural heterogeneity of the Holland Marsh was also blamed by some for the seeming inability of growers there to develop into a more formidable collective force. The reeve of King Township, complaining of the absence of cohesion within the struggling Holland Marsh Growers' Co-operative Exchange, noted, "It's hard going on the marsh, except for the Italian settlers, who ship direct to the city in their own truck and cut out the commission agent."[29] Going even further, a long-time Marsh farmer by the name of A. Nienhuis opined, "When you have Dutch, English, Germans, Italians, Ukrainians, and others, it's hard to get them together in a united front without determined leadership – and we haven't had that."[30] Making matters worse, the spiritual leader of the Marsh and an executive on the struggling Growers' Co-op, W.H. Day, died suddenly in his field in July 1938.[31]

Perhaps not surprisingly, then, the Growers' Co-op was struggling just a year after being formed. Its rules specified that the farmers who had signed on to the agreement (roughly 140 of the 160 operating in the area at that time) had to sell their produce through the exchange. But those who did not join (as well as many who did) were accused of "bootlegging" vegetables to wholesalers.[32] Meanwhile, those who did sell through the struggling co-op felt that they were not being fairly treated. According to one of them, William Valenteyn, representing a group of disgruntled farmers: "Some of us sent produce to the growers' association for which we got nothing in return. In other cases, we received not 10 per cent of the value of our crops. Some of us still have money owing from the association."[33]

While this first attempt at organizing the farmers of the Holland Marsh struggled to unite a relatively heterogeneous crop and cultural base, it also failed to address the farmers' central concern – the extent to which commission agents were able to profit at their expense. Indeed, tempers seemed to flare precisely because those agents were still largely in control of profits, despite the presence of the marketing board and the Growers' Co-op. Dennis Nolan, a Marsh farmer and ex-reeve of Bradford, was quoted as saying that the commission agents were "cutting [the farmers'] throats" and had the Marsh growers "at their mercy, and they're taking full advantage of that fact."[34]

In the end, the tumultuous first attempt to establish a marketing board for the geographic region of the Holland Marsh and to forge a unified farmers' organization fell apart about a year after it began. The official reason the Ontario Farm Products Control Board gave for revoking the first marketing board's license was that too many farmers were selling outside the Growers' Co-op's infrastructure, not only an indictment of the co-op's effectiveness but also a clear and punishable violation of the board's rules.[35] But the relative heterogeneity of the crops, the increasing desperation of the farmers, and the influence of latent cultural antagonisms certainly played a part in the dissolution of the marketing board and the Holland Marsh Growers' Co-operative Exchange. Not until seventy years later, in 2008, was there another attempt to launch a similar organization, the Holland Marsh Growers' Association (HMGA), although it is more an advocacy organization than a marketing board.[36] To date, no other marketing board exclusively based in the geography of the Marsh has been established. Nevertheless, the HMGA does provide some support to farmers and has helped develop local markets by leveraging recent popular interest in locally produced food.

Ultimately, the late 1930s represented a nadir of sorts for agriculture in the Holland Marsh. While individual farmers would struggle over the decades, never have the conditions of deprivation been as systemic and widespread as during those years. In part, this is because of the protective measures Marsh farmers were able to institute after 1940, demonstrating a point scholars have made clear: agriculture is rarely (if ever) completely capitalist – liberal-state policy modifies capitalist agriculture in ways that insulate the industry and farmers from the harshest effects of unfettered capitalism. At the same time, however, the organizations enabled through liberal-state policy and other forms of interventionist state support helped drive the continued transformation and manipulation of biophysical nature in the Holland Marsh. The kinder, gentler capitalism in the fields of the Marsh have masked, to some degree, the ecological contradictions of production, though these would surface in the decades to come.

Wartime Sacrifice, Social Supports, and Physical Infrastructure Produce Stability in the Holland Marsh

With the Second World War in full swing, a number of developments significantly affected the production of crops, farming practices, and the agricultural landscape in the Holland Marsh. First, perhaps learning from the false starts of the 1930s, growers became far more successful at organizing the social infrastructure they needed to support the development of markets and their survival as farmers. As a result, the 1940s saw the strengthening of provincial supports and the introduction of important local ones. With strengthened social networks came the ability to advocate for and organize important infrastructure projects. New transportation networks and the emergence of nascent storage and cooling technologies allowed Marsh growers to transform the freshness of their produce from a vulnerability into an important asset. Second, given the country's importance as a provider of calories during the Second World War, Canadian farmers were gaining strength as a respected and powerful cultural bloc, despite the simultaneous demise of the Co-operative Commonwealth Federation, their political protest party.[37] For farmers in the Marsh, the war provided not only hungry markets for their overabundant crops but also a chance for growers (many of them newcomers) to "prove" themselves as valuable, contributing members of Canadian civil society. Both the cultivation of credibility and the development of social and physical infrastructure during the wartime and immediate postwar years were crucial to stabilizing farming in the Holland Marsh.

Through the materiality and discourse of war, food and farmland became deeply entwined with state making through nationalism and antifascism. As consumers of food, most civilians were expected to endure shortages of staples such as oils, butter, grains, and meat while making do with what was at hand. As producers of food, farmers were expected to endure shortages of labour, materials, and machinery. From the growers' perspective, the sacrifices were significant: During the 1943 harvest, for example, Marsh farmers collectively lost an estimated $20,000 a day to rot and overripening for want of labour to harvest their crops.[38] The hundreds of students who lived in wartime work camps in the Marsh from late summer until school started in September were recalled to the fields in 1943 after classes had resumed. F.W. Davis, manager of the Ontario Farm Service Force, asked that three hundred of them be allowed to return: "It will be impossible for these crops to be harvested unless those students who have been working on farms during the summer return for another two weeks."[39]

Partly resulting from the growers' hard work and partly from the cultural, political, and material importance of food to the war effort, agriculture as a noble, even heroic, pursuit displaced far-less-flattering narratives framing rural people as inferior to their urban counterparts. The lowly "Marsh Muckers" emerged as crucial contributors to society in the eyes of the public. Wartime rhetoric became entangled with agriculture and catapulted farmers and farm workers onto the discursive front line. During the 1943 planting season, farmers "organized themselves into a sort of mobile commando unit, a sort of combined operations force, and as a field dries, no matter on whose farm, this commando unit swoops on it with tractors and horses, and gets it turned over and seeded in short order."[40] In the wartime firmament, such collective action was understood as essential, and farmers were celebrated for displaying the kind of selfless teamwork required to win the war, both at home and abroad. Popular culture and media were quick to use military rhetoric to emphasize their contributions. In 1941, newspaper ads also called on women to join the fight in the fields as a way of helping the beleaguered people of Britain: "Unless pickers are forthcoming, 8,000 bags of onions will remain unharvested. Here is an opportunity for women who have been sympathetic about Britain's onion plight to give a helping hand in Canada's program to release food for Britain."[41]

The role farmers played in providing food domestically and abroad certainly had a role to play in Canada's emergence as a middle power by the end of the conflict. At the same time, the homefront duties of war gave recent immigrants a chance to demonstrate their patriotism to their new communities while providing the state with an opportunity to conscript these new arrivals into the trappings of nationalism. The (largely) European diasporas in the Holland Marsh were celebrated for seizing on the opportunities to contribute: "Holland Marsh settlers are proving themselves second to none in Canada when it comes to patriotism, according to Victory Loan campaigns . . . Germans, Czechs, Italians, Romanians, Russians, Poles, Scandinavians and many other nationalities live in peace on the marsh and are showing their loyalty in this campaign, although incomes were poor up until this year."[42]

The emergence of the Marsh farmers (and their rural counterparts elsewhere) as respected, contributing members of society can be understood as part of a broader process of the rise of a "modern countryside."[43] The use value of farmland and the political power of its inhabitants became readily apparent particularly during the Second World War, shifting slightly the dynamic between the city and the countryside. Liberal notions of an ordered, productive, and profitable rurality, coupled with a need for calories at home and abroad, animated state-making projects, making farmland and farmers an important part of the postwar transition. After their struggles of the previous decade, the international crisis of the conflict and the national response to it helped Marsh farmers find some stability in the 1940s.

This stability was further facilitated by an emerging period of agricultural modernization during the decade, foreshadowing the emergence of the "green revolution" of the 1950s. The Canadian economy was just starting to pull out of the Great Depression, and stocks of most food commodities had been exhausted due to wartime's double pressures – on the one hand, an increase in demand to meet the soldiers' caloric needs, and on the other, a decrease in supply, at least initially, as the agricultural sector figured out how to maintain production with significantly less experienced (and even inexperienced) labour.[44] In any case, the remaining farmers and workers were expected to increase production so that the Canadian government could meet its food-export obligations while ensuring that the domestic population still had enough to eat.

Despite (or perhaps because of) farmers' struggles to launch supportive social infrastructure throughout the 1930s, the OFA transformed in the 1940s and 1950s into a permanent, robust, and integrated farm-advocacy organization. This largely progressive and successful period of the organization's history was ushered in during the spring of 1940, when members voted to allow membership to women and women's farm organizations. At the same time, there was a shift to decentralize power as the OFA sanctioned and supported the development of county-level decision-making bodies across the province. The early 1940s also saw it establish young people's committees in each county and a province-wide federation newspaper designed as a communication and learning tool. Perhaps most importantly, in 1944, the OFA was enshrined as an officially recognized association under the Agricultural Associations Act. This enabled it to obtain the power, in 1946, to collect membership fees, providing a stable funding mechanism and allowing the organization to develop its programming and advocacy work.[45]

Despite never coming to fruition, some Marsh farmers attempted to organize their own growers' union in 1948 and 1949. They expressed four familiar issues they wanted addressed by the union: fair marketing protocols to prevent the unscrupulousness of commission agents; a reduction in the price spread between what producers received and what consumers paid; a uniform inspection protocol throughout the province; and legislated floor prices for agricultural commodities.[46] Ultimately, the union failed to materialize in any meaningful sense, seemingly due to lack of support and interest. The principles motivating the organizing group, however, were carried on partially by other active farm organizations, including the OFA.

Another important development for farmers across Ontario was the launch of the National Farm Radio Forum, a joint initiative between the Canadian Broadcasting Company, the Canadian Association for Adult Education, and the Canadian Federation of Agriculture. With the motto "Read, Listen, Discuss, Act," the forum ran across Canada throughout the agricultural offseason between 1941 and 1965. It was designed to bring farmers together to collectively learn and engender social activism through the rapidly expanding new medium of radio. In addition to radio programming on various topics of concern to growers across the country, printed educational materials were mailed out to registered participants in advance of each broadcast to facilitate discussion in local groups. At its peak in 1949, the forum had over twenty-one thousand individuals registered as participants and had inspired the establishment of sixteen hundred local discussion groups.[47]

Within this emerging farmer-friendly milieu of the Second World War and immediate postwar era, momentum was clearly strong for social organizing among farm organizations, both federally and provincially. For growers in the Holland Marsh, still recovering from the collapse of their earlier efforts to establish a marketing board and co-op in the mid-1930s, there was inspiration to be had in the success of organizations beyond the canals. Beginning in the 1940s, Marsh farmers returned to social organizing, but this time around, they focused their efforts more explicitly and intentionally on the development of physical infrastructure.

By the late 1930s and early 1940s, innovations in cold-storage technologies were emerging in areas of intensive horticultural cultivation in the United States, notably California, as well as within the muck-crop areas of the Great Lakes basin such as Kalamazoo and Celeryville.[48] The introduction of reliable, affordable, and widespread cold storage had a profound effect on the production of crops in the Holland Marsh. (These socionatural dynamics are discussed in greater detail in Chapter 4.) While almost every farmer eventually would have his or her own cold-storage facility, in the early and middle 1940s, the technology was still very expensive and, as a result, largely inaccessible. The costs were prohibitive for all but the most commercially successful growers, meaning that, for the vast majority of Marsh Muckers, access to cold storage meant banding together despite crop and cultural differences.

In 1946, 158 of the roughly 500 growers in the Holland Marsh pooled financial resources to develop the Bradford Co-op Storage plant.[49] Drawing also on support from enabling federal legislation, including the Cold Storage Act and the Co-operative Marketing Loan Act, the federal and provincial governments each provided grants covering 30 percent of the cost to build the facility, leaving the farmers to cover the remaining 40 percent. A 1945 report to the York County Council unsurprisingly "pointed out that in view of the tremendous loss of vegetables through lack of proper storage, this plant would be of great value."[50] At its peak, the plant had the capacity to store up to fifty thousand crates of vegetables at a time, representing a significant capability to manipulate supply and avoid a glutted market. The Bradford Co-op also contained an ice-packing plant, which allowed farmers to ship their produce farther afield of the Marsh than previously possible. Having the capacity to put crates of vegetables on ice before shipping significantly lengthened the amount of time produce could be kept fresh and, therefore, the distance over which they could be shipped. This meant that Marsh farmers were no longer solely dependent on the Toronto market. Indeed, in 1946, lettuce from the Holland Marsh was, for the first time, consumed from Saskatoon to Halifax.[51] Another private facility, which other farmers could access for a fee, was also opened in 1946, the Holland River Gardens Company. Equipped with an icing and shipping wing, it could allegedly ice an entire railcar of produce within minutes.[52]

Other important physical infrastructure projects were started in 1946, including the construction of Highway 400. Up until then, the only road linking the Holland Marsh with Toronto (and markets beyond) was the increasingly congested Yonge Street. Contrasted with the "narrow brush mattresses of the muskeg of the marsh," the new four-lane superhighway would enable motorists "to sail across the wet flatlands at 50 miles an hour."[53]

Unfortunately for the growers of the Holland Marsh, development of the new physical infrastructure they viewed as their salvation was much slower moving than the natural cycle of the seasons and the seemingly ever-increasing yields pouring out of the fields. During the wartime and immediate postwar years, rock aggregate for concrete could not be mined fast enough to keep up with demand across the province, resulting in massive delays in various construction projects, including the completion of Highway 400, which would not open until the early 1950s. Marsh growers, meanwhile, lacked the financial resources to build as much storage as they needed, stuck in a cycle perpetuated by price: As long as wholesale prices remained so low, farmers would not have the financial resources or access to the credit required to build more storage and cooling facilities, yet they would not be able to control the wholesale price by manipulating supply until they had access to more storage and cooling facilities. The storage shortage was so acute that the Ontario government began making various publicly owned buildings available for produce storage, including several at the Canadian National Exhibition in Toronto.

Still, throughout the late 1940s and early 1950s, supply remained stubbornly prolific, largely uncontrollable, and thus mostly unprofitable. This remained particularly true of the more perishable, less storable vegetables, including lettuce. Eventually, Holland Marsh growers would cease growing lettuce almost entirely, somewhat reluctantly ceding the market to subsidized growers in Quebec. Yet during the 1940s and 1950s, the clumsy process of specialization – an incipient imperative of the mass industrialization of the agricultural sector during the era – was still playing out in the fields. Before the farmers finally gave up on growing lettuce in the Marsh, much of it was ploughed back into the fields because it was cheaper than storing and shipping it. As one reporter described it,

> According to the men who grow vegetables, selling lettuce at the price they receive from wholesalers (two cents a head) is an absolute losing proposition. In their fields they have enough lettuce to make every housewife happy, at half the current price (10 to 15 cents) – but somewhere between the time their product is dumped on the wholesaler's floor and the time it appears in a grocery store window, the price of lettuce is in line with everything else. It's high enough to keep Mrs. Toronto going all out on lettuce. Thus a surplus builds up.[54]

Despite the problematic nature of lettuce – or rather their problematic relationship with it – Marsh farmers were increasingly meeting the needs of "Mrs. Toronto" by the early 1950s. Though there was no unified organization to animate the collective concerns of all growers there, progress was still being made on developing necessary physical infrastructure – roads, storage, and icing plants. While still in embryonic form, these emerging technologies and infrastructure allowed the farmers greater control over the supply of their crops. Instead of glutting the local market with produce every fall, they were beginning to have the capacity to release it gradually, increasingly able to manipulate how long their crops would stay fresh and thus how far they could be transported. Growers were confronting and (partially) transcending the biophysical limitations of their crops, thereby expanding the scope and number of markets available to them. Marsh farmers were no longer dependent only on the local market but could reach willing buyers across the country, from "Mrs. Saskatoon" to "Mrs. Halifax."

The Holland Marsh was, if somewhat stubbornly, becoming the vision Watson and Day had foreseen – a highly specialized area of horticultural production churning out high-quality yields through the application of modern technologies. A 1949 issue of *Trade and Transportation* feted "the hardworking, industrious folk" of the Marsh with a special issue: "They are expert gardeners. They are specialists. They produce nothing but vegetables."[55] Included in the issue was a letter from then prime minister Louis St. Laurent addressed to the "people of an important Canadian industry."[56] He commended the Marsh farmers for "the manner in which they have so vigorously and successfully cultivated what was formerly a waste and apparently useless land. The extent to which they have co-operated in the application of scientific methods and in the use of modern equipment has resulted in a great benefit to the country."[57]

Conclusion

By the early 1950s, the social and physical infrastructure the Holland Marsh farmers had struggled to develop was yielding two important benefits. First, they had begun to harness the freshness of their produce as a profitable biophysical attribute. Freshness was improved to the extent that muck crops were arriving at their destinations in better shape than at any point in the history of Marsh agriculture, despite travelling greater distances. Previously a vulnerability, it was transformed into an asset to be leveraged by the farmers. Moving into the 1950s, the notion of freshness became both a material reality and a discursive strategy mobilized to develop markets, both locally and farther afield. The factors contributing to this development – social organizing and physical infrastructure – are lost within more conventional approaches to the history of agriculture. Indeed, the notion that freshness is a produced socionatural attribute is largely taken for granted. Without liberal-state interventions in the form of enabling policy and funding supports, Marsh farmers would have continued to face profound instability. Second, the earlier liability of volume was also transformed into an asset through the application of emerging technologies. Enabled by the development of improved cold-storage transportation and upgraded transportation infrastructure, the dispersal of produce over time created a kind of artificial scarcity across space. While originally bound to nearby markets (essentially the Greater Toronto Area), improvements in transportation allowed Marsh crops to be sold as novelty items in Halifax, Saskatoon, and New York. With the horizon of these new markets, Marsh produce also became a scarcer commodity in the Toronto area.

But as a result of the farmers' work to control certain biophysical characteristics of their crops, ecological contradictions of the agricultural enterprise in the Holland Marsh would soon begin to surface. This period, extending into the twenty-first century, was arguably (and tragically) ushered in by the Hurricane Hazel flood of October 1954. Lives were lost, harvests were decimated, and fields were washed away. Yet despite the torrent of news coverage and commentary on the devastation wrought by the hurricane, no one thought to point out that the so-called natural disaster was, in at least equal measure, social in character. In other words, the Marsh had ceased to become – at least discursively – a marsh. To the farmers (and their customers in Toronto and across the continent), the Marsh was emerging as a sophisticated and technological landscape of food production. As *Maclean's Magazine* put it in 1953, it had emerged as the "biggest kitchen garden in the country . . . a dreary stretch of ancient lake bed . . . [transformed into] . . . a black goldmine."[58] The busy struggling of a farm community over two decades – through social organizing and physical infrastructure projects meant to wrangle profits out of their produced natures – had effectively erased the memory of the Holland River valley, the wetlands, and the actual marsh. The first nature of the Marsh had been transformed into a socionatural agricultural landscape. Yet the contradictions on which this transformation relied would soon be revealed. The infamous 1954 hurricane underscored in dramatic fashion the folly of ignoring the contradictions of nature's production.

CHAPTER 4

Agricultural Modernization, Ecological Contradiction, and the Production of Instability, 1954–80

By the early 1950s, the vision of the original Holland Marsh boosters had seemingly come to fruition. The disparaging imagery of the "dismal swamp" had been thoroughly expunged from popular imagination, replaced by a sanitized imaginary of domesticated, albeit slightly unruly, crops. At the same time, the materiality of the landscape had similarly been tamed. The disorderly wetland had been torn apart, drained, canalized, and reassembled into orderly fields producing steady, plentiful vegetable yields. Meanwhile, hungry and profitable markets were springing up across Canada and the United States, made increasingly accessible by nascent storage and shipping technologies and providing an increase in demand for market-garden crops Marsh farmers were only too happy to meet. In short, by the 1950s, the domesticated "smiling farms" promised decades earlier had seemingly arrived.

While on the surface farming had never been better in the Holland Marsh, seeds of future challenges were being sown. From the early 1950s onward, the cultural and political clout growers had held in previous decades began to wane substantially in the context of a broader pattern of rural restructuring. Farming as something the majority of a large rural population did was about to change significantly. As the rural population declined and fewer farmers owned increasingly larger farms, a period of agricultural rationalization took hold. Following these broader national and global trends in agriculture during the era, growers in the Marsh would embrace the tenets of an aggressively productivist agriculture – the mechanized, chemical-dependent farming of the green revolution, with the promise of increased yields and the elimination of unpredictability.

The postwar agricultural system sought a "radical simplification" of farming and farmland administration in order to make it "more directly apprehended, controlled, and managed."[1] This system of "high-modernist agriculture," as some have called it, was mobilized through attempts to mechanize and standardize processes in order to produce a more uniform, predictable biophysical nature. Within this context, the trend was toward the development of more durable crops, more efficient farming practices, and flatter, more extensively drained and irrigated fields. The emergence of high-modernist agriculture would also usher in a shift in scale. While farming had been "global" in a nominal sense for centuries, the extent to which it now moved from a local to a globally integrated enterprise shifted substantially.[2]

The Holland Marsh, however, while subject to these broader trends in the political economy of agriculture, would remain somewhat insulated from them. The strengthening imperatives of global trade and multinational monopolistic chemical and seed companies would affect the Marsh, but that influence refracted through the specificity of the muck socioecology. The Atlanticist food order characterized by government support (public investment and enabling legislation) for mass production, mass consumption, and global trade of agricultural products constitutes only part of the broader historical development of the Marsh during the 1950s, 1960s, and 1970s. These grand trends in the political economy of agriculture applied unevenly in the Marsh, given the manifest difference in the crops grown there. Although carrots and onions would come to be globally traded commodities, in the immediate postwar years, muck crops were not nearly as integrated as grains and oil seeds.

As the Holland Marsh farmers adopted, translated, and adapted the emerging edicts of an increasingly productivist and globalized agriculture, they could not escape the associated ecological contradictions. The negative externalities and undervalued costs of chemical inputs and a reliance on a rapidly expanding network of markets would come to have alarming consequences on Marsh farmers and on the surrounding environment. The ecological contradictions of intensive, chemical-dependent agriculture would manifest themselves in ways specific to the Marsh, ultimately resulting in the imposition of new regulations and protective measures as an era of environmental politics emerged.

Celebrations heralding the beginning of a new era of agriculture wrested from the unpredictability and limits of biophysical nature belied the ecological contradictions just below the veneer. In 1953, the Lake Simcoe Conservation Club successfully petitioned the Ontario government to ban further development of the part of the Holland Marsh that extends north beyond Yonge Street (or Highway 11): "Any further development of the marsh as farmland will lead to the extinction of nesting and spawning grounds. The natural resources have decreased alarmingly. Further agricultural development will lead to the complete extinction of all fish and wildlife in the marsh."[3]

This kind of conservationist sentiment had surfaced around the Holland Marsh much earlier. Dr. D.A. Bentley, head of the Department of Biology at both the University of Toronto and the Royal Ontario Museum, raised some concern that the original draining of the Marsh would result in the loss of important bird habitat. In a 1926 column in the *Toronto Daily Star,* Bentley pointed out that there had been no research (nor anything included in Baird's engineer report) about the how draining the area would affect the resident wildlife. Ultimately, Bentley concluded: "I do not think, however, that there is any cause for alarm in Ontario yet.... There is still a great deal of territory where birds of these types may find a living."[4] In contrast to this fairly reserved expression of concern, a far-more-critical voice of the initial drainage plan emerged about a decade later.

Bride Broder, a columnist for the *Globe,* wrote a scathing condemnation of the draining of the Holland River valley in 1937, standing in stark contrast to the overwhelmingly prevalent sentiment of the time:

> . . . the clearance of the Holland marshes looms as one of the great and inexcusable mistakes – to call it by no harsher name – of those who have the right to say what shall, and shall not, be done with this territory or that. The drying up of the great cisterns that nature provided for the slaking of the thirst of the country around them, has been criminally wasteful so far as the present is concerned; it has been actual theft from the future. Also – and this should have been considered – good gardeners know that bog land, while it yields an almost tropical luxuriance in the first season or two . . . , having no substance, does not last.[5]

Her vivid indictment condemns the drainage project as an unmitigated environmental catastrophe, robbing future generations of the inherent benefits of the wetland. Her reaction is at least in part a result of what many others ignored (willfully or otherwise) – that muck soil degrades rapidly, becoming less productive not long after being brought into production and eventually subsiding completely.

To be sure, the ecological troubles of the kind implied by Bentley and made explicit by Brode began to surface in the early 1950s. And with the introduction of chemical-dependent farming in the Holland Marsh, "environmental" concerns moved beyond the conservationism of these critiques, becoming instead internalized matters of human health, safety, and livelihood. Yet even before these ecological externalities unaccounted for in the popular celebration of Marsh agriculture, the arrival of Hurricane Hazel served to underscore the hubris of the original boosters. This storm dramatically emphasized the point that nature could never really be conquered – certainly not as it was widely presumed to be.

Hurricane Hazel and Nature's Revenge

With crops rolling off the fields as though from a well-oiled conveyor belt, farmers in the Holland Marsh could be forgiven for forgetting about the fundamental biophysical character of the geological landscape of the pre-agricultural wetland. Indeed, by the early 1950s, the Marsh had been thoroughly separated (at least discursively) from its material referent and had emerged as the quintessential example of modernist, profitable agriculture. The fortune of the muck growers was such that, just over a year before they were in desperate need of charity as a result of their own catastrophe, Dutch farmers there were doing well enough financially to send $100,000 to aid flooded farmers in the Netherlands.[6]

The summer before the storm, Holland Marsh growers were being feted for their exemplary yields and innovative applications of technology. Farmers from across the province descended on the Marsh in the summer of 1954 for a tour hosted by the fledgling Ontario Soil and Crop Improvement Association. Participants observed a phantasmagoria of bursting fields and state-of-the-art packing facilities.[7] Poised on the "threshold of becoming the nation's salad bowl," as the *Globe and Mail* enthused just three months before the hurricane struck the area, the bounty resulting from the Marsh farmers' ostensible victory over biophysical nature was about to be shared across the country: "Man's victory over limp lettuce with construction here of the first vacuum cooling plant for leafy vegetables in Canada will soon make it possible for housewives in Vancouver and Halifax to buy lettuce as fresh and crisp as the day it left the prolific market gardens of the district."[8]

In the midst of the harvest of yet another bumper crop, the storm gathered in early October 1954, as many of hurricanes do, in the Caribbean Sea. After causing significant damage to a handful of island nations and parts of the Eastern Seaboard of the United States, Hurricane Hazel arrived in southwestern and central Ontario on October 15, 1954. Initial weather reports indicated that the storm would dissipate on arrival in the province; however, the reverse was true. The storm intensified and stalled over central Ontario for the better part of two days. Winds of up to 110 kilometres an hour were recorded in the Greater Toronto Area as Hazel dropped nearly 300 millimetres of rain.

The economic toll was immense, with some estimates putting the cost of the storm damage for Ontario at over $100 million (equivalent to $1 billion in 2020).[9] According to Ontario Ministry of Agriculture documents, Holland Marsh farmers claimed crop losses of nearly $2 million (or roughly $19 million today).[10] Hazel's human toll was even more brutal, leaving thousands of families across central Ontario homeless, and eighty-two people dead. In the Marsh, one person was killed, and the damage to the fields and farming infrastructure was nothing short of catastrophic.

Given the wetland geology of the area, much of nearly 300 millimetres of rain that fell from Hazel was simply absorbed into the peat, muck, and porous bedrock – at least initially. When the Holland Marsh became supersaturated and the broader Lake Simcoe watershed was unable to absorb any additional rainfall, water began to back up and furious flooding occurred. One long-time resident recounted how sudden the flooding was:

> I was 15 years old. I was at home with my dad, and it had rained really hard for about two and a half days. But everything was still stable at 6:30. At 6:45 the neighbour and I were out digging trenches between the houses and the water was up to our knees already. It was instantaneous. Our cellar filled with water, almost to the top step, in half an hour. Three or four young guys, one guy had a driver's license, we drove out to the road, and the water hadn't really risen that high. It had risen, but . . . [w]e watched the water rise up to the 400 [the highway]. And the cars were starting to stop. And the church. The church, Springdale, floated about a mile into the bank of the 400. . . . It raised the water level so fast that farmers had only about 10 minutes to choose between to take the tractor or the truck, which was going to be more useful. It was unbelievable.[11]

The water descended on the farmland from all directions as Lake Simcoe overflowed and backed up the Holland River toward the Marsh. The canal and its pump system were clearly outmatched, while the dykes were easily shredded by the torrent of water. A postmortem of the events found that thousands of baskets and crates of harvested vegetables acted as a kind of buckshot, propelled by the force of the water and aiding it in blasting through the dykes. Within hours, the entire Holland River lowlands had once again become a lake. As the *Toronto Daily Star* put it three days later, "Swollen and ugly the river rose, washed away banks and dykes, homes and machines, smashed the puny works of man's years of toil and created a lake, bringing the valley in full cycle back to its starting point."[12]

As weather events typically are, Hurricane Hazel was framed as a "natural" disaster. But of course the storm was only a disaster to the extent that it damaged "man's puny work" – in as much as it affected human settlement – revealing the social character of the storm. The reporting in the days following, understandably angry in tone, reproduced a discursive binary between nature and society through a demonization of the former and a lionization of the latter. The discursive and material distancing of the Holland Marsh from its natural origins – a project decades in the making – had been eliminated in just hours. Interestingly, some familiar disparaging language returned to circulation with respect to the landscape. According to one observer, from the air, the Marsh "resembled nothing so much as a huge, sluggish, mud-laden pond. . . . [T]he water lies, inert and paralyzing, over the richest farmland in Canada."[13]

The incursion by biophysical nature – especially water here – was clearly devastating to the Marsh farmers. They had spent the better part of three decades constructing a landscape specifically designed to control water. The canal system, the bridges and overpasses, the dykes, and the intricate network of drainage ditches were all victims of the flood in their eyes. As "the muddy waters spilled over the proud highway that was once the province's main road to the north," more than the fields or decades of work to physically transform the landscape were being washed away – the Promethean vision of Day and the early Marsh boosters was at risk, along with the livelihoods it had come to support.[14] As one headline put it, Hazel had turned "prosperous market gardeners [into] penniless refugees."[15]

Efforts to regain control over the profitable fields were swift and decisive. Vehicles, hay bales, and other detritus left in the wake of the storm were used to reinforce Highway 400 into a massive dyke, used to hold the water west of the highway at bay while the water east of it was pumped out toward Lake Simcoe.[16] Within days of the flood, pumps were flown in from around Canada to begin the drainage work. For nearly a month and a half, an army of machines pumped out 170,000 gallons of water per minute, twenty-four hours per day.[17] Once the fields were sufficiently drained, "operation mop up" commenced, a military-style undertaking to remove the mountains of water-logged, decaying vegetables; shattered houses and barns; and other debris. The provincial deputy minister of public works determined that this was "too onerous, odorous and unpleasant a task to be done manually," so a fleet of heavy and high-powered equipment, along with two thousand contract workers, were brought in to clear the fields.[18]

Redraining the Holland Marsh was heralded as an "engineering miracle." Although millions of bushels of onions, carrots, and potatoes were lost, the entire area was drained before the water could freeze, saving the following year's season.[19] Indeed, some farmers even managed to salvage some crops that had been

FIGURE 4.1. Water returns to the Holland Marsh. From Bradford West Gwillimbury Local History Association, *Governor Simcoe Slept Here* (2006).

put in storage before the storm hit. Decades-old concerns re-emerged, however, as biophysical nature in its pathogenic form (cholera and other water-borne disease) was feared to have returned after the flood through the waterlogged vegetables. Ultimately, after a mild public-health scare, the Ministry of Health ruled saleable "all vegetables which are normally cooked before eating, e.g., beets, potatoes, carrots," while those typically eaten raw were directed to be destroyed.[20] Both the provincial and federal governments provided rapid and abundant financial aid, temporary housing, and cleanup support. By the following spring, the vast majority of farms and farmers were prepared for the new growing season.

In the aftermath of the flood, the provincial government established the Carswell-Shaw Commission to appraise the overall damage from Hurricane Hazel and to make recommendations to avoid similar levels of devastation in the future from other (inevitable) storms and floods. The commission made a number of recommendations that demonstrated an appreciation for the socio-natural character of the disaster, including putting a moratorium on building in flood plains and establishing green-belt areas in the Humber River and Etobicoke Creek valleys. It further recommended that the main dyke in the Holland Marsh be raised forty-five centimetres and widened enough to allow the farmers' houses to be rebuilt on top, not in the low fields where they had been originally.[21]

The surprisingly activist recommendations from the Carswell-Shaw Commission can be understood, in part, as a function of the remarkable extent of the damage left in the wake of the hurricane. Hazel was a powerful storm that caused significant damage throughout the Caribbean, the United States, and Canada. Its severity gave political leaders, policymakers, and farmers cause to reexamine human-environment relations. But the recommendations of the report are also part of a broader context of conservationist thought percolating throughout Ontario during the late 1940s and early 1950s, foreshadowing farmland-preservation policies to come.

The Ontario Conservation and Reforestation Association, founded in 1936, had been instrumental in successfully lobbying the provincial government for the first conservation legislation in the province.[22] In the early 1940s, the Conservative government, cleaving to the left in response to growing popular support for the social-democratic Co-operative Commonwealth Federation, established the centralized Department of Planning and Development, which included the Conservation Branch. Later, in 1946, the Conservation Authorities Act was drafted to provide guidance and funding for municipalities to create local conservation authorities based on watershed geographies.[23] This led, in 1951, to the formation of the Upper Holland Valley Conservation Authority – the precursor to the current Lake Simcoe Region Conservation Authority – with jurisdiction over the Holland Marsh.

Despite the catastrophic damage from the hurricane, the commission's recommendations, the institutional presence of the conservation authority, and the conservationist sentiment of the era, very little changed in terms of farming practice in the Holland Marsh. Within a year of the storm, human habitations in the Marsh – not situated on the embankments, as the commission had recommended – had returned, perhaps even grown. Very little dyke work, save for the most necessary repairs, was completed. The thought of abandoning farming in the Holland River valley was all but unthinkable. Indeed, by 1955, the Marsh had become the exemplar of Ontario agriculture once again, held up as a template for wetland development from the shores of Lake Huron to the bog lands of northern Ontario.[24] Just five months after the catastrophic flooding in the Marsh, a Conservative Party member from Temiskaming, A.R. Herbert, regaled the Ontario legislature with his Promethean vision for northern Ontario, "a large area of some hundred square miles where black muck of the type originally found at Bradford await but draining and clearing to become productive of the same type of vegetables grown so profusely at the Holland Marsh."[25]

The crops emerging from the muck fields had simply become too prolific and profitable to consider interventions detrimental to their production. At the same time, the speed and determination of the Marsh farmers to clean up the damage from Hurricane Hazel seemed to add to the lore of the area. The Marsh emerged from this event solidified as a reference point for archetypal muck-crop farming, finally a mythical equal to Celeryville or Kalamazoo. The lessons available from Hazel, however, were not part of the conversation. A group of "industrious new Canadians from Holland and Belgium," for example, were busy converting a "waste land" of a duck-hunting preserve near Lake Huron "into rich market garden plots" just a year after the devastating flooding, death, and destruction wrought by the hurricane in the Marsh.[26]

An editorial in the *Toronto Daily Star* just a few years later gushed excitedly about the "black gold rush" occurring in the Marsh. This celebratory piece put a fine point on the pace of the Marsh's transformation, while speculatively gesturing at the frontiers of muck-crop farming:

> Thirty years ago you could shoot wild ducks in the heart of the Holland Marsh, south of Bradford, and nobody would hear your shots. Twenty years ago you could buy land in the newly drained wilderness at a few dollars an acre and build a shack far from your nearest neighbour. Today you have to

> pay over $1,000 for that acre and chances are you'll live in a streamlined house as modern as Metro Toronto, complete with TV, maybe a couple of sleek new cars, and friendly neighbours all over the place. Tomorrow, if you want to join the black gold rush, you may have to buy land at the bottom of what is now Lake Simcoe.[27]

In the end, Hurricane Hazel – the anniversary of which still inspires a handful of romantic news stories mourning the death and destruction it caused and heralding the ultimate triumph of humans over nature – only served to reinforce the perspective that the landscape could be controlled. More than this, the storm fortified the view that the landscape *should* be productive and profitable above all else. Perhaps Hazel's gravest sin was to reintroduce an unpredictable "nature" back into the Holland Marsh – a trespass the farmers, with ample support from the state, worked diligently to rectify. The fields emerged post-Hazel as more thoroughly expunged of their natural origins as farmers redoubled their efforts to sculpt the landscape into something somehow outside of nature. By the late 1950s, the smiling farms imaginary was as strong as ever, with the fields emerging as a thoroughly technologized landscape, replete with fancy cars and colour TVs "as modern as Metro Toronto." The clear message was that, despite Hazel's unwelcome incursion – or in part perhaps because of it – the Holland Marsh was a sanitized, safe, and modern site of food production – a Ford-like factory in the fields.[28]

Post-Hazel Renewal and the Triumph of Specialization

The timing of the Holland Marsh's emergence as a highly productive agricultural landscape, while perhaps coincidental, was not incidental. In many ways, farmers there were following the conventional lead in an era of productivist agriculture in full swing by the mid-1950s – a capital-intensive approach to agriculture-cum-celebration of science and technology in the pursuit of stability, intensification, and increased yields. While profits and yields soared as a result, chemical, technology, and machine-dependent farming also ushered in the productivist treadmill – a reliance on capital-intensive inputs begat a further reliance on capital-intensive inputs.

The introduction of new technologies during this era was a strategy for overcoming the "cost-prize squeeze," a situation in which the combined costs of production outpace increases in farm income.[29] Growers confronted with this typically have two options, either lower production costs or increase yields. Many farmers choose to employ both tactics. As agricultural scholar Anthony Winson observes, the typical strategy for escaping from the cost-price squeeze results in a further reliance on machines and chemicals:

> For the most part, the forces pushing net farm income down were met by attempts to increase the volume of production on the farm with the "tractorization" of agriculture and a dramatic increase in the use of chemical sprays, it becomes possible, at lease for some, to work much more farm land without raising the input of increasingly expensive farm labour. The incorporation of ever greater volumes of chemical fertilizers and other inputs, such as hybrid seed varieties, helped boost yields per acre.[30]

Within the Holland Marsh, these pressures took on a greater acuity, given the intensive (rather than extensive) character of cultivation. At least part of what makes muck farming so profitable is the scarcity of available land. The number of muck-soil hectares under tillage at any given point is a fraction of those of mineral soil under production across Ontario. This point was not lost on the Marsh farmers of the late 1950s. Postwar suburban expansion coupled with a rural landscape already largely under production served to compel would-be farmers and agricultural speculators to set their sights on new conquests for drainage. Given an increasingly crowded southern and central Ontario, the frontiers of agriculture were seen to lie at the bottom of untouched swamps and lakes.

Yet muck-crop speculators eager to start the pumps were confronted with a shifting ecological paradigm, one in which the Conservation Authorities Act made it difficult, indeed largely impossible, to turn wetlands into new fields. Increasingly, the state was intervening in unfamiliar ways by placing limits on how and where farmers could operate. A shift in the character of conservationism was providing a counterpoint to farming as an activity of land stewardship. While Day and the early Marsh boosters were seen to be "improving" the land with underdrainage – providing a service by bringing the land into production through cultivation – by the late 1950s and early 1960s, there was a change to the contours of "environmentalism." Partly as a result, the era of muck-crop farming as a kind of *extensive* agriculture in Ontario had come to a close. No longer could new land, whether just down the road or at the bottom of a swamp, be easily had in Ontario, meaning that farmers were forced to focus on *intensive* farming – getting the most out of the land they did have.

With so few opportunities for investing in the creation of more land, Marsh farmers, for the most part, turned toward investing in their existing land as a way of increasing production and profits. Investments in intensification were made in various ways in the Holland Marsh, but the driving force behind the

FIGURE 4.2. Shifting nature and composition of crop cover, 1954–2009.

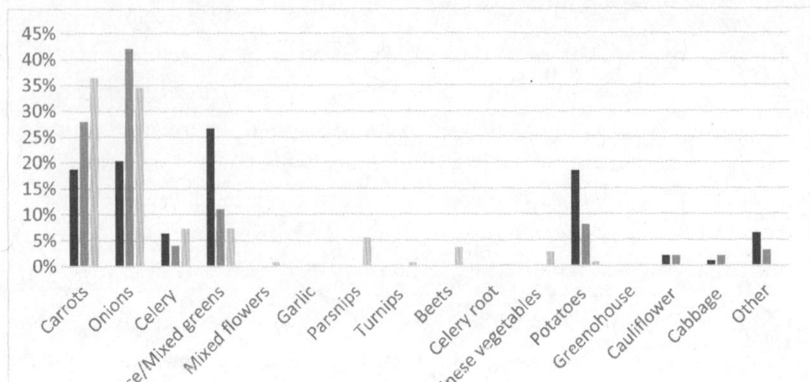

SOURCES: Department of Agriculture, "Holland Marsh Vegetables" (1954), Archives of Ontario, Hurricane Relief, Holland Marsh, 1954–56, B355358; Ontario Department of Agriculture and Food, "Announcement: Special Committee to Study Holland Marsh" (1967), 2, Archives of Ontario, ARDA – Holland Marsh 1967–70 B388426; Planscape, 2009.

pursuit of profits was crop specialization. The form that biophysical nature took (crops) and the social configurations of agriculture in the Marsh began to shift to accommodate this specialization. Put differently, what was grown and how it was grown began to shift fundamentally in the mid-1950s. Indeed, a novel field of plant breeding – phytoengineering – emerged in the 1950s, the explicit intention of which was to design more uniform and durable produce. As two exponents of phytoengineering noted: "Machines are not made to harvest crops. . . . In reality, crops must be designed to be harvested by machine."[31]

Figure 4.2 illustrates the extent to which the crop base in the Holland Marsh has changed since the 1950s. The dramatic shift in lettuce production provides a vivid example. While in 1954, more land in the Marsh was dedicated to lettuce than any other crop, very little of it is grown there today. What little lettuce production that does remain is not the robust iceberg variety popular in the 1950s and 1960s, but rather mixed greens and mesclun mix, a lettuce with a much different sociocultural and political-economic profile.[32]

As lettuce production migrated from the Holland Marsh, almost all of it landed in Quebec. It is not clear why farmers there (or the provincial government, through supportive subsidies and legislation) seemed to pursue this market to the extent it did – a fact that reinforces the need for far more scholarly work on the histories of various agricultures across Canada. But it is clear that Quebec did actively pursue this specialization and quickly became by far the most prolific lettuce-growing province in Canada. In 2011, as an example, Quebec produced 70 percent of the greenhouse-grown lettuce in Canada.[33]

For a time, however, the Holland Marsh was a lettuce juggernaut, shipping produce across Canada and throughout the United States. Some of the older farmers there remember the transition away from lettuce and point specifically to provincial legislation as the driving force behind the change:

> We all used to do lettuce and celery. When I married Tony [Bake], we grew lettuce and celery too. But slowly, there's only about 2 or 3 farmers out here now, because Quebec kills us, because the province of Quebec understands the importance of feeding people, and they subsidize their Quebec farmers. So they can push it into our markets cheaper because they're gonna get subsidized.[34]

Others point to ostensible qualities of the relatively fresher muck soil in Quebec compared to the longer-farmed Holland Marsh muck:

> Quebec had much newer soil than we did, and so they had better quality. But for some reasons we had better celery quality than they did, but I don't know the reason for that and I don't think they do either. So we tend to have better celery than they do, but they have better lettuce. There used to be 2,000 acres of lettuce grown here at one time.[35]

While crop specialization has increased over time, cultivation in the Holland Marsh was in some ways an exercise in specialization from the very beginning. The original boosters did not drain the land with the intention of growing grain or tomatoes or with the thought of raising cattle or sheep. The Marsh was always intended for growing primarily carrots, onions, and, to a lesser extent, celery. This is due, in part, because Day and the early boosters learned from muck croppers in Michigan and Ohio that these crops leveraged the biophysical and biochemical attributes of the soil and temperate climate to a greater extent than did others. The soft, peaty dirt is much gentler on carrots and onions during harvest. The tighter-packed, granular mineral soil tends to be more abrasive than muck soil, causing microscratches on these subterranean vegetables as they are pulled from the earth and resulting in shorter storage life. Beyond this, there are a number of reasons that make carrots and onions not only particularly well suited to muck soil but also productive crops to grow together. One long-time muck-crops researcher has noted:

> Onions and carrots actually are almost perfect rotation crops. It would be hard to pick ones that are better. One's a monocot, one's a dicot; the root structures are different; the chemicals, the insecticides, the insects and diseases are completely different; the herbicides you use on them are almost entirely different. But, you're rotating, you know; one year it's onions, one year it's carrots.[36]

The so-called natural advantages of the Holland Marsh and the extent to which specializing in carrots and onions seems like an obvious choice is predicated, however, on the productivist assumptions of capitalist agriculture. Specialization is, after all, first and foremost an accumulation strategy.[37] It typically makes sense, within the logic of capitalist agriculture, to concentrate production on a particular crop in as much as it is a way of rationalizing production and therefore maximizing profits. In other words, there is nothing inevitable about the produce grown in the Holland Marsh, but rather it is the result of social and natural processes. Muck soil can support a wide variety of other crops, but none fit both the biophysical and biochemical conditions of the soil and climate *and* the social constraints of profit quite so well as carrots and onions.

It was this socionatural confluence that caused an acceleration and intensification of crop specialization toward these two crops in the Holland Marsh from the 1950s through the 1970s. It was a decisive shift facilitated by a move toward a more industrial form of agriculture at a time when a fledgling agro-industrialism was beginning to have a profound influence on how food was grown, processed, sold, transported, and consumed. Science, technology, and capital were deployed in the fields and beyond in order to rationalize production, reduce risk, and increase sales. The speed and magnitude with which biophysical nature was being transformed in the Marsh increased considerably under the escalating demands of profit. The production of nature there was about to become far more intensive than it had ever been.

Research, Markets, and Marketing in the Making of Muck Crops

The Experimental Station for Organic Soils was established in the Holland Marsh in 1946. Now called the Muck Crops Research Station, the facility has run essentially as an extension program of the Department of Horticulture at the University of Guelph since it began, save for the few years it operated under the auspices of the Ontario Ministry of Agriculture and Food.[38]

The station extended and formalized the presence of the University of Guelph as established by Professor Day in the very earliest days of the Holland Marsh. The nearly continual presence of formalized research there is unique for agricultural areas in Canada. There are a handful of other research stations across the country, and most provincial governments do have some form of research-based agricultural-extension programs. None of these, however, are dedicated in quite the same way to such a specific, niche form of production targeting such a relatively small geographical area.[39]

The station's work ramped up in the late 1950s and early 1960s, and focused largely on plant pathology, pest management, and cultivar trials.[40] Although its research has always been primarily applied work, meant to be manifest in the fields of the Holland Marsh, it has rarely been directly commercial. Within the broader political economy of global agriculture, the Marsh is of negligible value. So while the station does do some fee-for-service research for seed, fertilizer, and pesticide companies, the results are only very narrowly applicable in an applied sense (that is, only to other muck soils) and thus largely valueless within the logic of global agribusiness.

Yet within the Holland Marsh, the work of the station has been significant on a number of fronts, the most important of which is through the cultivar-trials program, which began in the early 1960s. Although commercial interest in plant germplasm dates to at least the late nineteenth century, the biotechnology revolution in agriculture arrived much later.[41] Famously, in 1951, James Watson and Francis Crick succeeded in identifying and isolating deoxyribonucleic acid, DNA, the crucial genetic material that, among other things, transmits genetic information responsible for inherited traits. In the millennia previous to Watson and Crick, agriculturalists slowly adapted crops (either intentionally or not) through the selection of seed from plants with desirable qualities – high yielding, robust to cold, resistant to drought, and so forth. With the discovery of DNA and the subsequent development of techniques to manipulate it, scientists could begin creating changes in seed germplasm by direct manipulation at the molecular level.

While the station does not conduct genetic modification onsite, their cultivar trials are designed to test genetically modified seeds on behalf of various companies. Every spring it will typically grow dozens of different kinds of carrots and onions to test which ones perform best. The seeds, supplied by various companies that pay to have the station run these cultivar trials are designed to express various profitable traits.[42] Both time and form are particularly important in this respect. As farmers in the Marsh were swapping out lettuce for carrots and onions in the late 1950s and early 1960s, the fledgling cultivar trials were facilitating a further specialization within this narrower crop selection. Not only were fewer *kinds* of vegetables being grown but also fewer *varieties* of each vegetable. As demanded by an increasingly commercialized, industrialized agriculture of the 1960s, desirable traits in cultivars moved away from taste toward uniformity, colour, resistance to pests, durability in storage and shipping, and rapid growing time. One long-time, multigenerational farmer candidly admitted:

> One of the things [about] . . . a carrot grown in the muck, peat, mostly muck peat type soil, [it] is a lot tastier than anything else you get out there. If you grow the right variety. Unfortunately, we're growing varieties that you could drop on the floor and the carrot won't break, because we mechanically harvest and all that. It looks nice, but it doesn't taste all that great sometimes. Most of our carrots, some of our carrots, I wouldn't even eat them. It's just got that . . . . [T]hey look great, but they don't have the taste. Then other varieties that we grow, man, I can't stop eating them. But you grow them because that's what the store [buys] . . . [T]hey like a nice looking carrot right?[43]

The station does not formally endorse any particular cultivar, though grades are assigned for discrete qualities (uniformity of shape, colour, overall appearance) as well as overall performance (storability, durability) for each. In addition, qualitative descriptions of the mature vegetable are provided for each trial. The evaluation notes for the trial of a brand of carrot seed called Achieve included these comments: "Good length & width, Good smoothness, Good weight, Tapered & full tips, Good appearance, Uniformity of shape a little uneven, Fair exterior colour but a little uneven, Extra-large core size, Cavity spot slightly noticeable, Poor to average interior blending, Red ring around core (40–80%), Translucency throughout the core (20–80%)."[44]

The results of the cultivar trials are presented at the annual Muck Vegetable Growers Conference and are also compiled into a hefty annual report published by the University of Guelph. The farmers' process for deciding which seeds to grow from year to year is based on a variety of calculations, with great weight given to the results of the station's cultivar trials. It is very unlikely that a farmer would use seed that had not been through this process and equally as unlikely that a manufacturer would attempt to introduce a new variety of seed into the Marsh without having it tested first. In this respect, the station can be understood as an intermediary between the broader political economy of seed manufacture (and agribusiness more generally) and the Marsh farmers.

The presence of the station is in many ways the embodiment of the productivist ethic gathering during the late 1950s and early 1960s. It functioned (and continues to function) as a site of translation between the global imperatives of commercial, industrialized agriculture and the in situ specificity of muck-crop farming. In addition to the cultivar trials, the station also conducts "minor use" testing on chemical fertilizers and pesticides. With funding from Agriculture and Agri-Food Canada, it examines the applicability and efficacy of various pest and nutrient treatments – chemicals originally designed for use on larger-scale cash crops, such as corn or soybeans – on muck crops. There is no financial incentive for the manufacturers of agrochemicals to go through the lengthy process of registering a product for use on a crop of niche production, so the state facilitates this by paying research stations to do the work. In this respect – through minor-use testing on carrots and onions – the Muck Crops Research Station has made a significant contribution to the attempts to build stability not only in the Holland Marsh but also beyond to other muck-crop areas in Ontario, Quebec, and elsewhere.

Consumer Tastes and the Postwar Diet

Attempts to optimize nature in the Holland Marsh also emerged, at least in part, beyond the fields. The postwar years brought a significant shift – qualitatively and quantitatively – in consumer demand. At the dinner table, this was expressed as a demand for an idealized form of prepackaged freshness and convenience. As nature's biophysical form was manipulated into uniformity through phytoengineering, it was also increasingly sculpted to meet consumer expectations of freshness, nutrition, and authenticity, characteristics easily discursively fused onto the carrots, onions, and celery grown in the Marsh.

Increasingly, consumer expectations were mediated through the emergence of retail grocery chains and mass-market advertising. In the case of the food from the Holland Marsh, large chain stores invoked science in advertisements as a way of adding gravitas and authority to their claims of freshness. An ad typical of the era, from the grocery chain Dominion, reads: "Science assures you quality-controlled freshness.... Through scientific quality-control aided by 'round the clock refrigeration' ... Dominion is able to maintain the exclusive standard of freshness your family deserves!"[45] Ads like these had the effect of semiotically reinforcing the notion that the Marsh had transcended its murky origins to emerge as a domesticated and sanitized site of scientific food production.

More than this even, the implication is that freshness, while perhaps a characteristic inherent to vegetables, exists insufficiently in nature. Only through the application of science and technology can its full potential be realized.

For farmers in the Holland Marsh, there was some limited truth to this productivist narrative. As growers began shipping to markets farther away in order to avoid glutting local markets and driving down prices, time (particularly in the beginning) was not on their side. Unlike cash crops that hold value with relative stability over time – grains and oil seeds that can be easily stored for long periods of time – the fresh produce rolling off the Marsh fields has a much shorter shelf life and is much heavier and trickier to ship, all of which makes its transport more expensive. Time as a characteristic of biophysical nature – how long it takes a given piece of produce to lose freshness – became a serious concern for Marsh farmers within the context of shifting consumer expectations in the postwar years.

Through a combination of cultivar trials, which sought to breed traits that would extend a vegetable's shelf life and make it more resistant to damage during harvest and transport, and improvements in packing, shipping, and storage technologies, growers were able to manipulate their crops to be more resistant to time and space. These interventions ensured, or at least increased the chances, that the carrots, onions, and celery emerging from the Marsh met the expectations of consumers in an increasingly competitive marketplace. Indeed, long before the contemporary Holland Marsh Gold branding scheme had been conceived, "Holland Marsh" was a term very often leveraged as a competitive advantage. Invoking the Marsh was a way of semiotically fusing idealized notions of a sanitized, modernized nature to vegetables through advertising. Carrots became "Holland Marsh carrots" and onions "Holland Marsh onions" in order to capitalize on the natural imaginary of the area – very carefully crafted and purged of the invocation of wetlands, swamps, mosquitoes, and the like. During this era of high-productivism, consumers wanted their nature with a dose of sterilizing modernism.

As farmers organized production around meeting commercially mediated imaginaries of what various crops ought to look like, they were altering the composition of biophysical nature within the Marsh. And as they sought to do so in as efficient and profitable way possible, they also transformed their own material practices.

Modernization and Mechanization in the Holland Marsh

Emerging high-tech crops and shifting consumer expectations in the immediate postwar period created changes to the material practices of farming in the

Holland Marsh. Since the very beginning, the materiality of the muck landscape had demanded customized applications of technology. Mass-manufactured equipment tended to be too large and heavy for the boggy fields of the Marsh. The typical tractor was unfit for a variety of reasons – the chassis was too heavy, the axles were too narrow, and the tires were too thin, among others – all of which would result in it sinking into the muck, which happened many times in the earliest years of farming in the Marsh. As a result, many of the machines used there, from spraying equipment to onion harvesters, were often heavily modified by Marsh farmers. The specific mechanical demands of the muck soil have even spawned a cottage industry of sorts, with at least two light-equipment modifiers operating within the boundary of the canal.

Previous to the era of high productivism, however, agriculture in the Holland Marsh was largely a low-tech, stoop-labour family affair. Many made do working two- or five-hectare parcels of land, by hand, and selling their produce to packers in the Marsh or to grocers in Toronto. But as demand increased, costs rose, and growers looked to produce a more efficient, uniform biophysical nature, farming changed significantly in the Marsh. Two companies, in particular, were responsible for ushering in the productivist paradigm to farming in the Marsh in the early 1960s – Federal Farms Limited and Hardee Farms.

Perhaps unsurprisingly, nonfarmers from Toronto founded both companies. Philip and Morris Latchman formed Federal Farms Limited in 1948, while Abraham Dees, a "farm-born city slicker," founded Hardee Farms Limited in 1954.[46] In 1970, Federal Farms would restructure in an attempt to deal with cash-flow issues and emerge as Federal Diversiplex Limited. Later that decade, in 1978, Federal Diversiplex and Hardee would merge, creating COBI Food Services Incorporated, a food manufacturing and distribution company still in operation, though with no discernable presence in the Holland Marsh. While their tenure was short, Hardee Farms and Federal Farms had a significant and lasting effect on the Marsh.

Both Dees and the Latchman brothers were considered "collar and tie" farmers, more businessmen than agriculturalists, feted in the popular and industry press for bringing "sophistication" to farming and making the "muck bloom" through "super-mechanization."[47] The Latchmans' bona fides came from their background as middlemen – buying low in and around the Holland Marsh and selling high in Toronto. They were disciples of the new freshness and marketing paradigms and wanted to turn the Marsh into a climate-controlled conveyor belt of picture-perfect carrots, onions, and celery. In an address to a group of financiers and financial analysts in New York City in 1962, Morris assured the crowd, "please remember that we are not farmers in the business of farming. We are merchandisers in the business of farming. We were experienced in product movement, marketing and distribution in the vegetable industry long before we planted our first stalk of celery."[48]

Both Hardee and Federal poured vast amounts of capital into farming in the Holland Marsh in an effort to rationalize and modernize production to the greatest extent possible. Indeed, overextending cash flows and alienating themselves from potential investors would ultimately undo both companies. In the early 1960s, however, both were flush with capital. Hardee Farms owned over $5 million worth of muck fields, spread throughout the Marsh, southern Quebec, and parts of Florida. They also owned state-of-the-art processing facilities in both Canada and the United States. Foreshadowing the financialization of agriculture to come, Hardee raised the capital required for such prolific holdings by becoming, in 1960, the first farm business in Canada to be publicly traded on the Toronto Stock Exchange.[49]

Federal Farms, meanwhile, owned about 450 hectares in the Holland Marsh, a significant landholding given that most farmers operated on five-to-ten-hectare plots in the 1960s. Even today, many families there make due with forty-to-eighty-hectare tracts of land. Federal also processed roughly half of the produce grown in the Marsh, as well as vegetables from around North America at their facility there, then shipped to supermarkets throughout Canada and the United States. Indeed, in the early 1960s, Federal's main business was to supply supermarket chains with "a constant, day in day out source of fresh vegetables for their shelves, in enormous quantities."[50] In an audacious media stunt meant to display its agricultural mastery, Federal Farms became the first company to ship Marsh produce overseas, sending two thousand cases of celery to Britain in 1963.[51]

Both companies aggressively sought to transform the Holland Marsh through research and development and the introduction of emerging technologies. Hardee's activities in this respect were largely centred on water management in muck soil through the development of a hydrological system that could allegedly "keep one step ahead of alternating floods and droughts."[52] The operation was designed with the ability to oscillate between drainage and irrigation, able to meet both demands with a single system. The company also developed techniques to manipulate water levels to warm the muck soil when there was risk of frost or unseasonably cold weather.

Federal's innovations, arguably more significant and lasting, resulted in some fundamental changes in the ways in which produce in the Holland Marsh is processed, distributed, and sold. Three in particular have left an indelible mark

FIGURE 4.3. Bushel baskets (A) were supplanted by the now omnipresent pallet box (B). A, courtesy of the Bradford West Gwillimbury Public Library; B, by the author.

on muck-crop farming in the Marsh. First, one of the most enduring contributions of Federal was its adoption of the pallet box, which Latchman argued "revolutionized production" in the Marsh and "made high-speed, efficient production line operation possible."[53] Although the pallet box is now omnipresent on the Marsh landscape, previous to 1960 all produce there was stored in either bushel baskets or light wooden crates (see Figure 4.3). Before the pallet box, vegetables were handpicked and dropped into these baskets and crates. These were then picked up, again by hand, and carried over and lifted on to a flatbed trailer. The baskets would then be brought to either a processing or storage facility. For storage, they would be lined up in rows or sometimes very carefully stacked, though this was risky, given the flimsy materials with which they were made. In the processing facility, they would be moved around and emptied by hand, then sent back into the fields to be refilled. This was all done manually because neither the bushel baskets nor the crates were conducive to mechanization, for a tractor or forklift could not pick up and move a bushel basket without crushing it – besides, using a piece of heavy machinery to pick up a bushel basket of onions is overkill when a worker can easily do it manually. In short, the baskets and light crates were incongruent with mechanization.

On the other hand, the pallet box was custom designed for the era of mechanization. Its adoption considerably sped up the process of harvesting, and transportation and storage became far more efficient. Importantly, the boxes also enabled mechanical harvesting. Once Federal brought the pallet box to the Marsh, onions and carrots could be mechanically harvested directly into the container, which was already loaded onto a flatbed trailer. With a holding capacity of roughly a tonne, each pallet box can be offloaded with a forklift and whisked away to either a storage facility or a processing line. In storage, they can be vertically stacked without damaging any produce and in such a way as to take advantage of nearly every square metre of storage space.

The most important consequence of using the pallet box, however, was the effect it had on the speed of production. The laborious process of filling, moving, and packing bushel baskets and light crates by hand was eliminated. Suddenly, a tonne of onions could by swept away by a machine, moved around with ease, processed, stacked in cold storage, or loaded onto a truck with the pull of a lever. As Morris Latchman proudly put it, "For the layman, the best analogy I can draw is this: the pallet box has been to Federal Farms, what the airplane has been to travel."[54]

The second important innovation Federal introduced to the Holland Marsh was vacuum cooling. The company did not invent the technology, but it was the majority owner of Brad-Vac Cooling Company Limited, the first vacuum-cooling plant of its kind in Canada. Through this subsidiary, Federal was also the Canadian patent-rights holder for a cooling technique used primarily on lettuce and celery. All vegetables begin to degrade the moment they are harvested. Once the "field heat" is removed, however, the degrading process slows considerably. The quicker a vegetable can be cooled, the less it will degrade. Brad-Vac initially had the capacity to chill eight thousand heads of lettuce in twenty minutes in the early 1960s, in the process extending their shelf life from two to three days to five to seven days. This represented an enormous competitive advantage for the farmers who could afford to use the facility.

For lettuce, in particular, this was a revolutionary technology. A fickle, delicate, and labour-intensive crop was made far more robust by the advent of rapid cooling. Indeed the Brad-Vac plant made it possible for Marsh farmers to seek markets for their produce far beyond the Greater Toronto Area. By the early 1960s, Federal was shipping lettuce across a wide swath of North America, from the Rocky Mountains to Newfoundland and Labrador and throughout the eastern and midwestern United States. As Morris Latchman estimated in a speech to Wall Street financiers, "With Brad-Vac, our market has expanded from two million people to 100 million."[55]

A third technology that fundamentally changed farming in the Holland Marsh was polyethylene. Similar to the vacuum-cooling process, food-grade plastic wrap helps prolong the freshness in vegetables. By the late 1950s, many Marsh farmers and businesses were wrapping everything from lettuce to carrots and onions in polyethylene. As with the pallet box and rapid cooling, Federal Farms did not invent food-grade polyethylene, though they did have the capital to become an early adopter of the technology and certainly served to popularize its use throughout the Marsh. Using plastic wrap to prepackage vegetables was primarily a way for farmers to appeal to discerning postwar consumers and the ascendant grocery chains looking for freshness (or at least the appearance of it). The plastic packages were convenient for the chain stores to purchase and display and attractive to customers in an era of modern, sanitized consumerism, giving a sense of uniformity, predictability, and freshness. Polyethylene helped expunge just a little more of the feral "nature" from the produce of the Marsh. As Morris Latchman put it, "our idea was that packaged vegetables should be of consistent quality year-round – just like a can of soup is consistent, no matter what season."[56]

Each of these interventions, in their own way, was ultimately meant to produce a "better" nature – a fresher, more durable, more attractive, and ultimately more standardized and predictable consumer product. Although they may not have understood it as such, Dees and the Latchman brothers were dealing in the complexity of the production of socionatures. The innovations they introduced to the Holland Marsh were meant to transcend the limitations of biophysical nature and conventional farmland while trading on an imaginary of modernized crops in an effort to shape and appease postwar consumer demands for sanitized freshness.

By the time Federal Farms and Hardee Farms merged in the late 1970s, the Holland Marsh had been transformed into an industrial-agricultural landscape, a highly mechanized and rationalized space producing increasingly homogenous crops. But transformations of this kind are rarely benign. Instead, capital and technology-heavy investments tend to be accompanied by an inherent contradiction – the so-called negative externalities of production. As the first industrialists of the Marsh were ostensibly modernizing the fields, they were also inadvertently accelerating the degradation of the very conditions they required for production.

The Gathering Contradictions of Agricultural Modernization

If business was good on the Holland Marsh previous to Hurricane Hazel, it was spectacular a decade after the storm. Weather persisted as a minor irritant from time to time and had some minor effects on seasonal yields and price, but the many technological, capital-intensive investments made were managing to control the biophysical nature of the fields enough to allow for widespread profits. But if these were the halcyon days of the Marsh, the peace and profit belied the growing contradictions of productivist, chemical-heavy, and intensive agriculture.

Indeed, by the mid-1960s, social and ecological relations in the Holland Marsh were showing signs of stress. Shifting labour demands there, as a result of mechanization and the associated proliferation of packinghouses, eliminated jobs in the fields but created them in the factory. Federal Farms and other companies, including River Gardens and United Farms, engaged in a noteworthy and very public battle with unionized employees striking for better conditions and wages. The increasingly powerful companies attempted to invoke a still-existent clause in labour law that denied farm labourers the right to collectively organize and bargain. The Ontario Labour Relations Board ruled against them, however, determining that packinghouse employees were not farm workers since they did not actually work on farms.[57] Its decision in the original case filed by Federal Farms read, in part, "With respect to its plant operations the Board finds that the respondent is not engaged in agriculture or horticulture but rather that the respondent is engaged in a commercial enterprise of preparing vegetable produce for market."[58] In other words, the employees who worked in the processing facilities and packing plants were factory workers and thus had the right to organize their labour and collectively bargain with the employer. This victory, while important, was ultimately temporary. Within years of the ruling, the imperatives of global agriculture would result in the consolidation and elimination of many processing and packing facilities in the Marsh and throughout Ontario. The recent closure, then partial reopening of the tomato processing plant in Leamington, Ontario, puts a fine point on the continued instability of Ontario-based vegetable processing in an era of global, industrialized agriculture.[59]

In addition to labour strife, other socioecological issues emerged in the 1960s. For the first time in the history of the Holland Marsh, there was concern for the muck soil itself. There had been fleeting anxiety subsequent to Hurricane Hazel (and other minor flood events) over the fact that the soil was carried from the western part of the marsh toward the eastern end as the water drained, creating an unequal distribution of wealth, as it were. These concerns were quickly allayed as the piles of muck were evenly distributed with trucks and tractors. By the mid-1960s, however, the fears were more systemic, related to the longer-term sustainability of the soil. In 1963, the Ontario Agricultural College (OAC) at the University of Guelph found that the muck was subsiding at a rate of 3.3 centimetres per year, "a high rate of subsidence," especially given that the ground was frozen solid five months a year.[60] The authors emphasized that this rate equalled around 30 centimetres every ten years, "a substantial and serious loss of organic soils whose average depth is 3ft [nearly 92 centimetres] or less."[61]

Researchers posited that a well-designed water-management program could reduce the rate of soil loss and extend the productive life of the Marsh. In 1967 (after yet another significant flood), a special committee was struck, headed by a coauthor of the subsidence study, Dr. Ross Irwin. It was charged with the task of studying "all aspects of the drainage of the Holland Marsh, notably, (1) pumping facilities, (2) interior centre drainage (Holland River), (3) interior main drainage network, (4) use of drainage and irrigation water, (5) dykes, (6) soil depletion, [and] (7) flood control."[62] It is unclear what, if anything, ever materialized from this or the proposed study. It is telling however that the special committee, which was assembled specifically to investigate the problem of subsidence in the Marsh, was not instructed to investigate the role of farming and cultivation activities. Subsidence is, after all, a distinctly socionatural phenomena – the product of water and wind erosion and the natural decay of organic matter in the muck soil, though hastened significantly by the human activities of intensive cultivation. The committee members clearly prioritized farming preservation over farmland or landscape preservation.

Other ecological contradictions were beginning to be exposed by the late 1960s and early 1970s as well. Following growing concern regarding the use of chemical pesticides inspired by Rachel Carson's ground-breaking 1962 monograph, *Silent Spring,* the use of DDT was severely restricted in Canada on January 1, 1970. Biologists were debating the extent to which the bioaccumulation of DDT in fish in Lake Simcoe was cause for concern, but researchers were having trouble securing funding from the provincial or federal governments to study the actual Holland Marsh soil for signs and implications of harmful pesticides.[63] A lifetime resident of Bradford offered a powerful anecdote about pesticide use on the Marsh during this era:

> Well, it requires a tremendous amount of fungicides and a tremendous amount of insecticides to grow the crops they do. Me, personally, two friends of mine I went to high school with . . . were at a place out near the 400. And for that time in the 1950s they really were paying well. I was too young, I couldn't get a job. And I'm glad I didn't. If I did, I would be dead now, I think. Because they carried the weed killer in the sprayer on their back. And they never wore a shirt. And their bodies took on the liquids. One guy died in his 40s and the other guy died when he was 55. Both died of liver failure, you know. And they used open tractors and sprayers. Even now we walk on one of the canals, my wife and I. And if you see a tractor two miles away or a mile away, you can smell that stuff.[64]

Although the Marsh was initially given special permission by the provincial government to continue using DDT after the onset of the January 1970 ban, eventually, the chemical was disallowed everywhere. Regardless, a variety of other sources of contamination were already beginning to be highlighted as problematic in and around the Marsh. From health risks associated with parathion, a chemical used to replace DDT, through to nitrogen and phosphorus runoff causing algal bloom outbreaks on Cook's Bay and Lake Simcoe, the ecological contradictions of muck-crop farming were becoming increasingly apparent.[65]

Not to be overlooked, issues related to the discursive and material expansion of the Greater Toronto Area began to appear in the Holland Marsh in the 1970s. Real-estate ads from the growing town of Bradford boasted of newly built homes "only minutes from Hwys 400 and 85. Situated on a 2-acre lot with a magnificent view of Holland Marsh."[66] Torontonians, meanwhile, were urged to explore the "other Yonge Street" – the section that grazes the northern end of the Marsh – in the weekend section of the *Toronto Star*.[67] These physical corridors linking the city with the Marsh – Yonge Street and Highway 400 – so often used to move produce, were increasingly used to facilitate a growing leisure economy of day-tripping Torontonians. Idealized, bourgeois conceptions of pastoral agriculture bumped up against the reality of an urbanizing countryside – one day-tripper noted in a letter to the editor their "shock and dismay" at seeing a billboard erected on the side of Highway 400 in the Marsh, which imposed a "disastrous effect [on the] beautiful landscape."[68]

These emerging conflicts at the intersection of peri-urban agriculture and suburban expansion compelled the province, for the first time, to hire researchers to investigate land-use planning and agricultural acreage. The growing realization that suburban expansion was bumping up against farmland, with urban residents using the countryside as a recreational amenity, by the late 1970s, led the province to begin taking the issue of farmland preservation seriously for the first time.[69]

Conclusion

Beginning in the mid-1950s, the contradictions of the attempts to fully rationalize, standardize, and sanitize production in the Holland Marsh began to manifest in and around the fields. The dramatic events of Hurricane Hazel provided an opportunity for a recalibration of agriculture there, though instead efforts to tame the landscape were redoubled, and the techniques of modernist, productivist agriculture were intensified. At the same time, a nascent environmentalism was emerging, leading the provincial and federal governments to begin understanding wetlands as places to conserve, not drain and farm, while also directing more scrutiny at the practice of industrialized, chemical-intensive agriculture.

Without the option of simply making more farmland – one available in decades previous – farmers sought to get more out of existing land, to make nature work "harder, faster, and better."[70] Innovations introduced to the Holland Marsh by Dees and the Latchman brothers sought to harness biophysical nature in order to intensify production, increase control, and ultimately maximize profits. At the same time, commercially mediated imaginaries of nature played into the material changes in the fields as farmers responded to an emerging postwar food aesthetic.

By the 1970s, the contradictions of capitalist agriculture began to manifest in earnest. As growers intensified production, they also deepened the extent to which they were drawing on the conditions of production – the soil was subsiding, the water was contaminated, and the health of the human and nonhuman ecologies were beginning to decline. In sum, the emerging socionatural, political, and economic challenges the Holland Marsh was facing heading into the 1980s were symptoms of the gathering contradictions of an unsustainable, capitalist agriculture coupled with the ascendant pressures of an urbanizing countryside. Productivist farming had resulted in more profit on the Marsh, but it also created an agriculture that was more dependent on capital, chemicals, and proprietary research and technology. Any recollections of the Marsh as a wetland or lessons from Hurricane Hazel were, by the late 1970s, distant memories. Production continued to increase unabated, though the socioecological contradictions kept piling up.

CHAPTER 5

A Legacy of Contradictions

Crisis and the (Re)production of the Holland Marsh, 1980–Present

THE INDUSTRIAL LOGIC UNDERPINNING global agriculture beginning in the late 1940s hit full stride by the late 1990s. Capital-intensive, input-reliant, and long-haul agriculture of the so-called green revolution emerged as the de facto approach to farming in the last decades of the twentieth century. Increasingly, this operative logic was becoming edict – farmers unwilling to subscribe to the rules of industrial agriculture had little chance of success. Technologies developed in the 1960s and 1970s related to seed manipulation and cooling, storing, and shipping fresh produce had been improved and widely dispersed by the 1980s, making "distance and durability" the new pivot of an emerging global agricultural system.[1] By the early 1980s, produce from the Holland Marsh was whipping around the world in ways Professor Day would not have dared dream.

A new international division of agriculture emerged during this period, catering to year-round access to fresh produce for affluent consumers in the Global North coming from farms largely in the Global South.[2] As agricultural capital relocated to climates in which two or even three harvests of fresh produce per year could be had, a host of what food and agriculture scholar Harriet Friedmann has labelled "New Agricultural Countries" emerged.[3]

This resulted in traditionally more perishable crops becoming more fully integrated into global exchange markets than they ever had been before, meaning that Holland Marsh farmers were brought into competition with growers from around the world. The uneasy reality of trade liberalization created downward pressure on prices due to low-cost carrot and onion imports from California and later China. Pressures from rapid suburbanization, increasing (and increasingly public) concerns over pollution and contamination from the fields, the compulsion to adopt new technologies, and a dramatic shift in regional regulatory regimes have all complicated the prospect of muck-crop farming over the past forty years.

A profound change in the Holland Marsh, beginning in the 1980s, is the extent to which the area became subject to external scrutiny, including, importantly, the arrival of farmland-protection policies. Previously, farmers in the Marsh, while a curiosity to many outsiders, were able to operate largely free of public scrutiny. But this rapidly changed for two reasons. First, negative externalities of intensive agriculture began to manifest themselves in the fields of the Marsh and beyond. As human and nonhuman health deteriorated in and around the area, state and quasi-state actors moved in to regulate and impose limits on agricultural production there. The liberal state, in other words, came to amend its laissez-faire position with respect to farming and began imposing restrictions on production in the fields of the Marsh – an attempt to mitigate the contradictions of nature's production. Second, the rapid suburbanization of the countryside brought the city closer to the Marsh and vice versa, both materially and semiotically, thus creating points of tension between the rural farmers and their urban consumers. In this respect, land-use planning and local urban politics became intimately entangled with food and farming.

The growers' strategy (gamely facilitated by burgeoning corporate research, development, and biotechnology sectors) for coping with these colliding pressures has been to find ways to enlist biophysical nature in the agricultural process in ever more efficient ways – a search to control biophysical nature with increasing precision in order to get the very most out of the declining soil. Higher-than-average crop yields have been a feature of Marsh agriculture since Day's first test plots. But the political economy of agriculture was far different in the 1920s than it was in the 1980s and beyond. As farming in the Marsh approached the new millennium, the stakes for choosing the right seeds, pest treatments, and crop-monitoring regime were never higher.

Yet while the pressures of capitalist agriculture permeated the Holland Marsh, it was an uneven, incomplete infiltration. Despite the best efforts of a multitude of farmers, engineers, and planners to corral, contort, and control the biophysical landscape over the decades, nature continued to be unpredictable. Weather was too wet or too dry, too hot or too cold. Water transgressed dykes, backed up pumps, and flooded fields. Equally important, social and material limits in the form of conservation regulation and legislation, starting in earnest in the early 1990s, have also shaped the production of nature in the Marsh. The politics of environmental conservation and rehabilitation have imposed a new production paradigm, led to material changes in the fields, and even called into question the future of farming in the Holland Marsh.

Menacing Fields and the Unmaking of "Smiling Farms"

By the early 1980s, the contradictions of chemical-dependent capitalist agriculture were beginning to be exposed in the Holland Marsh. The generous use of synthetic fertilizers, fungicides, and pesticides over the decades had led to some decidedly undesirable yields that were beginning to affect the health of the land, water, and people in and around the Marsh. The pathologies – symptomatic of the widespread adoption of productivist agriculture – were revealed to an increasingly anxious public in a litany of dire news headlines throughout the early 1980s. In the first few years of the decade, the bad news from the Marsh was seemingly endless, and headlines departed distinctly from the "smiling farms" narrative of the original boosters in the 1920s. The more alarming of them: "Holland Marsh Widely Polluted, Report Says"; "Simcoe's Fishing Future Gloomy"; "Birth Defects High in the Holland Marsh"; and "Probe Rural Birth Defects."[4]

These reports displaced the idyll of milk-fed, hardworking farmers and high-yield carrots and onions with a far-bleaker tale of toxic farms, polluted lakes, dying fish, and human birth anomalies. The emerging disasters seriously challenged the identity of the Holland Marsh as a unique local getaway or as a site of pristine, natural peri-urban farming. Instead, its biophysical nature was cast as a threatening, menacing force, demonstrating once again the tangled discursive and material character of the production of nature.

The Holland Marsh's bucolic imaginary began to be challenged in earnest when a Newmarket-area pediatrician contacted the York Region's medical officer of health in the summer of 1978 to express his concern over "the apparent high number of congenital anomalies among infants born to families in the Holland Marsh area."[5] At the officer's request, researchers at the University of Toronto and various regional health authorities conducted a feasibility study to determine whether a full-scale community-health survey of the Marsh area should be launched.

Even before these medical authorities caught on, evidence of chemical contamination had already been mounting. A peer-reviewed article published in the *Journal of Economic Entomology* in 1978 found high levels of DDT, banned a decade previous, in the soil and water of the Holland Marsh.[6] To be clear, this was not the result of recent use, but rather a legacy of the pesticide's prior use. That it remained in perceptible concentrations long after the ban went into effect is a testament to the chemical's persistence. Additionally, the organophosphorus compounds ostensibly designed as safer alternatives to DDT (many of which, including parathion, malathion, and diazinon, have been banned or restricted in recent years) were discovered to be rapidly accumulating at dangerous levels in the water and soil of the Marsh and beyond. The findings from this 1978 study were more or less confirmed by Ministry of Environment scientists in an in internal, unpublished memo.[7]

Despite accumulating evidence of chemical contamination, finding that the differences in congenital abnormalities in the Holland Marsh and the control areas were "statistically significant," and determining that the Marsh (in particular West Gwillimbury) was a "high risk" area for birth defects, the authors of the feasibility study ultimately concluded that an exhaustive community-health survey was not warranted.[8] Instead, they seemed to opt for a "wait and see" approach. Meanwhile, presumably to cast some doubt on the findings that the Marsh constituted a high-risk area for birth anomalies while distancing themselves from the potential fallout, officials at both the Ministry of the Environment and the Ministry of Agriculture publicly challenged aspects of the very study they had a part in producing.[9] This is perhaps not surprising, given that the ruling provincial Conservative Party of the day was not filled with keen environmentalists. In addition to challenging the more troubling aspects of the report, the opposition Liberals also publicly called out the provincial government in the summer of 1981 for abandoning plans to clean up Lake Simcoe.[10]

The reasons for not pursuing the matter further, while perhaps partly political, cannot be attributed entirely to the unreceptive political climate. Proving causation in clusters of noncommunicable disease is a notoriously challenging scientific proposition, even within in the contemporary context.[11] The authors of the report indeed pointed out that the data were "tentative," given the small sample size (495 total births in and around the Holland Marsh) and duration of the study (a five-year period between 1973 and 1978). James Williams and his four coauthors admit that "there is a body of scientific thought in the literature calling agricultural chemicals, particularly organophosphorus pesticides, into question," though they continue, "No direct link between the chemicals and congenital anomalies has been demonstrated."[12] They could have determined in their feasibility study that the abnormally high number of birth anomalies in the area constituted a ready empirical case to test the hypothesis that organophosphorus pesticides have no effect on infant health. They could have also concluded that additional study was warranted, given that the incidence of birth anomalies within the Marsh was statistically significant. Instead, they determined that further attention was not warranted, a position seemingly encouraged by officials from the Ministry of the Environment.[13] Given the improbability of ever being able to determine causation in a case such as this, and the resource-intensive character of conducting an environmental-cluster analysis of noncommunicable diseases, it is not surprising that the researchers would recommend no further investigation into the matter, regardless of the political tenor of the day.[14]

Williams and his colleagues do share an original causal hypothesis, one that may hint at the extent to which the wartime image of the Holland Marsh farmers as homefront heroes in previous decades had been replaced in the 1980s by a far-less-flattering narrative. They note that their initial assumption was "that patterns of intermarriage among families" in the Marsh was a risk factor for birth abnormalities, a hypothesis eventually dismissed due to "the apparent ethnic diversity of the area." In other words, their initial working hypothesis was that endemic intermarriage and inbreeding among Marsh residents had led to the high rates of birth anomalies, a supposition that exposes a gross misunderstanding of the social and cultural history of the Marsh.

In any case, the five researchers ultimately concluded that the burden of conducting a full-scale community-health survey outweighed the potential benefits: "Community surveys of potential risks and hazards are difficult to design in terms of rigorous scientific requirements, costly to execute, they may involve hundreds of people, and, they take time. In summary, the results of the study indicate that a community survey of risk factors is neither warranted nor feasible."[15] Despite the decision to not undertake further *public* study, the Ministry of the Environment did commit to continued monitoring of water and soil samples.[16] Regulatory changes were forthcoming in the early 1980s, but the political reaction to the 1981 report reveals that, at least in the beginning, the provincial government was reluctant to address – even publicly acknowledge – the existence of environmental degradation and contamination in the area. Conceivably, this reluctance was at least partly a result of wanting to protect the image and the industry of the Holland Marsh. In an era of high unemployment, agriculture remained a steady economic driver in Ontario.

Yet despite the apparent efforts of the governing Conservative Party and others, containing the ecological deterioration in the Holland Marsh was difficult, given the unpredictable character of biophysical nature and its disregard for ostensible boundaries. The considerable efforts made by the early boosters to physically partition the Marsh from its immediate surroundings with a canal were, inevitably, incomplete. In reality, the canal system only ever *appeared* to sever the Marsh from the surrounding landscape. Attempts to control the environment were not as complete as may have been assumed. The Marsh remains very much physically connected to adjacent areas, particularly the Lake Simcoe watershed, through the flow of surface and groundwater. The ostensibly necessary socionatural interventions required of capitalist agriculture – using pesticides, fungicides, and fertilizers to protect and boost yields – "underproduced" the immediately surrounding ecology, as James O'Connor might put it. Through the process of production, farmers were destroying the conditions necessary for further production, including, potentially, their own health. Human and nonhuman well-being within the Marsh suffered, but the negative externalities of industrial farming inevitably moved beyond its boundaries. Water served as a vector, enabling the agricultural chemicals to transgress the borders of the canal system via the Holland River and groundwater flows. And as the industrial inputs spilled out of the Marsh, the health of Lake Simcoe and its greater watershed declined steeply.

By the early 1980s, Lake Simcoe was suffering a very public death. Its water was becoming hypoxic – starved of oxygen. This was particularly true of Cook's Bay, the southernmost part of the lake and the direct catch basin of the Holland River.[17] Researchers pointed to dangerously high levels of phosphorus in the water and very clearly implicated farming in the Holland Marsh as a significant source of the contamination.[18] A key ingredient in fertilizer, phosphorus was polluting Lake Simcoe and accelerating the growth of algae, which were metabolizing dissolved oxygen in the water at an unsustainable rate. This resulted in significant flora and fauna causalities, ultimately threatening the freshwater fishing industry in the area.

While health matters in the Holland Marsh at this time were largely invisible, aside from the occasional news story, fertilizer runoff was far more conspicuous. As elevated levels of phosphorus exited the Holland River, large algal blooms blanketed the surface of Cook's Bay and southern parts of Lake Simcoe. These blooms were not only threatening the health of the lake's flora and fauna – and the viability of the local freshwater fishery – but also an ugly nuisance for the increasing numbers of urban recreationists and holidaymakers. Local boosters had begun positioning Lake Simcoe as a vacation destination closer to home for Torontonians in light of a flagging economy, high interest rates, and increasing gas prices. Algae, "creeping across the bays, fouling the water and coating shoreline rocks with oily green slime," was more than just an ecological issue – it was not good for business.[19] Efforts to transform Lake Simcoe into a getaway for the urban middle class were severely undercut by the green, slimy, transmogrified water.

The collective public finger pointed at the Holland Marsh. To be fair, there were other contributing sources across the watershed, including urban effluent (sewage, soap residues, and the like, especially from the burgeoning towns of Aurora and Newmarket), within the lake's watershed. The net result, in any case, was a three-fold increase in phosphorus levels from estimated presettlement rates.[20] Decades of overfertilizing had finally come to a crisis point. The provincial government, still reluctant to be seen as putting "the squeeze on farmers" or of favouring an "agricultural-economic trade off," wanted to find solutions that did not interfere with agricultural production.[21] As a result, the issue was largely left unaddressed until well into the early 1990s.

Increasingly, however, non- and quasi-state actors were beginning to have more influence in public and private matters, including environmental health and agriculture. In the early 1980s, the Lake Simcoe Region Conservation Authority (LSRCA) spearheaded the Lake Simcoe Environmental Management Strategy.[22] This was an initiative meant to address the ailing ecological health of the lake. There was here, undoubtedly, a symbiosis of sorts: The budding LSRCA put itself at the centre of a very public debate about the health of Lake Simcoe in light of government inaction, boosting its own brand while addressing the broader ecological issue. The strategy featured a series of reports on the lake's health, many of which focused specifically on the dynamics of phosphorus leaching from the muck soil of the Holland Marsh.[23]

Phosphorus interaction with mineral soil was fairly well understood, but in the mid-1980s, very little was known about how the element interacted with (and importantly leached from) muck soil. Researchers with the LSRCA found that the Holland Marsh fields were indeed saturated with phosphorus from overfertilization and that it was leaching into Lake Simcoe. But they also found two significant complicating factors unique to muck soils. First, as the muck breaks down, or subsides, organically (as it inevitably does), phosphorus is created. Although this is considered to be of "minor significance" under normal conditions, with phosphorus levels already so damagingly high from fertilizers, any additional amount was too much.[24]

Second, researchers found that as the muck subsides, the effect is a greater concentration of phosphorus per unit of soil – that is, the existing amount of phosphorus, plus the phosphorus created during the process of subsidence, now exists in an overall smaller volume of soil. This is significant – "a serious concern for the future" – because the higher the concentration of the mineral in a given volume of soil, the more readily it leaches.[25] So, while the phosphorus problem in the Lake Simcoe watershed was largely caused by agricultural activity, it was exacerbated by muck-crop farming specifically.

By the early 1990s, and as a direct result of the work conducted by the LSRCA, programs to reduce phosphorus loading were implemented. An ongoing focus has been on determining how much external phosphorus is required in muck-crop fertilizers, an issue the Muck Crops Research Station continues to study. Coupled with national bans on phosphate additives in laundry soap and other consumer products and ongoing monitoring of levels in its waters, Lake Simcoe has seen a significant reduction overall in recent decades, though work to reduce phosphorus runoff continues.[26]

The initial public and eventual political concern over pollution levels in the Holland Marsh and phosphorus levels emanating from it contributed to two developments that would have significant consequences for agriculture in the area. First, pressure from the public and from nonstate actors resulted in increased scrutiny of farming practices in the Marsh. This was spurred on by public concern for the ecology of the Marsh and its surrounding area. This would eventuate in the implementation of various legislative and policy interventions meant to regulate farming there by both state and nonstate actors. As regional environmental sensibilities evolved throughout the 1980s and 1990s, the Marsh was pulled into a regional geography of conservation and featured prominently as a site in the province's conservationist agenda. Second, and as an attempt to maintain competitiveness in the global trade of horticultural crops, ecological modernism flourished in the Marsh. Farmers, private businesses, and the state doubled down on modernist, techno-optimistic notions of the production and control of biophysical nature in attempts to build a better, more efficient, and more ecologically sound nature.

Socionature, Regulation, and Conflict: Smiling Farms 2.0

Efforts aimed at rehabilitating the material ecology and the ecological reputation of the Holland Marsh began in earnest just as the city and countryside were becoming increasingly intertwined, both materially and discursively. On the one hand, the urban areas and supportive infrastructure around the Marsh – present since its initial draining – were rapidly expanding outward, bringing the city ever closer, as it were. On the other hand, nature's imaginary – the idealized agricultural pastoral – began to be leveraged by Marsh farmers, boosters, and developers in new ways. Whether invoked to sell carrots, onions, or peri-urban real estate to urbanites, "nature" in the Marsh has been heavily conscripted in recent years. In effect, these efforts have brought (at least discursively) the countryside closer to the city.

At the same time, rehabilitating the Holland Marsh's reputation as a safe, natural area of agricultural production has also relied on a contradictory discursive move – an imaginative distancing of the Marsh from proximate urban areas, especially Toronto. In the 1990s, the Marsh was redefined in contrast to urban areas – those working to rehabilitate its ecological reputation attempted to recuperate some of the wildness the earlier boosters worked so fastidiously to expunge from the fields in the first place. The Marsh as urban getaway, or a "natural" agricultural landscape, has no appeal if it is seen to be toxic. Yet while notions of an external and pristine nature in the Marsh have been exhumed to sell produce in Toronto and empty house lots in Bradford, it is a patently different kind of biophysical nature than the historical, pre-agricultural variety. This new conception of nature has come with a litany of material regulations and technological caveats stipulating new ways of being and interacting with the fields and crops.

Within the Holland Marsh, the politics of nature's production have typically been enabling – that is, liberal-state policies have provided supportive regulation and legislation to allow farming to occur (as an obvious example, allowing the conversion of the wetland in the first place). But, more recently, agriculture in the Marsh has been affected and shaped by a shifting liberal-state intervention of the kind Karl Polanyi observed over eighty years ago.[27] Liberal economic state policy, when confronted with the contradictions of its productivist polices, tends toward interventionism. This double movement, as Polanyi put it, created tensions in the fields of the Marsh and resulted in important social and material changes to nature's production.

Institutions, rules, regulations, and legislation have always been pertinent in the Holland Marsh, particularly since the introduction of agriculture there (recall the original enabling legislation of the Ontario Municipal Drainage Aid Act). But as part of the more general trend of external forces penetrating the Marsh, beginning particularly with the movement to restore its ecology and ecological reputation in the mid-1980s, there has been a considerable increase in the regulatory and institutional presence. Various ministries, departments, and organizations, both state and nonstate, are all attempting to shape biophysical nature according to their various prerogatives and normative conceptions of what the socioecological constitution of the Marsh ought to be. Jamie Reaume, then executive director of the Holland Marsh Growers' Association, put a fine point on the matter in a 2014 prebudgetary presentation to the provincial Standing Committee on Finance and Economic Affairs:

> I deal with basically twenty-three ministries. I always laugh about the fact that I deal with twenty-three provincial ministries, fourteen federal ministries, two conservation authorities, one county and one region that really

> don't get along very well, five municipalities, and I have a myriad set of regulatory regimes that we all have to fall under. That is very hard for the farmers.[28]

Regardless of the actual number of ministries, authorities, regions, rules, and regulations having some jurisdiction within the Holland Marsh, the qualitative effect is clear: Farmers are extremely frustrated by what they see as unnecessary interference to their livelihoods. For current-day Marsh growers, most of whom grew up helping their parents and grandparents on the farm, this increased regulation is something that has happened over the course of their adult lives – rather rapidly, in other words. One disgruntled farmer summarized the general sentiment: "We're overregulated. All these authorities. It's getting crazy. . . . [T]alk to the other guys. . . . [E]verybody wants to regulate you to death. For what?"[29]

A good number of regulatory changes since about 1995 are related to environmental and land-use management – in part, as discussed above, to restore the ecology and ecological reputation of the Holland Marsh. Perhaps not surprisingly, then, these rules and regulations tend to be the ones that most complicate the farmers' lives. Among them, a recent initiative by the provincial Ministry of the Environment to monitor water taken for irrigation in the Marsh has been particularly contentious. Ontario requires, with few exceptions, any company or organization that uses more than fifty thousand litres of water per day to obtain a permit and track their usage. Marsh farmers see this as needless meddling because their fields are surrounded by water, and drought has never really been an issue for them. As one long-time grower put it:

> We've now had since 1934, Lake Simcoe; that has never failed. . . . [W]e've been irrigating out of there for 80 years . . . and now they want us to let them know how much we get out of there. Maybe in the future they want to control it? And that's good for areas where people are running out. But let's worry about that if Lake Simcoe were to dry up and we would have to control it. We don't need any permits for that. And it's just a government regulation that's useless.[30]

Along similar lines, the LSRCA has a number of initiatives clustered largely around protecting and restoring water quality in the Holland Marsh and beyond, work enabled by the passing of the Lake Simcoe Protection Act in 2008. From phosphorus monitoring and reduction programs to riparian protection programs meant to reduce the amount of soil erosion on the banks of the canal and silt transference, the LSRCA has had an increasingly prominent role in shaping nature in the Marsh. Not surprisingly, its role in the socioecological politics of the area has been fraught at times. The introduction and privileging (through incentives and programs) of a particular, normative socionatural perspective lies at the heart of the enmity.[31] As an example, in a 2009 "report card update," the LSRCA gave the West Holland River a grade of D for phosphorus concentration. Within the Holland River subwatershed, the authority clearly fingers agriculture – specifically in the Marsh – as the culprit of ecological distress and demise: "Impacts from the agricultural areas include the removal of riparian vegetation; the input of sediment-laden sediment which impacts both water quality and the habitat of fish . . . the use of large volumes of water for irrigation, and the changes to the hydrology of the system by the artificially maintained polder system; channelization."[32]

According to the Ontario Ministry of the Environment, only 4 percent of the phosphorus now entering Lake Simcoe originates in the Holland Marsh. This suggests that the Marsh is a very small contributor, though it is worth pointing out that it is the only source, of the five noted, identified with such specificity. All other agricultural activity in the watershed, as an example, is folded into "watershed streams," which includes "streams or tributaries that include the runoff from urban, rural and agricultural areas in the watershed."[33] So, while a 4 percent contribution may not seem significant, the LSRCA has deemed it noteworthy enough to single out – a point that has not gone unnoticed by Marsh farmers.

Perhaps more poignantly, the ministry identifies the Holland Marsh as problematic as a result of its current socioecological configuration as fields. Referring to wetlands as "natural heritage features" in the "Lake Simcoe Phosphorus Reduction Strategy," the ministry emphasizes that they "help to regulate water quality by filtering contaminants and retaining excess nutrients before they reach water sources." It further points out that the "loss of key natural heritage features and shoreline areas along Lake Simcoe has impaired the ability of the natural heritage system to perform these multiple functions."[34] In other words, had the marsh of one hundred years ago, which ostensibly performed these water-quality services, not been turned into an area of intensive agricultural production, phosphorus levels in Lake Simcoe would be much lower. The Marsh, then, is a double culprit, according to the ministry. First, agriculture there is responsible for adding to the overall phosphorus load in Lake Simcoe through the overapplication of fertilizers, soil subsidence, and the like. Second, it has resulted in phosphorus from other sources not being removed from the hydrological ecology. As a general remedy, the protection plan calls for the safeguarding of existing wetlands and remediation and restoration of "natural areas or features."[35] In other words, the ministry's discourse seems to suggest that it would prefer to see the Marsh returned to a pre-agriculture state.

This perspective seems to clash with that of another central institutional and regulatory presence in the Holland Marsh – also an appendage of the provincial government – the Greenbelt Act (2005). This pioneering legislation enshrines a variety of protections for the rural countryside generally and for agricultural land specifically. The protected greenbelt area – the largest of its kind in the world – encompasses a large swath of land that curves around the so-called Golden Horseshoe of Lake Ontario, from the Niagara Escarpment in the south to the Oak Ridges Moraine in the northeast.

The regulatory regime of the Greenbelt Plan includes a distinctive delineation for agricultural land, Specialty Crop Area (SCA). At the moment, there are two such designated areas in the province – the Niagara Peninsula Tender Fruit and Grape Area and the Holland Marsh. According to the province's documents, the Niagara area was afforded special status "based on provincial soil and climate analysis of current and potential tender fruit and grape production areas." The Marsh, meanwhile, was given the designation based on a fairly vague description, including "provincial muck soil analysis and current agricultural production in the region."[36]

Functionally, the SCA designation includes rigorous land-use parameters and restricts the ability of regional and municipal governments to redesignate land uses in the Marsh. Only "normal farm practices and a full range of agricultural, agricultural related and secondary uses are supported and permitted."[37]

The definition and implications of the SCA were updated recently in a Provincial Policy Statement (PPS), the preeminent land-use planning and development mechanism in Ontario. Currently, an SCA is, in part, "designated using guidelines developed by the Province, *as amended from time to time*." Also according to the latest PPS, these areas are described as places that grow "tender fruits (peaches, cherries, plums), grapes, other fruit crops, vegetable crops, greenhouse crops, and crops from agriculturally developed organic soil."[38]

The recent policy statement also outlines conditions under which activity other than farming can be conducted within an SCA. The extraction of mineral-aggregate resources is allowable, according to the 2014 PPS, "provided that the site will be rehabilitated back to an agricultural condition." But if full restoration cannot be achieved, mining and associated development is still permitted provided "there is a substantial quantity of high quality mineral aggregate" in the area.[39]

Despite the ostensible intentions of the Greenbelt Plan to protect the countryside generally and farmland specifically, there remains an economic caveat that reveals an instrumentality to how the province conceives of biophysical nature and landscapes. It is not surprising, for example, that the two SCAs – afforded the most comprehensive protections – are also among the most profitable agricultural lands in Ontario. Similarly, mining and aggregate extraction are highly profitable ways of exploiting land and, likely for this reason, allowable, even privileged, within a supposedly ecologically protected zone.

Operationally, the greenbelt legislation affects the farmers' land in at least two ways. First, it freezes the development rights of landowners within each designated area and prevents them from "freely disposing of their property in the marketplace." Second, it imposes a new "positive obligation" on landowners by requiring them to provide or to continue providing "environmental amenities."[40] The expectation within the logic of the plan is that amenity services will be present in the countryside as a consequence of restricting its development. The onus, in this respect, is placed on the farmers.

In this regional environmentalism as expressed through the Greenbelt Plan, the imaginary (or ideology, as Neil Smith has put it) of nature is on full display. There is no mention of subsidence at all within the plan or the SCA legislation. Indeed, it seems as though the sociocultural perceptions of the muck soil have superseded its biophysical reality. In other aligned reports sponsored by Friends of the Greenbelt, the idea that muck is a sturdy, unassailable substance is regularly reproduced. Shelley Petrie and three colleagues write that the Holland Marsh is protected "because of its soil quality and importance in Ontario's agricultural history" while making no mention of subsidence.[41] Jessica Bartram, Susan Lloyd Swail, and Burkhard Mausberg, meanwhile, bring up the inevitability of subsidence (though they do not use the technical term) in only one paragraph of a thirty-three-page report on the challenges of Marsh agriculture. Yet even then, they casually write off any immediate consequence of subsidence by suggesting that the soil will be "stripped of its fertility in 100 to 200 years."[42] Neither of these reports mentions the subsidence estimates of either McDonald and Chaput or Mirza and Irwin.

As the muck soil continues to subside, it is unclear what the effect will be on the conditions of private-poverty ownership in the Holland Marsh. Many there insist that the area will always remain agricultural land due to the SCA designation and its location within a flood plain. These claims, however, can be scrutinized. First, provincial legislation and the legal basis of property are both impermanent and changeable, and there is no guarantee that, as the soil continues to subside, the SCA designation will remain in place. Beyond this, the most recent PPS indicates, as noted, that the Marsh or any other SCA can be mined for high-quality mineral materials, if present. Furthermore, no remediation of the SCA is required if the extraction process renders "restoration of pre-extraction agriculture capability unfeasible."[43] Suggesting that the area is a flood plain as a way of rationalizing that it will never be built on, meanwhile, underappreciates the fact that the Marsh is already a built environment highly tuned to managing water levels.

For the farmers, the introduction of the Greenbelt Plan has been received, for the most part, as yet another set of rules and regulations that might eventually have some effect on them. Many also see it as a potential and partial element protecting their agricultural livelihoods. Area residents typically invoke the idea that the Holland Marsh is in a flood plain as evidence that it will always remain agricultural land. Some now understand the protections afforded to agriculture under the plan as further proof of the immutability of agriculture in the Marsh. As one farmer, who refers to the protections for the Oak Ridges Moraine, an area protected by the greenbelt, explains: "Well first off, we're not really worried it's going to be taken over by development, because it's zoned for agriculture. And it's also in a flood plain. And it's also a green area, Oak Ridges Moraine, as well. So it's protected from industry."[44]

Optimism is almost a job requirement for farming, given the vagaries of weather, markets, and dozens of other factors likely to intervene in one's livelihood and income throughout the course of any given year. So it is not surprising that most growers in the Holland Marsh feel that agriculture will always exist there. They might admit that muck-crop farming may end but are confident that the transition to mineral-soil and greenhouse farming (which has already begun) will provide them the opportunities and lifestyle afforded by the muck soil. But such optimism in this case may be misguided. The protective measures currently afforded by the Greenbelt Act, like those of any piece of legislation, are impermanent and subject to political machinations and election cycles; they may very well change. The current definition of the Marsh as a designated SCA is premised, in part, on the uniqueness of the muck soil. But as the muck subsides, leaving only mineral soil, the question of whether it will continue to be a protected agricultural area is a very valid one. Mineral-soil farming is not as profitable as muck-soil farming – the financial calculus vis-à-vis peri-urban development may one day tip in favour of the latter. Ultimately, the question of whether agriculture will remain in the Marsh over the next one hundred years is impossible to answer at this point. How biophysical nature is defined and produced, and what kinds of biophysical natures are privileged, will all be central to the future of Holland Marsh agriculture.

The City, Countryside, and Crops: Contradictions and Conflicts in the New Nature of the Holland Marsh

High interest rates, escalating housing prices, and the pursuit of cheap land ignited a building boom in the hinterlands of the Greater Toronto Area beginning in the early 1990s. On the south side of the Holland Marsh, the boundaries of Aurora, Newmarket, and Vaughan began to creep northward, while on the north side, those of Bradford and Barrie expanded southward. More recently, discussions have emerged within the Bradford City Council to encourage commercial and industrial development on either side of Highway 400.[45] While the Marsh will continue to be a protected SCA (at least for now), building as close to it as possible – to maximize the utility of Marsh produce and to create employment closer to Bradford and the urbanizing hinterland – is emerging as a high priority. As one Bradford politician put it:

> They'll never build on the Marsh. The only development I championed was putting employment on either side of Highway 400. My argument is, people can say, "Oh, either side of the 400 is valuable farm land." Well that ship sailed when you paved it over with 6 lanes of highway, so now let's maximize the utility of that massive piece of infrastructure, so you can actually put a business there, or businesses plural there. You hop on an interchange, and you get to the largest market in the country in, you know . . . from our border to Steeles Avenue is 20 minutes. I measured it. I know these things.[46]

Local job creation is a key priority for many urban politicians in and around the Holland Marsh. Given the mechanization and consolidation of agriculture in recent years, it now employs far fewer people than it once did – farm populations are diminishing, an appreciable trend since at least the 1980s.[47] At the same time, beginning in roughly the early 1990s, housing developers in Bradford, capitalizing on relatively cheap land, began luring homebuyers to the area with the promise of the "Bradford bonus," proximity to the Marsh and "a pleasing mix of . . . small-town charm and big-city conveniences."[48] This double pressure – an increase in urban population and a decrease in agricultural work – created the impetus to make nonfarm job growth a key priority in the area.

The west part of Bradford, in particular, has experienced intensive suburban development in recent years. A new commercial and retail development,

FIGURE 5.1. Sprawling city meets the fields. New luxury homes and burgeoning subdivisions on the edges of the Holland Marsh increase demand for new roads, water service, sewage disposal, power generation, and the like. By the author.

consisting of dozens of stores and straddling both sides of Holland Street West, now anchors significant residential neighborhoods of hundreds of homes directly adjacent to it. Increasingly, the pull of this commercial-retail power centre draws residents from across Bradford, threatening ongoing efforts to revitalize the downtown core. A couple of blocks from the development centre, at the intersection of Holland Street West and Professor Day Drive, sits a brand-new library, archives, and community centre, providing further amenities on the west side of town.

These changes in and around the Holland Marsh – the accelerated material and discursive urbanization of the rural landscape throughout the 1980s and 1990s – are emblematic of Terry Marsden's idea of the "consumption countryside." While Marsden's focus lies in Europe, his observations are instructive to North America. As a host of broadly political economic trends emerged in the 1990s, including intensified neoliberal globalization, new information and communication technologies, and the de/reregulation of state activities, the countryside was pulled into an increasingly globalized, and urbanized, society – or rather the increasingly globalized and urbanized society began to extend into the countryside. As a result, according to Marsden, rural areas became "progressively less self-sufficient, self-contained and sectorally controlled, and ever more open to the wider forces (economic, social, political) shaping . . . global development."[49]

As Bradford expanded, other villages in the area grew into towns, and towns nearby into cities, a host of infrastructural needs emerged, ranging from road improvements and expansions to sewage-treatment facilities, garbage dumps, and power plants. This is the often invisible (to urban residents) shrapnel spiraling out of urban development. Yet to farmers in the Holland Marsh, the pressures of this growth around them have had material consequences on their trade. In some instances, these frustrations have occurred over idiosyncratic issues. In one recent case, farmers became agitated by the inability to make a left turn out of the Marsh toward one of the main packing plants in Bradford because traffic has become so heavy in recent years. Given that they often make multiple trips per day and, more importantly, depend on selling their produce to the packing houses in a timely manner, being held up by traffic is no small inconvenience. Eventually, the issue was resolved when a local politician succeeded in having a traffic light installed at the intersection in question. Nevertheless, residual resentment regarding local roads remains.

In other cases, issues garnering wider attention have arisen. Conflict over the siting of a gas-fired power plant within eyeshot of the Holland Marsh in 2008 was particularly fierce. According to the project proponents, Pristine Power's York Energy Centre was designed to be a peaking generation facility, meaning that it would only produce energy when the wider power grid required additional capacity. With the recent population growth in the area, however, energy is increasingly in high demand, which led many local residents to believe that the plant would run – burning gas and polluting their environment – far more often than officials claimed in their proposal.[50] Opponents argued that siting the plant so close to the Marsh and the south canal posed too great a risk to the ecological health and economic viability of the area should a fuel leak ever occur.[51] Beyond this hypothetical possibility, it was feared that the plant's emissions and the water requirements as a matter of routine operation would put the environment and nearby farms at risk. Growers felt that their concerns were misguidedly dismissed within a planning process that privileged the production of joules over the production of calories –as one farmer-blogger put it, "you can't eat energy."[52] Despite the angry opposition, construction of the plant and the associated infrastructure needed to bring in fuel and to distribute the generated power proceeded; it was completed in May 2012.

Growers, not surprisingly, typically oppose developments on the immediate margins of the Holland Marsh. Such projects are viewed as threatening incursions and have created anxiety within the agricultural community. As the farmers look from their fields up to the hills beyond, increasingly they see a colonizing urbanization that makes them feel as if they are "under siege."[53] As another Marsh farmer put it, "I feel like I'm beginning to farm inside a city."[54] With increasing numbers of urbanites looking for cheaper real estate and a pastoral lifestyle in the countryside, tensions increase. Such rural migrants buying land in the Marsh, perhaps even more than the commercial/retail/infrastructure developments in the highlands, are seen as direct threats to the fields. As one farmer observed,

> You get some people from the city, nothing against city people. We need city people, we love city people, however, when they're investing in real estate, they buy it and think, "Well, I can do whatever I want to with it." No, you can't. And they set up a business, or they start burying construction materials (in the fields). . . . You have people who will come out here, and they get 10 acres and a house and they pay half a million for it and think, "Oh my god, I've died and gone to heaven," because in the city you get a postage stamp and pay $500,000 for it.[55]

Part of the worry is that urbanites buying property in the Holland Marsh are increasing the spread of tenant-farmed land there and further adding to grower vulnerability. While no definitive aggregate data exists on land tenure in the Marsh, it seems that as nonfarmers move in to purchase property, increasingly, more fields are being rented out to the farmers than are owned by them. At the same time, differences in what each group values about the land have also become apparent. One long-time grower has seen an increase in this dynamic in recent years,

> You tend to rent some of other people's land with yours. But it's also hard to.... [W]hat's happened is that you have a house, a nice house, and a barn, a little outdated maybe.... It's almost useless for us to buy that, because we don't need that 300, 400 thousand dollar home, and that barn is just totally outdated, and we don't need that. And you get somebody from Toronto, and they say, "Oh, I like that house, I'd like to live here, and I get 5 or 10 acres of land." So sometimes it just goes to total strangers. And they just rent it out to you. Sometimes they try to farm it themselves, but that doesn't work. Well, they get a little bit of income. Say they paid $500 thousand for the whole thing, for 10 acres and the house and all that stuff. It doesn't pay for us to buy it.[56]

Urban aesthetics and imaginaries – in other words, the ideas and perceptions that "city people" have about nature – clearly also have a role in shaping the materiality of the Holland Marsh. Modern Torontonians moving to the Marsh, an ostensibly empty, open, natural landscape, make the same mistake that the original Marsh boosters did. Both the contemporary city people and the original boosters had perceptions about nature and landscape that erase important and ongoing histories. What was a First Nations' fishing grounds, cover for bootleggers, or an important part of a complex ecology was dismissed by the early boosters in much the same way that current-day agriculture and agricultural practices are often dismissed by urban notions of the rural.

Bradford residents, as an example, have been known to complain about the very fields they have chosen to live near – fields they have been drawn to based on a pastoral imaginary. Complaints from urban residents based on noise or odour have become fairly routine as a symptom of the colliding city and countryside. One farmer-advocate expressed her frustration in what she sees as the threat posed by urbanization:

> So we're not pumping pesticides into the water, the lake, or anything like that. Pesticides are being used for sure, but the products now are almost entirely reduced risk materials. There are a few exceptions. But the growers are doing a very good job of applying them properly, and managing them properly. But, when somebody's got their newborn baby out in their back yard, and they think they can smell something, you know, that doesn't help. So too much... urbanization close to the Marsh is always a threat.... Irrigating at night is the best time to irrigate, but you know the neighbors complain because the pumps keep them awake, and of course they have to irrigate when it's hot and dry, and people have windows open, unless they have air conditioners.[57]

Certainly, the expectation of all residents, whether urban, suburban, or rural, should be to be able to live free from the risk of chemical poisoning. And, of course, bringing concerns related to chemical pesticides to the fore, as did the Newmarket medical officer of health in the late 1970s, often can have important implications. Complaints from urban residents on the southern hills of Bradford about the odour of pesticide treatments are certainly justified – this is not meant to minimize them. But it is worth emphasizing that these conflicts arise precisely at the intersection – sometimes almost literally – of the fields and front yards. While this will undoubtedly result in a variety of longer-term implications, it is clear that farmers are already worried that it means the continuation of a broader, somewhat disconcerting trend – farm practices being determined by nonfarmers. As one long-time employee of the Muck Crops Research Station put it: "I think that's the biggest threat that . . . it's the pressure from people who aren't farming, to change farming practices or stop farming. So that's a pressure that I'm concerned about."[58]

The Evergreen Revolution and Building a "Better" Nature in the Holland Marsh

As these multiple farmland pressures – ecological, pedological, financial, and demographic – descend on the area, Holland Marsh farmers are responding in familiar ways. In the 1960s, mechanization was the tactic through which the paradigm of productivist agriculture was introduced. Fifty years later, the approach seems to be a technologization of farming, though the end goal remains the same – to extract profit from the muck soil and maintain a viable livelihood. The techno-optimism present in the Marsh throughout its history is seemingly being doubled down on as growers seek ways of insulating against the constant vagaries of weather and markets while surviving the more substantive issues of subsidence and suburbanization.

This technological zeal was on full display at the 63rd Annual Muck Vegetable Growers Conference, hosted by the Muck Crops Research Station and the University of Guelph.[59] Dr. George Lazarovits, director of research at A&L Biologicals, a private, for-profit agricultural research and diagnostics laboratory, gave an illuminating presentation titled "The New Era of Diagnostics and Biological Control."[60] Speaking to a crowd of close to seventy-five people (consisting of farmers, crop researchers, and agro-industry representatives), Lazarovits shared a story about Dean Glenney, a corn and soybean farmer in Dunnville, Ontario, a small town close to where the Grand River meets Lake Erie. He recounted how Glenney had noticed that the rows of corn and soybeans closest to the fence posts in his fields seemed to be more successful than those elsewhere. The stalks grew taller, the ears of corn were fuller and plumper, and the plants seemed more resistant to extreme weather conditions. Flummoxed initially, Glenney eventually speculated that the difference had something to do with the fact the soil of the rows closest to the fence posts was often not tilled as thoroughly as elsewhere. Hitting a fence post with a tiller can result in costly repairs to both the fence and the machine; rather than risk catastrophe, he would typically give the posts a wide berth.

Testing his hypothesis, as the story goes, Glenney began to till fewer hectares and, eventually, stopped tilling his fields altogether. When he seeded in the spring, he was careful to drive his seeder in the exact same spot from year to year in order to minimize soil compaction. An agricultural engineer by trade, Glenney even custom built a special seeding machine to minimize soil disturbance. He refers to this technique as "fence row farming," premised on leaving the soil as undisturbed as possible. As Glenney put it, "The secret is to just get out of the worms' way."[61]

Of course, no-till farming did not originate on Glenney's farm. The technique has been used around world as a counterpoint to mechanized farming for decades. Still, for the past few years, Glenney has been a quasi-celebrity among the farming community in Ontario. In 2015, he was even crowned "Soil Champion of Ontario" by the Ontario Soil and Crop Improvement Association. The attention he has been getting is, within the farming community, no idle curiosity. Glenney's fence-row farming, as Lazarovits pointed out in his presentation, has consistently generated corn and soybean yields twice the national average. He has been studying Glenney's farm and farming techniques in an attempt to isolate the science (and, thus harness the profit potential) of fence-row farming. Lazarovits claimed that his findings confirm recent speculation in the broader commercial-agricultural research sector that a third agricultural revolution is underway. As he put it to the conference attendees in early April 2014: "From 8000 BC to 1950 we went through the agricultural revolution. From 1950 to 2010 we went through the green revolution. And from 2010 to 2050 we're going to go through the *evergreen* revolution."[62]

The so-called evergreen revolution in farming is taking place in the rhizosphere, an ever-changing, curiously indefinable area at the root-soil interface. First identified by the German agronomist Lorenz Hiltner in 1904, the rhizosphere is a complex physical, biological, and chemical protean amalgam. It "is not a region of definable size or shape, but instead, consists of a gradient in chemical, biological and physical properties which change both radially and longitudinally along the root."[63] In other words, as roots grow, their chemical, biological, and physical properties change as does the character of their particular rhizosphere.

Scientists of various agriculture-related disciplines now believe the rhizosphere to be, in effect, the most important factor in plant health and crop yields. Not surprisingly, this has led to a burgeoning interest from those with a pecuniary interest in agriculture. Lazarovits speculates that through a prolonged period of nondisturbance, Glenney has developed a unique, robust microbial ecosystem uniquely adapted to corn and soybeans, one that stimulates a robust and tailored rhizosphere. Early results of his experimentation have demonstrated that the soil bacteria and pythium in Glenney's soil are fewer and far more uniform than in control soil, suggesting that Lazarovits's tailored-ecosystem speculation is on track.

As the alleged third agricultural revolution marches onward, some concerning and familiar arguments are recirculating. Indeed, the Indian agronomist Mankombu Sambasivan Swaminathan, considered by many to be one of the fathers of the green revolution, is now a chief prognosticator of the evergreen revolution. Analogous to its predecessor, the evergreen revolution is promising lower input costs, higher yields, and increased profit for farmers – and in the process farmland loss is being further destabilized as a legitimate concern as it was during the height of the previous period. But while the green revolution relied heavily on chemical inputs (fertilizers, pesticides, and the like) and genetic manipulation of seed germplasm, the evergreen revolution will allegedly improve on these past practices with better science, information, and technology. In some ways, the modernist proclamations of twentieth-century agriculture are simply being rearticulated through the science and technology of the twenty-first.

The failures of the agricultural green revolution typically go unspoken in the boosterist accounts of this putative third revolution. Yet it is worth recalling the many negative social and ecological consequences of technology-reliant, profit-driven agriculture. Agro-food system scholar and activist Jack Kloppenburg provides a useful list:

> These include the exacerbation of regional inequalities, generation of income inequalities at the farm level, increased scales of operation, specialization of production, displacement of labour, accelerating mechanization, depressed product prices, changing tenure patterns, rising land prices, expanding markets for commercial inputs, agrichemical dependence, genetic erosion, pest-vulnerable monocultures, and environmental deterioration.[64]

Yet many patterns of the green revolution are being reproduced by its successor, including an emphasis on ecological modernist and productivist notions of biophysical nature. While Glenney was content to simply get out of the way of the worms, as he put it, a whole host of commercial, profit-driven agricultural companies are scrambling to very much insinuate themselves in the rhizosphere through the manipulation of bacteria. As Lazarovits put it, "We have to figure out how to exploit these microorganisms to produce better crops."[65] He continued: "What we're hoping to do – and many companies are very interested in this – is to develop a method of bio-fertilizing plants, putting those good guys back in the soil. And if you can do that, it may take much less than the five or six years to get the growth promotion that Dean's site took."[66]

This is Glenney's "leave it alone" approach done in a hurry – an attempt to impose a capitalist time scale on a biophysical process in order to speed up the arrival of increased production. The evergreen revolution is emerging in ways familiar to the green revolution before it but refracted through the paradigms of just-in-time delivery, information and communication technologies, the Internet, and social media. And while understanding and, more to the point, manipulating rhizosphere ecologies are thus far incomplete projects, a new wave of science and technology, based on information and diagnostics, is already blanketing the growing fields.

Lazarovits's presentation on Glenney was well placed, given that the commercial appeal – and hubris – of this forthcoming iteration of agricultural activity is on full display at the annual Muck Vegetable Growers Conference. In some ways, his presentation was evocative of Professor Day's test-plot yield demonstrations eighty years previously. Of course, the particular technologies on display differ, yet each represents an attempt to harness biophysical nature through cutting-edge technologies for the purpose of demonstrating human mastery and increasing profits. In a departure from Day's presentations in the 1930s, the contemporary conference, designed primarily to bring muck-crop researchers and farmers together, heavily features commercial agrochemical, agro-technology, and agro-research companies. These businesses are willing to pay for access to the conference participants – potential customers – through presentation slots, trade show displays, and paid advertisements in the conference directory. The trade show portion of the conference, set up in an erstwhile hockey rink at the Bradford and District Community Centre, features a mix of agricultural equipment manufacturers, chemical and technology companies, seed companies, and farm-management companies. Regardless of the function, all of them emphasize the extent to which cutting-edge technology is an essential element of farming in the contemporary period.

Their technologies promise to reveal to farmers the *real* secret of farming, which is not to simply get out of the worms' way, as Glenney suggests, but to push biophysical nature aside. Ads for various technologies and agrochemicals featured in the conference guide are instructive. One such technology, Field Manager Pro 360, promises to let farmers "see [their] farms like never before." The product ostensibly enables them to probe below the surface of their fields with a stratified, analytic precision. The tacit pledge is that exposing the subsurface stratum will reveal important, commodifiable information to farmers.

Within the paradigm of capitalist farming, peering into the depths of one's fields is only useful in as much as it is profitable. Phostrol, a phosphorus-based fungicide manufactured by Nufarm, which similarly suggests that peeling back the skin and gazing into the very heart of biophysical nature can (perhaps should) similarly reveal undiscovered profit. Its ad features the image of a money-lined potato and strikingly demonstrates the extent to which the pursuit of profit through the exploitation of biophysical nature has become normalized. Perhaps not all farmers see their carrots, onions, and potatoes lined with twenty-dollar bills, but the normative implication here is that they should. DuPont, meanwhile, warns farmers, "This year in the Marsh, one move will make all the difference." The promise in its ad seemingly strips away the inherent contingencies of nature's production in the Holland Marsh – inclement weather, pests, floods, poor markets, and the like – reducing the determination of success down to the use of DuPont's fungicide. The operative notion here is precision – with one, almost clinical, sure-fire "move," Marsh farmers can be guaranteed of a profitable season.

The notion of precision is increasingly pervasive and influential within the agricultural sphere. While there is a rich tradition of (attempts at) controlling aspects of biophysical nature in the Holland Marsh – from the initial canal development to tame the landscape, to the introduction of cold-storage and shipping technologies, and so on – the precision paradigm strives for something beyond simple control.

Within the context of this green revolution 2.0, modernist notions of human control over biophysical nature have been redoubled – the expectation now is that biophysical nature is fully able to be manipulated, customized, and sanitized of uncertainty and unpredictability. As DuPont promises surgical-like precision with "one move," PlantProof claims to bring the kind of control previously only afforded to indoor greenhouse environments to the outdoor environment of the muck soil of the Marsh. Attempts are being made, in other words, to transcend the messy, contingent outdoors of the farm fields through a discursive and material transformation, with the intended result of an imposition of ultimate control.

The evolution of seeding in the Holland Marsh is emblematic of the desire to construct and control biophysical nature with ever more precision. While, initially, farmers in the Marsh, much like anywhere, would collect seeds each year to sow the following season, that practice has long since ceded to an international political economy of seed manufacturers. As one long-time Marsh grower recounted:

> They used to do that, in the very, very beginning for a little while. But that petered out pretty quick and it's all gone now. There are certain areas that really lend itself [*sic*] for growing, reproducing seed. And it's like a dry climate where they do that. And they also now have places in South America, so if they have a crop failure here, they still have a chance of getting the seed for you in South America. You got two chances. And, so, these seed companies have become multinational; they're just all over the world.[67]

Of course, the seeds now grown in the Holland Marsh have been modified, designed, and tested to express certain – profitable – characteristics, including uniformity, yield, weight, and the like. These are the seeds of the green revolution. Those of the evergreen revolution, however, typically undergo further processing, with a coating of growth-promoting, pest-deterring chemical material applied well before planting. Each seed is encrusted with an application of various chemicals – importantly, this coating is designed to give them a sculpted uniformity. The chemicals promote profitable growth, as has been the case for decades now, while the shape of the seed facilitates precision planting. In the high-stakes context of muck farming, the distance between seeds is a crucial consideration. Most farmers now use a variation of an air seeder, a device that controls planting with air pressure. Rather than allowing it to roll on a belt, as traditional seeders do, air seeders control the coated, uniform seed with a much higher degree of precision, allowing farmers to plant with great accuracy. As one grower who had recently converted to using an air seeder explained:

> You know, you wanna put 9.5 seeds per foot, well you can put 9.5 seeds per foot. Before you used to have to guess, you used to weigh the seed and do all that stuff. And still, depending on your speed and that, you're always off. Now, it's very accurate, you get a lot better crops.[68]

The pursuit of seed-application perfection is a tactical intervention, part of a broader strategy farmers employ in order to simply stay in business in an increasingly competitive sector and in the context of increasingly precarious ecological conditions. An additional motivation for precision specificity is the simple reality of the subsiding muck soil. The notion of simply walking away from the Holland Marsh and letting it return to whatever socionatural hybrid it might become if left fallow is out of the question. The strategy is to farm more carefully – with more precision – in an attempt to extend the profitable life of the muck soil, to get as much out if it as possible before the soil vanishes completely. There is an element of ecological stewardship here, to be sure, but the more immediate concern of simply staying in business is the priority.

In a similar vein, the use of diagnostic technologies in the Holland Marsh, while present for many years, has intensified recently. The Integrated Pest Management System run by the Muck Crops Research Station, versions of which are offered by all of the major seed and agrochemical companies operating in the Marsh, provides extensive field surveillance and feedback. While field scouts are still used by most pest-management programs – usually summer students literally walking the fields looking for outbreaks and infestations – drones are beginning to appear over the Marsh. Armed with high-powered cameras, these vehicles are the latest technology conscripted into the increasingly fevered world of crop surveillance. Although drone use is not yet mainstream in the Marsh, according to one farmer, the station has been experimenting with them as part of their system.[69]

Once a drone, farmer, or field scout has identified an infested site, the common practice now is to text message, email, or tweet a picture of it either to a specific office (the station or an agrochemical company) or to a wider community of farmers in order to identify the pest and devise a treatment. One farmer explained this process:

> You know, guys with their smart phones [go out] now, walking their crops, checking it. They see some kind of weed, take a picture of it, put it on Twitter, "What is this?" or they send it, they email it to their crop advisor at Cargill or wherever they get their inputs from, and they get back to you and say, "Oh you need this chemical, this crop protection treatment product." It's neat. You can get answers right away now, there's not that lag time. It's pretty neat – it's exciting stuff.[70]

Undoubtedly, the pursuit of precision has served to change, in some fundamental ways, the process of agriculture in the Holland Marsh. Farming is a fickle undertaking, even within the carefully built environment of the Marsh. The elimination of contingencies through manifold technologies – advanced pesticide treatments, rebuilding the canal, seed coatings, and air seeders – is, however, only ever partial and largely based on perception. The biophysical nature farmers want – pliable, predictable, and profitable – and the one promised to them by the purveyors of agricultural technologies and techniques remains, and likely will remain, beyond reach. Biophysical nature will continue to operate in uncontrollable ways, possibly through ever-evolving diseases and pests in the muck soil, perhaps through a storm of similar magnitude to Hurricane Hazel, and inevitably through the subsidence of the soil. Attempts to forestall and eliminate the variability, degradation, and downright surprising character of biophysical dynamics remain an important fulcrum on which the production of socionatures teeters.

Conclusion

The hubris of the green revolution resulted in a decidedly toxic socionatural amalgam in the Holland Marsh, leading to the emergence of a variety of socioecological contradictions during the last decade of the twentieth century. While initially obstructionist, or at least reluctant to be transparent about the extent and effects of chemical-dependent farming in the Marsh, the liberal state eventually became interested in regulating the production of nature in the area when Lake Simcoe's deteriorating ecological health led to public shaming. New rules and regulations on chemical and phosphorus use in the Marsh eventually changed the socionatural configurations beyond it; algal blooms are no longer as significant an issue now as they were in the late 1990s. As a legacy of this, the provincial government, through the Ministry of the Environment (along with the LSRCA) and the Greenbelt Act, has become increasingly implicated in the production of agriculture in the Marsh.

A close inspection of farming in the Holland Marsh, particularly since 1990, demonstrates the extent to which the liberal state, politics, and planning are active forces in remaking agriculture there. The imposition of water-taking protocols, the banning and restriction of certain pesticides, and the inevitability of subsidence – as examples – all commingle in sometimes cooperative, sometimes contradictory ways to coproduce farming in the Marsh.

The compulsion of competition and the struggle for livelihood has led many Marsh farmers to embrace the coming agricultural "evergreen revolution" promised by the burgeoning agro-technology and agro-research sectors. These industries claim the ability to create a more precise and profitable crop without the negative externalities of the green-revolution technologies. But as farmers, aided by the agro-tech sector, push to transcended the biophysical limits of crops in the pursuit of a stable livelihood, the spectre of James O'Connor's insights regarding the second contradiction of capital loom over them – intensive agriculture, regardless of the promises of emergent technologies, tends to damage the conditions it needs for ongoing production. How these contradictions will manifest remains to be seen, but that they will manifest seems nearly certain.

Holland Marsh farmers are at the centre of these divergent, competing conceptions of what kinds of biophysical nature are (or ought to be) produced in their fields. To be sure, they continue to pursue the most immediately profitable path possible. Increasingly, however, they are doing so in a regulatory and technological milieu rife with radically different normative conceptions of what biophysical nature in the Marsh ought to be. Farming continues – almost improbably – despite the crush of suburbanization, soil subsidence, and federal, provincial, regional, and municipal rules, regulations, and legislation. Yet inconsistencies in the kind of socionatures resulting from these myriad processes and protocols mean that growers operate in a radically ambivalent context. Despite decades striving for certainty and predictability, ultimately uncertainty and contradictions persist in the fields of the Holland Marsh.

CONCLUSION

W(h)ither the Marsh?

ON JANUARY 23, 2015, Avia Eek, a long-time Holland Marsh farmer and councillor for Ward Six in King Township, tweeted about a recent trip to the grocery store with her husband, Bill: "Bill & I did some grocery shopping tonight. 3# of #Canada #onions $1.99. Our #Farmers are getting $3.00 for 50# #disgusted."[1] Records from the *Toronto Daily Star* confirm that farmers were getting essentially the same price (between $2.85 and $3.25) for fifty pounds of cooking onions now as they did in the spring of 1958 – almost sixty years previous to Eek's tweet.[2] I found the *Toronto Daily Star* produce-market column a few months earlier, and when I saw Eek's tweet, I sent a reply highlighting the similarities in price: "@eekfarms, *Toronto Star*, March 1958. 50lb cooking, $2.85–3.25, crate of Spanish, $4.00–4.25. Almost 60 years ago."[3] I also included a digital reproduction of the original newspaper column. The exchange between Eek and I received a number of responses from other Twitter users commenting on the low onion prices, with thoughts and opinions on everything from the increased cost of production to the greed of the oil and gas industry undermining other key sectors of the Canadian economy. It was a quintessentially twenty-first-century discussion about some very old issues. The onion, an enduring agricultural product of the Holland Marsh since the very beginning, had gone digital.

The reasons for low onion prices in 2015 reflect a socionatural amalgam of persistent and emergent issues. On the one hand, 2014 was a bumper year for Holland Marsh onions, exceeding even the strong yields many in the area consider a standard. The local market was flooded with high-quality onions even before the problem was exacerbated by reemerging Cold War geopolitics. Responding to growing tensions with the European Union, the Russian government established a variety of trade embargoes, including the importation of onions. The drop in demand this created significantly impacted major producing markets in Europe, including the Netherlands, costing the sector there tens of millions of euros.[4] This complicated geopolitical impasse effectively created a glut of onions on the global market. Excess European supply spilled out around the world, including to the Caribbean, a key destination for Marsh produce.[5] A bumper crop locally and an excess supply in the global market combined to drive down prices, leaving farmers in the Marsh with a significant surplus of onions that they had great difficulty finding a market for.

Holland Marsh farmers of 2015 were thus confronted with a very similar problem as that of their forebears of the 1930s. When the Marsh was first brought into agricultural production in the early 1930s, supply far outstripped the demand of the local market, causing many to simply plough their crops back into the muck. In 2015, cold-storage, transportation, and advanced seed-germplasm-manipulation technologies were such that the crises of glut and price could be forestalled, though not indefinitely. By the late spring of 2015, the 2014 vintage onions in cold storage were approaching the end of their shelf life, which forced farmers to dump the crop for whatever price they could get, wherever they could get it – cutting their losses while figuratively ploughing the 2014 harvest back into the field. This vignette, unfortunate though it was for the Marsh farmers who, once again, were bearing the brunt of a disjuncture between supply and demand, encapsulates the dynamics I have attempted to highlight and articulate throughout this book.

Chronicling the histories of our areas of local agricultural production is important. While there are many rich community-produced histories of agriculture across Canada (including several on the Holland Marsh), there are far too few scholarly accounts of local and regional agriculture in Ontario, or even around Canada for that matter.[6] The profound effects agriculture has had on the fabric of Ontario has been captured to some extent through macro and national perspectives refracted largely through the staples-thesis lens. Yet these accounts cannot capture the local particularisms, stories, and cultures of the sundry agricultural regions across the province. Muck-crop farming, as a handy example, is scarcely mentioned in any of the canonical contributions of Ontario's agricultural history. Capturing the history of the Holland Marsh is crucially important to adding texture to our understanding of Canada's agricultural past, present, and future. It can help us move beyond thinking about agriculture (in the singular) and instead refocus on exploring the agricultures (in plural) that exist across the province and across the country. Local food systems will be increasingly more important in the months and years ahead, and it behooves us to know something about them.

One of the key issues the story of the Holland Marsh raises is the limit of the liberal state to stabilize small-scale domestic production. While the Marsh is a fierce economic driver, it sits in a relatively small car. The federal state is far more likely to intervene in matters related to canola, corn, or soybeans than they are to carrots or onions. Ontario has fewer levers to pull in terms of farmer-income stabilization, and the relevant municipalities scarcely have the resources to maintain the drainage system, let alone bail out Marsh farmers in times of intense downward pressures on price or (socio)natural catastrophe.

The liberal-state apparatus has undoubtedly supported the Holland Marsh – from enabling the initial drainage to developing the specialty crop designation, though this support has almost exclusively been within the domestic realm. Since the mid-1980s, there has been less state support in the form of agricultural income-stabilization programs as international trade agreements have emerged.[7] The tools available to municipal, provincial, and federal governments to support domestic agriculture are being dulled by international neoliberal trade policy. The 2014 crisis notwithstanding, the Marsh has largely been insulated – at least as it relates to prices – from the effects of global agricultural instability. It seems likely, however, that as emerging international trade developments continue to supersede and frustrate national and subnational policy, global politics will play a larger role in the Marsh in the years to come.

International developments in agro-technologies have had, arguably, a much more profound influence on the Holland Marsh than international politics thus far. From the adoption of ice-packing facilities, pallet boxes, and food-grade plastic wrap in the 1950s to the introduction of novel chemicals and seed varieties, the Marsh has relied on technologies developed internationally to enable and stabilize production. Even the dredger that cut the original canal system was a US import.

In some instances, individual farmers and investors (like the Latchman brothers) have introduced technologies into the Holland Marsh. In other cases, institutions have played a key role in the integration of agro-technologies. The Muck Crops Research Station, with its cultivar trials and minor-use testing of agrochemicals, has been instrumental in translating and adapting essential agricultural inputs developed within the broader political-economic milieu of global agriculture to the specific context of the Marsh.

The station has played a crucial role in the ongoing productivity and stability of the area. Its annual reports, as an example, provide farmers with important insight into the performance of seed, developed elsewhere, in the Holland Marsh. Similarly, the minor-use tests provide growers there (and muck-crop farmers elsewhere) a rigorous assessment of the efficacy and safety of agrochemicals developed for other contexts and purposes. But it may also be the case that translating these technologies to the context of the Marsh will lead to future instabilities. The ecological contradictions and consequences of chemical-dependent, monoculture farming are a continual, and destabilizing, spectre of contemporary capitalist agriculture.

These contradictions are partly driven by how "nature" is understood. Shifting perceptions of nature – an ever-evolving imaginary – has been a driving force of landscape change in the Holland Marsh. The cultural resonance of biophysical nature – what it means within a given time and place – is directly related with how it is conscripted into use. The same dismal swamp that was written off by a generation of colonial explorers was understood just years later as an opportunity to produce a landscape in the image of the liberal-state ideal of orderly, smiling farms. How the Marsh has been (mis)understood has had a profound influence on how it has been used and the shape it has taken.[8]

Of course, the materiality of the Holland Marsh's biophysical nature has played an equally decisive role in the history of the area. Running water, subsiding soil, crumbling dirt canal walls, rain, snow, and sundry other examples demonstrate that biophysical nature is not so easily ordered into smiling farms. The novel administrative bodies that have emerged to corral discrete aspects of material nature – the station for seeds, the Holland Marsh Growers' Association for the plants and fields, and the Holland Marsh Drainage Commission for the canal system – combine with these biophysical characteristics in the continual reproduction of its socionatural landscape.

It is also important to recall how liberal-state policy has served to shape agriculture and socionatures in the Holland Marsh. At times, the state has appeared to operate as a monolithically capitalistic force within the Marsh, supporting the initial destruction of the wetland and the contamination of the surrounding area for economic development and profit. From the early twentieth century to roughly the late 1950s, the state was (on the whole) supportive of whatever initiatives industry proposed for the area, from its initial drainage through to the chemical recklessness of the green revolution. Despite the apparent one-sidedness of its actions during this period, it is clear that the state was not a coherent, monolithic force. The dynamics James O'Connor anticipates in terms of the second contradiction of capitalism were implicit in the state's support of agriculture in the Marsh. While not evident initially, by the 1980s, the ecological externalities of intensive industrial agriculture in the area were manifesting in ecological catastrophe. Responses to these ecological contradictions and limits were imported into the very fabric of the state through various protective polices and production regulations. In other words, even when appearing to act as a unified, coherent force, the state's actions have been far more ambivalent and contradictory when looked at in a historical trajectory.

Over time, and in response to public outcries about the condition of the ecological health of the Holland Marsh and surrounding area, the state's presence there has become a much more obviously activist force. Any farmer is happy to share multiple ways in which the state regulates, impinges on, and restricts the conditions of production – from monitoring water taking and banning chemicals to food safety and traceability protocol, the state has erected multiple policies that change the way growers do their work.

The historicity of the Marsh demonstrates that ongoing socionatural change is fundamental to shaping its future context. The drainage of a wetland on the scale of the Holland Marsh for any purpose in contemporary Ontario is very unlikely. But in 1920s Ontario, it was heralded as an exemplary land-improvement project. The intervening century consists of a trajectory – by no means inevitable – of contingent historical moments. As the landscape has changed over the years, the institutional matrix of the state – its branches, ministries, and policies – implemented in the Marsh shifted in response. Similarly, what "nature" meant to various figures and populations throughout the past hundred years has been a dynamic and decisive force in how nature has been produced in the Marsh.

Indeed, in some respects, the history of the Holland Marsh pivots on the changeable character of its natural imaginary. The earliest colonial settlers to the area –John Simcoe and John Galt – imagined the marsh as a wasteland, "a mere ditch swarming with mosquitoes, flies, bullfrogs and water snakes."[9] Many years later, W.D. Watson would look out onto the same wetland and imagine fields teeming with crops and, in 1911, wrote evocatively to William Day about his "pride at the immense possibilities which lies in the scheme."[10]

The history of the Holland Marsh resists the imposition of either a declensionist or progressive narrative structure. It does not suggest that the ongoing imagining of the Marsh has resulted in the creation of either a vaunted pastoral sanctum or a devastated septic wasteland. The truth is rather messier than either of these edifices permits.

Still, there have been severe material effects – declensionist, even catastrophic in character – as a result of the production of particular kinds of nature in the Holland Marsh. The health of humans and nonhumans alike has suffered in and around the Marsh as a direct result of agricultural activity. The remaining ambiguities about its role in elevated levels of birth anomalies in the 1960s will likely never be conclusively resolved. But given that many of the chemicals used at the time have since been banned – precisely because they have proven to be detrimental to human and nonhuman health – it seems clear that farming in the Marsh did play some role. Neither birth anomalies nor vast algal blooms fit neatly into the smiling farms narrative, yet they are material truths to confront about the kinds of nature we produce through agriculture.

This ambivalence signals an ongoing tension in the Holland Marsh – at least since the popularization of environmentalist sentiment in about the 1960s – between "the environment" and farming. Most farmers would likely insist that they are stewards of the land because their livelihoods depend on the health of the land. Yet this clearly does not make every farmer an unmitigated environmentalist. Maintaining the land in a state amenable to agricultural production, in practice, usually diverges significantly from what many environmentalists would consider stewardship. Even a hypothetical agro-ecological variety of farming, within the context of the delicate muck soil, would be too destructive to be considered ecologically sound. Yet at the same time, growing vegetables does intuitively seem to be "environmentally friendly" in some respects. But how can this be reconciled within the context of the Specialty Crop Area (SCA) designation that remains substantively silent on the one thing most important to Marsh faming, the muck soil?

Part of the problem of evaluating the ecological consequences of the production of nature in the Holland Marsh is that, in order to do so, an arbitrary baseline of sorts has to be established – an imaginary time when the ecology of the area was ostensibly "better" than it is now. One approach is to assume that the Marsh's pristine apogee was at some point in its pre-agriculture existence, and every intervention since then has been tantamount to pulling another petal off of the rose. This, of course, is a far too linear conceptualization, one that disregards the subtler aspects of the production of nature revealed throughout these chapters. Yes, there has been ecological contamination of the human and nonhuman environment, however, it is also the case that harmful chemicals have been banned and discontinued, phosphorus levels have been moderated, and safer, healthier farming techniques have continued to emerge. In other words, protective social limits have been placed on the production of nature in the Marsh. If the basis of comparison is pathogenic or bacterial, one could make the argument that the area is actually cleaner now than it was previous to the introduction of agriculture, given that the risk of contracting cholera there now is virtually nonexistent.

This is not to let farming off the hook completely. As many have pointed out, the compulsion of capitalist, productivist agriculture is to seek profit above all else, which tends to be socially and ecologically unsustainable. There is a paradox here, framed in theoretical terms by O'Connor and others: capital needs nature to reproduce, but in reproducing, capital destroys the very nature it requires. The "negative externalities" of farming there (and elsewhere) continually lurk throughout the production process. In the case of the Holland Marsh, the contradiction is literally grounded: The more intensively the soil is farmed, the more quickly it subsides.

Farmers have been experimenting with growing lower-value mineral-soil crops as well as building more greenhouses on the edges of the Marsh, where the muck soil has all but disappeared. It is difficult to say how long it will be until all of the muck in the Marsh is gone, but that it will one day be gone, and that the process is occurring in earnest, are irrefutable facts. What then will become of the Holland Marsh? It seems likely that the deterioration of the muck soil will happen slowly enough to allow growers in the area ample time to adjust to the changes, should they want to, and to continue farming mineral-soil or greenhouse crops. But it also seems clear that the Marsh will be a very different place in the absence of that formidable biophysical, cultural, and economic substance that set it apart from the start.

Here again, appreciating the specific socionatural history of the area makes clear the limits of farmland-protection policies within the context of the Holland Marsh. The state's intervention in the form of the Greenbelt Plan legislation and its associated SCA designation seems, in this case, to be inadequate to the task of preserving the muck-crop farmland. The mineral soil beneath may last for generations, but it is not at all clear that the per-hectare returns from farming it would be enough to insulate the area against suburban development.

In 1961, popular historian Pierre Berton mused about the forthcoming half century in a *Toronto Daily Star* column. He envisioned a dystopian future of overpopulation and food shortages. By 1989, he envisioned the mayor of Toronto announcing that the city had 5 million inhabitants:

> This huge consumer market, he said, ensured the prosperity of the Queen City which had out-stripped the rosiest predictions of the demographers. A few people complained about the price of bread, that had risen to $5 a loaf because of the wheat scarcity, and there was some nostalgia, too, about the good old days of green vegetables. But it was generally agreed that the draining of the Holland Marsh and its conversion into a popular midtown apartment district had been a magnificent engineering feat. As the mayor said in his statement: "You just can't stop progress."[11]

Fifty years on from Berton's perfervid imaginings, urban development *is* rapidly filling the space around the Holland Marsh. As the muck soil subsides, it may be the case that the provisions afforded to the area under the SCA designation will also erode – there is nothing particularly distinctive about mineral soil, after all. Minimally, the end of the muck soil would have to result in an end – or at least rerationalization – of the SCA designation. Similarly, the subsidence of the muck will also erode the value of the land in the Marsh. According to a 2013 report, land there was valued at between $20,000 and $25,000 per acre (roughly between $50,000 and $60,000 per hectare).[12] To put this into perspective, farmland in southcentral Ontario can be had for as little as $9,500 an acre ($23,000 per hectare).[13] At the same time, former agricultural land rezoned for residential and commercial development in the area around the Marsh fetches as much as $54,000 an acre ($130,000 per hectare).[14] As regional populations grow, land becomes scarcer, and the distinctiveness of the Marsh erodes, Berton's predictions may still come to pass.

As the Holland Marsh faces the dawning of another geologic era – the Anthropocene – amidst the roiling chaos of climate change and COVID-19, its function as a node of local food production has never been more important. A broad consensus among food-systems scholars and advocates suggests that solutions to food-system challenges can be found in place-based efforts focused on strengthening existing links – and forging new ones – between eaters and growers.[15] Terry Marsden, a key scholar of the subject argues for an "eco-economy paradigm which re'places', and indeed relocates, agriculture and its polices into the heart of regional and local systems of ecological, economic and community development."[16] The director general of the Food and Agriculture Organization of the United Nations recently noted that relocalizing food systems is "critical to achieving the goal of eradicating hunger and malnutrition, guaranteeing more sustainable food systems which are also more resilient to the effects of climate change, and ensuring a healthy and nutritious diet for all."[17] In Ontario, the provincial government has recently encouraged communities to develop regional agro-food strategies to support long-term economic prosperity and community development.[18]

These are all positive developments and might signal that liberal-state policy may be moving beyond its productivist predilection. Confronting the past shortcomings of these approaches to agricultural production and farmland protection specifically, and the "management" of socionature more generally, are increasingly urgent projects. We need to think beyond such past ways to understand what effective farmland-preservation and food-systems policy consists of. While no answers are offered here, it does seem clear that solutions will not be found in either techno-centric or eco-centric approaches. Observing that all nature is produced is a far-different argument than suggesting that all nature is controllable, as techno-centrists believe. The folly in assuming that nature has been fully tamed has been revealed at many times throughout the history of the Holland Marsh. Given the fundamental need for food, reflooding it in an attempt to return the area to its pre-agricultural state, as eco-centric perspectives might suggest, is a similarly untenable solution.

Agro-ecological and regenerative agricultural practices are charting courses that seek to balance the pursuit of a robust yield against a broad concern for people and the environment.[19] These approaches demonstrate that there need not be a trade-off between production, ecological health, and social well-being. A central motivation of the original Marsh boosters – to provide fresh produce to local markets – well aligns with agro-ecology. Provisioning local markets in a socioecologically regenerative way, aimed at girding the local food system against the destabilizing effects of climate change, global pandemics, and other unforeseen crises, however, will require us to reexamine our relationship to, and governance of, the landscape. As we approach the one hundredth anniversary of the transformation of the dismal swamp, perhaps it is time to once again reimagine the smiling fields of the Holland Marsh.

NOTES

Preface

1. Rob Wallace, Alex Liebman, Luis Fernado Chaves, and Rodrick Wallace, "COVID-19 and Circuits of Capital," *Monthly Review,* May 1, 2020, https://monthlyreview.org/2020/05/01/covid-19-and-circuits-of-capital/.

2. A. Haroon Akram-Lodhi, "Contemporary Pathogens and the Capitalist World Food System," *Canadian Journal of Development Studies / Revue Canadienne d'études du développement* 42, 1–2 (2021): 18–27, http://doi.org/10.1080/02255189.2020.1834361.

3. Spectator Editorial, "Doug Ford Takes an Axe to Greenbelt Protections," *Hamilton Spectator,* December 10, 2020, https://www.thespec.com/opinion/editorials/2020/12/10/doug-ford-takes-an-axe-to-greenbelt-protections.html.

4. Canadian Press, "Half of Ontario's Greenbelt Council Quits in Wake of Chair's Protest Resignation," *Toronto Star,* December 6, 2020, https://www.thestar.com/politics/2020/12/06/half-of-ontarios-greenbelt-council-quits-in-wake-of-chairs-protest-resignation.html.

5. William Cronon, "A Place for Stories: Nature, History, and Narrative," *Journal of American History* 78, 4 (1992): 1349 (emphasis original).

Introduction

1. I invoke here William Cronon's towering environmental history of Chicago and the Midwest, *Nature's Metropolis: Chicago and the Great West* (New York: W. W. Norton, 1991).

2. Andrew Stewart, "The Zander Site: Paleo-Indian Occupation of the Southern Holland Marsh Region of Ontario," *Ontario Archeology* 41 (1984): 45–79.

3. Dorothy Cilipka, *The Holland Marsh: The Heart of Canada's Vegetable Industry* (Beeton, ON: Simcoe York, 2004).

4. John Galt, a surveyor for the Canada Company in 1825, quoted in Bradford West Gwillimbury Local History Association, *Governor Simcoe Slept Here* (Altona, MA: Friesens, 2005), 282.

5. John L. Riley, *The Once and Future Great Lakes Country* (Montreal and Kingston: McGill-Queen's University Press, 2014), 94, 95.

6. Dave Watson quoted in Ross Irwin, C.C. Filman, and R.G. Gregg, "Report of the Committee Appointed for a Drainage Engineering Study of the Holland Marsh Area, 1968," p. 2, Archives of Ontario, #3 ARDA – Holland Marsh, B388426.

7. "Plan to Transform Dismal Swamp Area into Smiling Farms," *Globe,* March 5, 1925, 2.

8. Raj Patel, *Stuffed and Starved: The Hidden Battle for the World's Good System* (Brooklyn, NY: Melville House, 2012); Stephen Pyne, "California Wildfires Signal the Arrival of a Planetary Fire Age," *The Conversation,* November 1, 2019, https://theconversation.com/california-wildfires-signal-the-arrival-of-a-planetary-fire-age-125972 (accessed November 10, 2019); Rob Wallace, *Dead Epidemiologists: On the Origin of COVID-19* (New York: Monthly Review Press, 2020).

9. Brett Clark and John Bellamy Foster, "Ecological Imperialism and the Global Metabolic Rift," *International Journal of Comparative Sociology* 50 (2009): 311–34.

10. Miguel A. Altieri, *Agroecology: Science and Politics* (Canada: Fernwood, 2017); Eric Holt-Giménez and Miguel A. Altieri, "Agroecology, Food Sovereignty, and the New Green Revolution," *Agroecology and Sustainable Food Systems* 37, 1 (2013): 90–102.

11. Alison Blay-Palmer, R. Sonnino, and J. Custot, "A Food Politics of the Possible? Growing Sustainable Food Systems through Networks of Knowledge," *Agriculture and Human Values* 33 (2016): 27–43; Alison Blay-Palmer, G. Santini, M. Dubbeling, H. Renting, M. Taguchi, and T. Giordano, "Validating the City Region Food System Approach: Enacting Inclusive, Transformational City Region Food Systems," *Sustainability* 10 (2018): 1680, http://doi.org/10.3390/su10051680.

12. The Soil Classification Working Group of Agriculture and Agri-Food Canada periodically publishes an exhaustive taxonomy of soil in Canada. The document was updated most recently in 1998. Organic soil is one of the orders of soil classification, which include "soils commonly known as peat, muck, or bog and fen soils." Soil Classification Working Group, *The Canadian System of Soil Classification,* 3rd ed. (Ottawa: Research Branch, Agriculture and Agri-Food Canada, 1998), chap. 9, para 2. The organic order is one of the more recent additions to the classification system, having been officially inducted at the 1965 meeting of the National Soil Survey Committee. See Darwin Anderson and Scott Smith, "A History of Soil Classification and Soil Survey in Canada: Personal Perspectives," *Canadian Journal of Soil Science* 91, 5 (2011): 680. I largely use the term "muck soil" throughout, though also occasionally invoking the more formal designation "organic soil" and at other times simply "soil."

13. Planscape, "Holland Marsh Agricultural Impact Study," August 2009, p. 10, https://www.greenbelt.ca/holland_marsh_agricultural_study (accessed November 17, 2014).

14. Jessica Bartram, Susan Lloyd Swail, and Burkhard Mausberg, *The Holland Marsh: Challenges and Opportunities in the Greenbelt* (Toronto: Friends of the Greenbelt Foundation, 2007), p. 1, https://d3n8a8pro7vhmx.cloudfront.net/greenbelt/pages/14663/attachments/original/1615839004/The_Holland_Marsh_Challenges_and_Opportunities_in_the_Greenbelt.pdf?1615839004 (accessed November 12, 2014).

15. "The Holland Marsh: Who We Are," Holland Marsh Growers' Association, http://www.hollandmarshgold.com/side-navigation/our-community/ (accessed December 15, 2014).

16. Planscape, "Holland Marsh Agricultural Impact," ii.

17. Ibid.

18. For more on the so-called agrarian debates, see A. Haroon Akram-Lodhi and Cristobal Kay, "Surveying the Agrarian Question (Part 1): Unearthing Foundations, Exploring Diversity," *Journal of Peasant Studies* 37, 1 (2010): 177–202. See also Robert Brenner, "Agrarian Class Structure and Economic Development in Pre-industrial Europe," *Past and Present* 70 (1976): 30–75; Robert Brenner, "The Agrarian Roots of European Capitalism," *Past and Present* 97 (1982): 16–113; Karl Kautsky, *The Agrarian Question* (London: Zwan, 1899).

19. Jack Ralph Kloppenburg Jr., *First the Seed: The Political Economy of Plant Biotechnology* (Madison: University of Wisconsin Press, 2005); Susan Mann, *Agrarian Capitalism in Theory and Practice* (Chapel Hill: University of North Carolina Press, 1990); Susan Mann and James M. Dickinson, "Obstacles to the Development of a Capitalist Agriculture," *Journal of Peasant Studies* 5, 4 (1978): 466–81.

20. Harriet Friedmann and Philip McMichael, "Agriculture and the State System: The Rise and Decline of National Agricultures, 1870 to the Present," *Sociologia Ruralis* 29, 2 (1989): 93–117.

21. I offer an extremely truncated discussion of food regime theory since I draw on it only sparingly in this study, though it remains useful to invoke for the broad framework of periodization it provides.

22. Friedmann and McMichael, "Agriculture and the State System," 95.

23. Harold Innis, *The Fur Trade in Canada* (Toronto: University of Toronto Press, 1930); William Mackintosh, "Economic Factors in Canadian History," *Canadian Historical Review* 4, 1 (1923): 12–25.

24. Frank D. Lewis and Malcolm Charles Urquhart, "Growth and the Standard of Living in a Pioneer Economy: Upper Canada, 1826 to 1851," *William and Mary Quarterly* 56, 1 (1999): 151–81; Peter A. Russell, *How Agriculture Made Canada: Farming in the Nineteenth Century,* vol. 1 (Montreal and Kingston: McGill-Queen's University Press, 2012).

25. Nathalie Cooke, ed., *What's to Eat? Entrées in Canadian Food History* (Montreal and Kingston: McGill-Queen's University Press, 2009); Dorothy Duncan, *Canadians at Table: Food, Fellowship, and Folklore: A Culinary History of Canada* (Toronto: Dundurn, 2006); James Murton, *Creating a Modern Countryside: Liberalism and Land Resettlement in British Columbia* (Vancouver: UBC Press, 2007); Shannon Stunden Bower, *Wet Prairie: People, Land, and Water in Agricultural Manitoba* (Vancouver: UBC Press, 2011).

26. Franca Lacovetta, Valerie J. Korinek, and Marlene Epp, *Edible Histories, Cultural Politics: Towards a Canadian Food History* (Toronto: University of Toronto Press, 2012).

27. Stunden Bower, *Wet Prairie,* 10.

28. Murton, *Creating a Modern Countryside,* 6.

29. Ian McKay, "The Liberal Order Framework: A Prospectus for a Reconnaissance of Canadian History," *Canadian Historical Review* 81, 4 (2000): 617–51.

30. Ibid., 618, 621.

31. See Cole Harris, *The Reluctant Land: Society, Space, and Environment in Canada before Confederation* (Vancouver: UBC Press, 2008).

32. McKay, "Liberal Order Framework," 645.

33. James Murton notes a qualitative distinction between liberals at the start of the nineteenth century and the more broadly progressive proponents of New Liberalism who emerged shortly thereafter. "Yet," he concludes, "though new liberals, and progressives more generally, wanted to understand the environment, their approach suggests that they still wanted to order and control it, and that their knowledge might not have extended much beyond general theories." *Creating a Modern Countryside,* 16.

34. Ibid., 13.

35. Donald Worster, *Rivers of Empire* (New York: Pantheon Books, 1985). Worster, of course, is writing here about the agricultural development of the American West.

36. Bruce Braun, "Producing Vertical Territory: Geology and Governmentality in Late Victorian Canada," *Ecemene* 7, 1 (2000): 15.

37. Braun, "Producing Vertical Territory," 41. See also James C. Scott, *Seeing like a State: How Certain Schemes to Improve the Human Condition Have Failed* (New Haven, CT: Yale University Press, 1998), 262.

38. Darren Ferry, *Uniting in Measures of Common Good* (Montreal and Kingston: McGill-Queen's University Press, 2008); Tina Loo, *Making Law, Order, and Authority in British Columbia, 1821–1871* (Toronto: University of Toronto Press, 1994); Berry Ferguson, *Remaking Liberalism: The Intellectual Legacy of Adam Short, O.D. Skelton, W.C. Clark, and W. A. Mackintosh, 1890–1925* (Montreal and Kingston: McGill-Queen's University Press, 1993).

39. Neil Smith, *Uneven Development: Nature, Capital, and the Production of Space* (Atlanta: University of Georgia Press, 2010), xi.

40. Ibid., 65.

41. Ibid., 71.

42. Ibid., 78.

43. Ibid., 81.

44. Noel Castree, "Socializing Nature: Theory, Practice, and Politics," in *Social Nature: Theory, Practice, and Politics,* ed. Noel Castree and Bruce Braun (Malden, MA: Blackwell, 2001), 1–21.

45. David Harvey, "Ideology and Population Theory," *International Journal of Health Services* 4, 3 (1974): 515–37.

46. Kay Anderson, "The Nature of 'Race,'" in Castree and Braun, *Social Nature,* 64–83; Derek Gregory, "(Post)colonialism and the Production of Nature," ibid., 84–111; Jane Moeckli and Bruce Braun, "Gendered Natures: Feminism, Politics and Social Nature," ibid., 112–32.

47. Nikolas Heynen, Maria Kaika, and Erik Swyngedouw, "Urban Political Ecology: Politicizing the Production of Urban Natures," in *In the Nature of Cities: Urban Political Ecology and the Politics of Urban Metabolism,* ed. Nikolas Heynen, Maria Kaika, and Erik Swyngedouw (New York: Taylor and Francis, 2006), 6.

48. Castree, "Socializing Nature," 15.

49. Erik Swyngedouw, "Modernity and Hybridity: Nature, Regeneracionismo, and the Production of the Spanish Waterscape, 1890–1930," *Annals of the Association of American Geographers* 89, 3 (1999): 445 (emphasis original).

50. Castree, "Socializing Nature," 13 (italics in the original).

51. William Boyd, Scott Prudham, and Rachel A. Schurman, "Industrial Dynamics and the Problem of Nature," *Society and Natural Resources* 14, 7 (2001): 555.

52. Ibid., 564.

53. Ted Benton, "Marxism and Natural Limits: An Ecological Critique and Reconstruction," *New Left Review* 178 (1989): 51; Noel Castree, "The Nature of Produced Nature: Materiality and Knowledge Construction in Marxism," *Antipode* 27, 1 (1995): 12–48.

54. "Eaton's Highlights Mink, Persian Lamb, Silver Fox," *Toronto Daily Star*, August 21, 1940, 33.

55. See, for example, Guy Debord, *The Society of the Spectacle*, trans. Donald Nicholson-Smith (New York: Zone Books, 1995); and Paige West, *From Modern Production to Imagined Primitive: The Social World of Coffee from Papua New Guinea* (Durham, NC: Duke University Press, 2012).

56. Castree, "Nature of Produced Nature"; Michael Redclift, *Frontiers: Histories of Civil Society and Nature* (Cambridge, MA: MIT Press, 2006); Gillian Rose, *Feminism and Geography* (Minneapolis: University of Minnesota Press, 1993).

57. Neil Smith, *Uneven Development: Nature, Capital, and the Production of Space* (Atlanta: University of Georgia Press, 2010), 11.

58. See also Matthew Gandy, *Concrete and Clay: Reworking Nature in New York City* (Cambridge, MA: MIT Press, 2002); and Maria Kaika, *City of Flows: Modernity, Nature and the City* (New York: Routledge, 2005).

59. That dominant understandings of nature and society tend to reinforce, rather than dissolve, the discursive and material boundaries between the two is a function of contemporary capitalism, according to Smith. Others have suggested a similar dynamic was implicit in earlier iterations of capitalism, early modernism, and was instrumental in propping up various technocratic regimes throughout history. See Gandy, *Concrete and Clay;* Kaika, *City of Flows;* and Erik Swyngedouw, "Power, Nature, and the City: The Conquest of Water and the Political Ecology of Urbanization in Guayaquil, Ecuador, 1880–1990," *Environment and Planning A* 29, 2 (1997): 311–32.

60. Shawn McCarthy, "Anti-Petroleum Movement a Growing Security Threat to Canada, RCMP Say," *Globe and Mail*, February 17, 2015. For a thorough list of attempts by the federal government to undermine the capacity of government scientists, see John DuPuis, "The Canadian War on Science: A Long, Unexaggerated, Devastating Chronological Indictment," *Confessions of a Science Librarian* (blog), May 20, 2013, http://scienceblogs.com/confessions/2013/05/20/the-canadian-war-on-science-a-long-unexaggerated-devastating-chronological-indictment/.

61. See, for example, the Mann-Dickinson thesis, which identifies the ways in which biophysical characteristics of nature prevent agriculture from being as thoroughly capitalist as other industries. Susan A. Mann and James M. Dickinson, "Obstacles to the Development of a Capitalist Agriculture," *Journal of Peasant Studies* 5, 4 (1978): 466–81.

62. Castree, "Socializing Nature"; Martin O'Connor, "On the Misadventures of Capitalist Nature," *Capitalism Nature Socialism* 4, 3 (1993): 7–40; Scott W. Prudham, *Knock on Wood: Nature as Commodity in Douglas-Fir Country* (New York: Psychology, 2005).

63. James O'Connor, "Capitalism, Nature, Socialism a Theoretical Introduction," *Capitalism Nature Socialism* 1, 1 (1988): 11–38.

64. For the root of this argument, see David Goodman and Michael Watts, "Reconfiguring the Rural or Fording the Divide? Capitalist Restructuring and the Global Agro-food System," *Journal of Peasant Studies* 22, 1 (1994): 1–49.

65. Mary Douglas, *Purity and Danger: An Analysis of Concept(s) of Pollution and Taboo* (London: Routledge, 1966), 36.

66. Ibid., 37.

67. Salvatore Engel-Di Mauro, *Ecology, Soils, and the Left: An Ecosocial Approach* (New York: Palgrave Macmillan, 2014), 3.

68. Piers Blaikie, *The Political Economy of Soil Erosion in Developing Countries* (London and New York: Longman, 1985); Piers Blaikie and Harold Brookfield, *Land Degradation and Society* (London and New York: Methuen, 1987).

69. Niek Koning and Eric Smaling, "Environmental Crisis or 'Lie of the Land'? The Debate on Soil Degradation in Africa," *Land Use Policy* 22 (2005): 4. Ironically, many have argued that the imposition of particular farming techniques by colonial governments seeded the resistant movements that culminated in national independence for some African nations. See Goran Hyden, *Beyond Ujamaa in Tanzania: Underdevelopment and an Un-captured Peasantry* (Berkeley: University of California Press, 1980); Fiona Mackenzie, *Land, Ecology, and Resistance in Kenya, 1880–1952* (Portsmouth, NH: Heinemann, 1998); and J. Forbes Munro, *Colonial Rule and the Kamba: Social Change in the Kenya Highlands, 1889–1939* (Oxford: Clarendon, 1975).

70. David Anderson, "Depression, Dust Bowl, Demography, and Drought: The Colonial State and Soil Conservation during the 1930s," *African Affairs* 83 (1984), 321–43; Mackenzie, *Land, Ecology, and Resistance in Kenya*; Dianne Rocheleau, Philip Steinberg, and P.A. Benjamin, "Environment, Development, Crisis, and Crusade: Ukambani, Kenya, 1890–1990" *World Development* 23, 6 (1995): 1037–51.

71. Konging and Smaling, "Environmental Crisis or 'Lie of the Land'?," 4.

72. Blaikie and Brookfield, *Land Degradation and Society.*

73. Engel-Di Mauro, *Ecology, Soils, and the Left*, 61–62.

74. Darwin Anderson and Scott Smith, "History of Soil Classification," 675–94.

75. Ibid., 676.

76. Blaikie and Brookfield, *Land Degradation and Society*, 1.

77. Engel-Di Mauro, *Ecology, Soils, and the Left*, 91.

78. Both Blaikie and Brookfield and Engel-Di Mauro insist on an approach that takes into account the socionatural historical context in analysis of land degradation.

79. Blaikie and Brookfield, *Land Degradation and Society*, 27.

80. Engel-Di Mauro, *Ecology, Soils, and the Left*, 93.

81. Michel F. Girard, "The Commission of Conservation as a Forerunner to the National Research Council, 1909–1921," *Scientia Canadensis* 15, 2 (1991): 19–40; Girard, "Conservation and the Gospel of Efficiency: Un Modèdel de Gestion de L'environnement Venu d'Europe?" *Histoire Sociale* 23, 45 (1990): 63–79.

82. Janet Foster, *Working for Wildlife: The Beginnings of Preservation in Canada*, 2nd ed. (Toronto: University of Toronto Press), 1998.

83. Stuart Udall, *The Quiet Crisis* (New York: Holt, Rinehart, and Winston, 1963), 54.

84. John Sandos, "Nature's Nations: The Shared Conservation History of Canada and the USA," *International Journal of Environmental Studies* 70, 2 (2013): 358–71.

85. Girard, "Commission of Conservation."

86. Ibid., 31.

87. James Robertson, quoted in Commission of Conservation, "Improving Canadian Agriculture," 1912, 6, https://archive.org/details/cihm_83706/page/n5.

88. James Robertson, quoted in Commission of Conservation, "First Annual Report of the Commission of Conservation," 1910, 43–44, https://archive.org/details/commissionconser1910cana.

89. Ibid., 44–45.

90. Ibid., 43.

91. Girard, "Commission of Conservation"; Sandos, "Nature's Nations."

92. Sandos, "Nature's Nations."

93. Aldo Leopold, *A Sand County Almanac: With Essays on Conservation from Round the River* (1949; reprint, Toronto: Random House, 1966).

94. Ibid., 172.

95. George Warecki, *Protecting Ontario's Wilderness: A History of Changing Ideas and Preservation Politics* (New York: Peter Lang, 2000).

96. In an early, noteworthy study, Ralph Krueger found that between 1951 and 1956, 730 hectares of land in the Niagara region was lost, which he tied directly to urbanization: "Thus, since 1951 it can be said that urban expansion has been occurring at the expense of fruit growing." Krueger, "Changing Land-Use Patterns in the Niagara Fruit Belt" (PhD diss., Indiana University, 1959), 130. He went on to a distinguished career at Laurier and Waterloo Universities.

97. Ibid., 3.

98. Wayne Caldwell, "Rural Planning and Agricultural Land Preservation: The Experience of Huron County, Ontario," *Great Lakes Geographer* 2 (1995): 23.

99. The CLI itself states: "Land capability for agriculture, forestry, wildlife, recreation, wildlife (ungulates and waterfowl) was mapped. Over 1000 map sheets at the 1:2,500,000 scale were created during the 1960s, '70s, and early '80s." Canada Land Inventory, National Soil Database, Agriculture and Agri-Food Canada, 1998 (last modified, September 15, 2015), http://sis.agr.gc.ca/cansis/nsdb/cli/index.html.

100. Michael Troughton, "Canadian Farmland – a Fluctuating Commodity," in *Farmland Preservation: Land for Future Generations*, ed. Wayne Caldwell, Stew Hilts, and Bronwynne Wilton (Guelph, ON: University of Guelph, 2007), 40–61.

101. Ibid., 53.

102. Ibid.

103. Michael Bunce, "Thirty Years of Farmland Preservation in North America: Discourses and Ideologies of a Movement," *Journal of Rural Studies* 14, 2 (1998): 237.

104. Ibid., 238.

105. Jesse B. Abrams, Hannah Gosnell, Nicholas J. Gill, and Peter J. Klepeis, "Re-creating the Rural, Reconstructing Nature: An International Literature Review of the Environmental Implications of Amenity Migration," *Conservation and Society* 10, 3 (2012): 270.

106. Leigh J Maynard, Timothy W. Kelsey, Robert J. Thee, and Panajiotis Fousekis, "Rural Migration: What Attracts New Residents to Non-Metropolitan Areas," *Community Development* 28, 1 (1997): 131–41; Bunce, "Thirty Years of Farmland Preservation," 239.

107. Bunce, "Thirty Years of Farmland Preservation," 241.

108. Ibid.; David Danbom, "Romantic Agrarianism in Twentieth-Century America," *Agricultural History* 65, 4 (1991): 1–12.

109. Bunce, "Thirty Years of Farmland Preservation," 242.

Chapter 1: The Production of Land, 14,000 BC–1925

1. A patch of now-protected prairie at Holland Landing was the site of a semipermanent trading post in the early to mid-nineteenth century. See John L. Riley, *The Once and Future Great Lakes Country* (Montreal and Kingston: McGill-Queen's University Press, 2014), 209.

2. Andrew Stewart, "Intensity of Land-Use around the Holland Marsh: Assessing Temporal Change from Regional Site Distributions," in *The Late Palaeo-Indian Great Lakes: Geological and Archaeological Investigations of Late Pleistocene and Early Holocene Environments,* ed. A. Hinshelwood and L. Jackson (Gatineau, QC: Canadian Museum of Civilization, 2004), 85–116.

3. Frederick M. Johnson, "The Landscape Ecology of the Lake Simcoe Basin," *Lake and Reservoir Management* 13, 3 (1997): 229.

4. John Chapman and Donald F. Putnam, *Physiography of Southern Ontario,* 3rd ed. (Toronto: University of Toronto Press, 1984).

5. For more on the landscape left behind after the glaciers, see ibid.; Anders Sandberg, Gerda R. Wekerle, and Liette Gilbert, *The Oak Ridges Moraine Battles: Development, Sprawl, and Nature Conservation in the Toronto Region* (Toronto: University of Toronto Press, 2004), 45.

6. Riley, *Once and Future Great Lakes Country,* 5.

7. Olina Volik, Francine M.G. McCarthy, and Nicholas L. Riddick, "Insights from Pollen, Non-pollen Palynomorphs and Testate Amoebae into the Evolution of Lake Simcoe," *Journal of Paleolimnology* 56 (2016): 146.

8. H. Dinel, P.H. Richard, P.E.M. Levésque, and A. Larouche, "Origine et évolution du marais tourbeux de Keswick, Ontario, par l'analyse pollinique et macrofossile," *Canadian Journal of Earth Science* 23 (1986): 1145.

9. Lake Simcoe Region Conservation Area, "Ecological Land Classification and Existing Land Use," 2005, https://www.lsrca.on.ca/Shared%20Documents/watershed_elc.pdf. See

also Lake Simcoe Region Conservation Area, "West Holland River Subwatershed Management Plan," 2010, https://www.lsrca.on.ca/Shared%20Documents/Subwatershed-Plans/west-holland-subwatershed-plan.pdf.

10. Barry G. Warner and C.D.A. Rubec, eds., Canada Committee on Ecological (Biophysical) Land Classification, National Wetlands Working Group, *The Canadian Wetland Classification System* (Waterloo, ON: Wetlands Research Branch, University of Waterloo, 1997), 3.

11. See Eunji Byun, Sarah A. Finkelstein, Sharon A. Cowling, and Pascal Badiou, "Potential Carbon Loss Associated with Post-Settlement Wetland Conversion in Southern Ontario, Canada," *Carbon Balance and Management* 13, 6 (2018), 1–12. In the absence of "presettlement" wetland maps, the authors use current soil maps as proxies for determining wetland class.

12. Paul Irvine, personal interview with author, September 25, 2013.

13. I discuss the dynamics of the muck soil in more detail in the Chapter 2. Suffice it to say for now that over millennia, the vegetative material built up because it decomposed so slowly due to low levels of oxygen in the water – hypoxia – typical of the water in wetlands. Once the land was drained, however, oxygen became abundant, kicking off rapid oxidization and decay of the peat. As the vulnerable organic material breaks down, it erodes away, eventually disappearing altogether and exposing the clay-based substrata.

14. Andrew Stewart, "The Zander Site: Paleo-Indian Occupation of the Southern Holland Marsh Region of Ontario," *Ontario Archeology* 41 (1984): 45–79; Peter L. Strock, "Research into the Pale-Indian Occupations of Ontario: A Review," *Ontario Archaeology* 41 (1984): 3–28.

15. Dillon H. Carr, "A Landscape Approach to Reconstructing Territorial Mobility during the Parkhill Phase in Southern Michigan and Ontario," *PaleoAmerica* 3, 4 (2017): 364–73.

16. Riley, *Once and Future Great Lakes Country*, 9.

17. Ibid., 15; Cole Harris, *The Reluctant Land: Society, Space, and Environment in Canada before Confederation* (Vancouver: UBC Press, 2008), 9.

18. Galt quoted in Harry Vander Kooij, "Holland Marsh," *Origins* 24, 2 (2006): 16. Elsewhere, Galt is quoted as referring to the Marsh as a "mere ditch swarming with bull frogs and rattle snakes," Albert VanderMey, *And the Swamp Flourished* (Surrey, BC: Vanderheide, 1994), 1.

19. A plaque at the Simcoe County Museum commemorates Holland's surveys of Upper Canada, resulting in the building of Yonge Street and various namesakes, including the Holland River; Holland Marsh; Holland Landing, a small village just east of the Marsh; and Holland Street in Bradford. See untitled plaque, Bradford West Gwillimbury Local History Association, 2005, 1. (Bradford West Gwillimbury Local History Association, *Governor Simcoe Slept Here* (Altona, MA: Friesens, 2005) – the plaque is featured in this collection.)

20. Quoted in Riley, *Once and Future Great Lakes Country*, 209.

21. Donald Worster makes this observation in the context of his book about John Muir, who spent a brief by formative time in the Holland Marsh area. Worster, *A Passion for Nature: The Life of John Muir* (New York: Oxford University Press, 2011), 94.

22. George Godwin, *Town Swamps and Social Bridges* (New York: Routledge, Warnes, and Routledge, 1859), 1.

23. Suzanne Zeller, *Inventing Canada: Early Victorian Science and the Idea of a Transcontinental Nation* (Montreal and Kingston: McGill-Queen's University Press, 2009), 4.

24. Ibid., 241.

25. Michael Redclift, *Frontiers: Histories of Civil Society and Nature* (Cambridge, MA: MIT Press, 2006).

26. C. Max Finlayson, Rebecca D'Cruz, and Nick Davidson, "Ecosystems and Human Well-Being: Wetlands and Water," Washington, DC: World Resources Institute, 2005, https://www.millenniumassessment.org/documents/document.358.aspx.pdf.

27. James Rodney Giblett, *Postmodern Wetlands: Culture, History, Ecology* (Edinburgh: Edinburgh University Press, 1996).

28. David Wood, *Making Ontario* (Montreal and Kingston: McGill-Queen's University Press, 2000), xviii.

29. Robert Leslie Jones, *History of Agriculture in Ontario, 1613–1880* (Toronto: University of Toronto Press, 1946). See also Wood, *Making Ontario.*

30. John Thorpe, "A Circular: Addressed to the Friends of Humanity," 1864, E1 B1 R4a S4 Sh1, Simcoe County Archives; Thorpe, "Beware of Strong Drink: A Circular Addressed to the Friends of Humanity," 1865, ibid.

31. "Police Making War on the Moonshiners," *Toronto Daily Star,* October 12, 1929, 2.

32. Dr. Eugene Haanel, chief engineer of the Division of Fuel Tests, gave testimony to the Senate Commission on Fuel Supply in April 1923. He suggested that 0.4 hectares (one acre) of the Marsh mined of its peat would yield 200 tonnes of fuel. The price per tonne was $3.50. Haanel estimated that there were 6,900 hectares (17,000 acres) of mineable peat there – a tantalizing prospect to be sure, though not as potentially profitable as agriculture. See "The Holland River Bog," *Globe,* April 7, 1923, 4. See also "County Council Wants Peat Bogs Developed: Committee Will Bring Matter before Provincial Government," ibid., January 26, 1923, 2.

33. "Plan to Transform Dismal Swamp Area into Smiling Farms," *Globe,* March 5, 1925, 2; "Large Cash Return from Marsh Region," ibid., January 2, 1931, 4; "Reclaiming a Marsh," ibid., October 20, 1933, 4.

34. Tully quoted in Gene Desfor, "Planning Urban Waterfront Industrial Districts: Toronto's Ashbridge's Bay, 1889–1910," *Urban History Review/Revue d'histoire urbaine* (1988): 80.

35. Paul Jackson, "Cholera and Crisis: State Health and the Geographies of Future Epidemics" (PhD diss., University of Toronto, 2011); Paul Jackson, "From Liability to Profitability: How Disease, Fear, and Medical Science Cleaned Up the Marshes of Ashbridge's Bay," in *Reshaping Toronto's Waterfront,* ed. Gene Desfor and Jennefer Laidley (Toronto: University of Toronto Press, 2011), 75–96.

36. See Linda Nash, *Inescapable Ecologies: A History of Environment, Disease, and Knowledge* (Berkeley: University of California Press, 2007), 5.

37. Jackson, "From Liability to Profitability," 80–81.

38. Winthrop quoted in Ann Vileisis, *Discovering the Unknown Landscape: A History of America's Wetlands* (Washington, DC: Island, 1999), 30.

39. Harris, *Reluctant Land,* 309.

40. Redclift, *Frontiers,* 18.

41. Giblett, *Postmodern Wetlands,* 14.

42. Ibid.

43. For more on landscape legibility, see James Feldman, *A Storied Wilderness: Rebuilding the Apostle Islands* (Seattle: University of Washington Press, 2011).

44. The Marsh was first used for commercial purposes starting around 1901, when marsh hay, or sawgrass, began to be harvested for various purposes, including mattress stuffing, packing for shipping fragile goods ("packing grass"), and rope making. See Bradford West Gwillimbury Local History Association, *Governor Simcoe Slept Here* (Altona, MA: Friesens, 2005), 283–84.

45. As the story goes, a Bradford grocer named Dave Watson invited Professor William Day to the Marsh to investigate the possibility of draining it for agriculture in 1909. Later that year, Day, Watson, and two other investors formed a syndicate and purchased 4,000 acres (roughly 1,600 hectares) of the wetland – facing some legal battles related to the purchase a number of years later. See ibid., 284–85.

46. Cavell, quoted in George Jackson, *The Big Scheme: The Draining of the Holland Marsh* (Bradford, ON: George Jackson, 1998), 17.

47. Riley, *Once and Future Great Lakes Country,* 81.

48. Jackson, *Big Scheme,* 16.

49. Harris, *Reluctant Land,* 258.

50. Redclift, *Frontiers,* 75.

51. Harris, *Reluctant Land,* 335.

52. For more on the crucial debates about whether, when, how, and to what extent agriculture is capitalist, see Robert Brenner, "Agrarian Class Structure and Economic Development in Pre-Industrial Europe," *Past and Present* 70 (1976): 30–75; Brenner, "The Agrarian Roots of European Capitalism," *Past and Present* 97 (1982): 16–113; Maurice Dobb, *Studies in the Development of Capitalism,* rev. ed. (New York: International, 1963); Paul Sweezy and Rodney Hilton, *The Transition from Feudalism to Capitalism* (London: Verso, 1967); and Ellen Meiksins Wood, *The Origin of Capitalism: A Longer View* (London: Verso, 2002).

53. When the Marsh was first drained, beginning in 1924, the entire area was divided into seventy-seven ownership parcels. Currently, there are roughly 740 ownership parcels. See Holland Marsh Growers' Association, "Holland Marsh Profile of Agriculture," 2020, https://edo.simcoe.ca/Shared%20Documents/Holland%20Marsh%20-%20Profile%20of%20Horticulture.pdf.

54. Bradford West Gwillimbury Council Minutes, February 4, 1911, Bradford West Gwillimbury Public Library, Art Janse Fonds, Holland Marsh Scheme, Stack 10, Drawer 2, Council and Commission Minutes.

55. "Holland Marsh to Yield Wealth," *Globe,* March 1, 1924, X13.

56. "Famous Old Holland Marsh Soon to Blossom as a Rose," *Toronto Daily Star,* October 23, 1916.

57. Watson quoted in Ross Irwin, C.C. Filman, and R.G. Gregg, "Report of the Committee Appointed for a Drainage Engineering Study of the Holland Marsh Area, 1968," p. 2, Archives of Ontario, #3 ARDA – Holland Marsh, B388426.

58. Willis Merriam, an agricultural economist at Washington State University, conducted a postmortem, of sorts, of the reclamation project. He confirms that the early Marsh boosters were right to dream of profits: "Economically it would appear that the Holland Marsh area is one of the most successful drainage reclamation projects on the continent." Merriam, "Reclamation Economy in the Holland Marsh Area of Ontario," *Journal of Geography* 60 (1961): 140.

59. Bradford West Gwillimbury Council Minutes, June 4, 1910, Bradford West Gwillimbury Public Library, Art Janse Fonds, Holland Marsh Scheme, Stack 10, Drawer 2, Council and Commission Minutes.

60. Jackson, *Big Scheme,* 37.

61. Bradford West Gwillimbury Council Minutes, March 4, 1911, Bradford West Gwillimbury Public Library, Art Janse Fonds, Holland Marsh Scheme, Stack 10, Drawer 2, Council and Commission Minutes.

62. Bradford West Gwillimbury Council Minutes, January 18, 1924, ibid.

63. Alexander Baird, "Holland Marsh Drainage Report, 1924," Simcoe Country Archives 2009-50 B4 R38 S6 SH2, 1.

64. "Holland Marsh to Yield Wealth," *Globe,* X13.

65. The Kalamazoo celery industry peaked in the 1930s and 1940s, just as production was ramping up in the Holland Marsh, particularly in the immediate postwar years. Shortly after that, the hardy Pascal celery that dominated the markets began to be grown in California. This decimated not only the existent industry in Kalamazoo but also other places like Celeryville, Ohio. Within a couple of decades, most farmers in the area had switched to growing bedding flowers. That the California celery industry was so robust likely drove down prices, even in Ontario, creating a disincentive for growers in the Marsh and possibly explaining in part why celery has remained such a marginal crop in the area, despite being a species particularly suitable to muck soil. Anthony Palmieri, "Kalamazoo Celery Patent Medicines," *Pharmacy in History* 39, 3 (1997): 113–17.

66. The book was reissued at least once, ten years later, in 1896, this time sponsored by the Union Seed Company.

67. Peter Schuur, *How to Grow Celery Anywhere: Giving the Principles Which Govern the Growth of Celery* (Kalamazoo, MI: Kalamazoo Celery and Union Seed, 1886), 3, http://www.biodiversitylibrary.org/bibliography/41692#/summary.

68. Day quoted in Jackson, *Big Scheme,* 41.

69. William Day, "Reclamation of the Holland Marsh, Bradford," *Canadian Engineer* 52, 7 (February 15, 1927): 211–15.

70. In 1964, the OAC was amalgamated with the Macdonald Institute and the Ontario Veterinary College to form the founding nucleus of the University of Guelph.

71. William Day, *Principles and Tillage and Rotation,* Ontario Department of Agriculture Bulletin 156 (Toronto: Department of Agriculture, 1907), https://archive.org/details/cihm_83782; Day, *Farm Underdrainage: Does It Pay?,* Ontario Department of Agriculture Bulletin 174 (Toronto: Department of Agriculture, 1908), https://archive.org/details/cihm_83727; Day, *Farm Drainage Operations,* Ontario Department of Agriculture Bulletin 175 (Toronto: Department of Agriculture, 1909), https://archive.org/details/bulletinsfromon15818oonta; Day, *The Farm Water Supply,* Ontario Department of Agriculture Bulletin 367 (Toronto: Department of Agriculture, 1918), https://archive.org/details/bulletinsfromon15818oonta. Day has an impressive array of namesakes, including a building at the University of Guelph and a school and two roads in the Bradford area. Additionally, there is a brass sign dedicated to him in front of the Bradford City Hall.

72. Day, *Farm Underdrainage,* 1.

73. Ibid.

74. "Drainage Demonstration," *Witness-News,* April 28, 1910, Local History Collection, Bradford Library.

75. Jackson, *Big Scheme,* 43. Jackson speculates that Watson left due to being discouraged by the lack of success the syndicate had in obtaining financing for the project.

76. Anthony Winson, *The Intimate Commodity: Food and the Agro-Industrial Complex in Canada* (Toronto: Garamond, 1992), 23.

77. Municipal Corporation of the Township of King v. The Municipal Corporation of the Township of West Gwillimbury and the Municipal Corporation of the Village of Bradford, Bradford West Gwillimbury Public Library, Art Janse Fonds, Holland Marsh Scheme, Stack 10, Drawer 2, Issues between Marsh Townships.

78. Mitchell and Blacklock point out that there have been over 150 amendments to the Drainage Act since its inception and that the law has largely been assembled piecemeal in response to various problems and issues as they arose. The following discussion of drainage law is based on M. Mitchell and J. Blacklock, *History of Drainage Statutes of Ontario (1853–1973)* (Toronto: Ontario Legislative Assembly, Select Committee on Land Drainage, 1973), 1–47.

79. Ibid., 27.

80. Municipal Corporation of the Township of King v. The Municipal Corporation of the Township of West Gwillimbury and the Municipal Corporation of the Village of Bradford, 104.

81. Ibid., 100–104.

82. The federal government remained largely uninterested in preserving wetlands from agricultural reclamation until the 1980s. Currently, there are a range of regulatory and process mechanisms in place to protect wetlands from development, though in practice, they continue to experience incremental transformations. See Bruce Mitchell and Dan Shrubsole, *Canadian Water Management: Visions for Sustainability* (Cambridge, ON: Canadian Water Resource Association), 1994; and Dan Walters and Dan Shrubsole, "Assessing Efforts to Mitigate the Impacts of Drainage

on Wetlands in Ontario, Canada," *Canadian Geographer/Le Géographe Canadien* 49, 2 (2005): 155–71.

Chapter 2: The Production of Fields, 1925–35

1. While commercial production was still a number of years off, 1930 marks the year that Day's test plot was put into full production, the results of which were shared widely with the media.

2. Ross Irwin, "Drainage Law" (Toronto: Ontario Department of Agriculture, 1967), Archives of Ontario, #3 ARDA – Holland Marsh, Correspondence of the Minister of Agriculture and Food, 1967–1970, RG 16-1, B388426.

3. See, for example, James Murton, *Creating a Modern Countryside: Liberalism and Land Resettlement in British Columbia* (Vancouver: UBC Press, 2007); Shannon Stunden Bower, *Wet Prairie: People, Land, and Water in Agricultural Manitoba* (Vancouver: UBC Press, 2011).

4. Mark Fiege. *Irrigated Eden: The Making of an Agricultural Landscape in the American West* (Seattle: University of Washington Press, 1999); Stunden Bower, *Wet Prairie.*

5. William Day, *Farm Underdrainage: Does It Pay?,* Ontario Department of Agriculture Bulletin 174 (Toronto: Department of Agriculture, 1908), 24, https://archive.org/details/cihm_83727.

6. Ibid.

7. Ibid., 15–16.

8. Ibid., 16–17.

9. "Famous Old Holland Marsh Soon to Blossom as a Rose," *Globe,* October 23, 1926, n.p.

10. George Jackson, *The Big Scheme: The Draining of the Holland Marsh* (Bradford, ON: George Jackson, 1998), 69.

11. Bradford West Gwillimbury Local History Association, *Governor Simcoe Slept Here* (Altona, MA: Friesens, 2005), 281.

12. Ibid.

13. William Day, "Holland Marsh Gives Wonderful Results," 3, Bradford West Gwillimbury Public Library, Joe Saint Fonds, Holland Marsh, vol. 1, pt. 310, JSC v.1-310–16.

14. Ibid., 2.

15. Ibid., 3.

16. "Large Cash Return from Marsh Region," *Globe,* January 2, 1931, 4.

17. "Reclaimed Marshes Yield Crops Valued at $26,000," *Toronto Daily Star,* December 30, 1930, 22.

18. "Plan to Transform Dismal Swamp Area into Smiling Farms," *Globe,* March 5, 1925, 2.

19. In the summer of 1928, a lyrical piece of writing appeared in the lifestyle section of the *Globe,* in which "The Homemaker" waxes eloquently about a leisurely drive she took out to the countryside, noting especially "the level verdure of the Holland Marsh

spread a long strand of beauty where it lay." See The Homemaker, "Among Ourselves: Mary Ann's Drive," *Globe,* July 5, 1928, 10.

20. "Large Cash Return from Marsh Region," 4; "Reclaimed Marshes Yield Crops Valued at $26,000," 22.

21. "Reclaiming a Marsh," *Globe,* October 20, 1933, 4.

22. The moniker was recently showcased in the title of a Holland Marsh advocacy video, *The Marsh Mucker's Tale* (2013). Similarly, the Holland Marsh Gold brand, associated with the advocacy group Holland Marsh Growers' Association, alludes to the monetary value of the soil. Simply put, the soil has resonated (and continues to resonate) throughout the popular imagination as a result of media reports and other cultural representations.

23. Soil Classification Working Group, *The Canadian System of Soil Classification,* 3rd ed. (Ottawa: Research Branch Agriculture and Agri-Food Canada, 1998), 5.

24. Unlike flora or fauna taxonomies, soil taxonomies are not universal. While the Canadian system is informed by soil taxonomies developed in the United States and by the United Nations, it remains distinct. As an example, muck soil such as that found in the Holland Marsh is classified as "organic soil" in Canada and as "histisol soil" in the United States. Not surprisingly, and similar to the Canadian experience, the soil-classification work of other jurisdictions is housed within departments of agriculture; in the case of the United Nations, it is the Food and Agriculture Organization.

25. Soil Classification Working Group, *Canadian System of Soil Classification,* 2.

26. John R. McNeill and Verena Winiwarter, eds. *Soils and Societies: Perspectives from Environmental History* (Isle of Harris, UK: White Horse, 2006), 3.

27. A relational taxonomy, the Von Post Scale of Humification, was developed to categorize the extent of decomposition of plant material in organic soil. The scale ranges from H1 (completely undecomposed peat moss) through to H10 (completely decomposed). An additional metric represents the moisture level of the plant material and ranges from B1 (dry) through to B5 (very wet). See Lennart von Post, "Sveriges geologiska undersöknings torkinvenstering och några av dess hittils vaana resultant," *Svenska Mosskulturfören Tidskr* 36 (1922): 1–27; and Randall Kolka, Stephen Sebestyen, Elon S. Verry, and Kenneth Brooks, eds., *Peatland Biogeochemistry and Watershed Hydrology at the Marcell Experimental Forest* (Boca Raton, FL: CRC, 2011).

28. Mary Ruth McDonald and Jim Chaput, "Management of Organic Soils," Ministry of Agriculture, Food and Rural Affairs, 1998, http://www.omafra.gov.on.ca/english/crops/facts/93-053.htm. The Muck Crops Research Station is effectively a joint satellite office of the University of Guelph and the Ontario Agricultural College. It has been in operation almost as long as crops have been harvested in the Holland Marsh.

29. Ibid.

30. Some of the earliest research on muck soil, published in 1933 by the Research Branch of the federally funded Agriculture Canada, perhaps not surprisingly was designed to investigate how applicable various types were for commercial agricultural production. The first research on subsidence of muck in Canada seems to have come later on in the decade, published out of the Sainte-Clotilde Experiment Substation in

Quebec. T.H. Anstey, "One Hundred Harvests: Research Branch, Agriculture Canada, 1886–1986," *Historical Series, Research Branch, Agriculture Canada* 27 (1986): 143–44.

31. Cameran Mirza and Ross W. Irwin, "Determination of Subsidence of an Organic Soil in Southern Ontario," *Canadian Journal of Soil Science* 44, 2 (1964): 253.

32. McDonald and Chaput, "Management of Organic Soils" (emphasis added).

33. Ibid.

34. William Day, "Reclamation of the Holland Marsh, Bradford," *Canadian Engineer* 52, 7 (February 15, 1927): 213.

35. See, for example, Ross Irwin, "Soil Subsidence of the Holland Marsh," Engineering Technical Publication 126034, School of Engineering, University of Guelph, 1976; Gerald Walker, "How the Holland Marsh Community Developed," *Canadian Geographical Journal* (August/September 1977): 42–49; and Frank Sercombe, "Holland Marsh," *Hamilton Spectator,* Saturday, July 27, 1970, 23.

36. Wilton Consulting Group, "Holland Marsh 2028," 2018. http://hollandmarshgold.com/uploads/1/7/2/8/17281360/hollandmarsh_sustainabilitystrategy_final_sept2018.pdf (page removed).

37. Day, "Holland Marsh Gives Wonderful Results."

38. Bradford was incorporated from a village to a town in 1960. In 1991, Bradford and West Gwillimbury Township were amalgamated to become the town of Bradford West Gwillimbury.

39. Jenni Dunning, "Should Holland Marsh Boundaries Be Moved?," *New Market Today,* April 16, 2019, https://www.newmarkettoday.ca/local-news/should-holland-marsh-boundaries-be-moved-1377849.

40. Art Janse, "Cleaning the Canals: A Report to the Holland Marsh Drainage Committee," August 3, 2006, Bradford West Gwillimbury Public Library, Art Janse Fonds, Holland Marsh Scheme, Council and Commission Minutes, Stack 10, Drawer 2.

41. Art Janse, "Holland Marsh Drainage Scheme," n.d., ibid., Reports 1, Stack 10, Drawer 2.

42. Frank Jonkman, Margaret Black, and Art Janse, "Submission for Funding Holland Marsh Drainage Scheme," ibid., Issues between Marsh and Townships, Stack 10, Drawer 2.

43. Art Janse, "Re: Cleaning the Canals, a Letter to King Council," ibid.

44. Drainage Act RSO, 1990, c. D.17, 76(1).

45. Superior Court of Justice, In the Court of the Drainage Referee, Town of Bradford-West Gwillimbury v. Township of King, Town of East Gwillimbury, Town of Caledon, Town of Newmarket, and Town of New Tecusmeth, 2002, 10–11.

46. Ibid., 5.

47. Ibid., 30.

48. K. Smart Associates Limited, "Holland Marsh Drainage System Canal Improvement Project 'Text' Volume 1" (2010), https://www.hollandmarsh.org/Docs/Drains/TheProject/Volume%201%20-%20Text.pdf.

49. Case quoted in "North York MPP Hurls Fraud Charges: Drainage Scheme at Holland Marsh Comes under Fire," *Globe,* February 2, 1932, 1.

50. Ibid.

51. Ibid.

52. "Writ Threatened by D. Paul Monro against Mr. Case," *Globe,* February 3, 1932, 1.

53. Kennedy quoted in "Townships Urged to Investigate Marsh Project," *Globe,* February 6, 1932, 13.

54. Widdifield quoted in "Drainage Inquiry May Be Dropped, Judge Intimates," *Globe,* March 10, 1932, 11.

55. Evans quoted in "Drainage Inquiry May Be Suspended," *Globe,* March 14, 1932, 12.

Chapter 3: Crops, Markets, and the Production of Stability, 1935–54

1. Susanne Friedberg, *Fresh: A Perishable History* (Cambridge, MA: Belknap Press of Harvard University Press, 2009), 178. For vivid fictionalized accounts of this dynamic, see John Steinbeck's *The Grapes of Wrath* (1939) and *Of Mice and Men* (1937), which memorialize the sociocultural and material fallout of the Great Depression on labour, especially in California.

2. Statistics Canada, CANSIM, "Net Farm Income," 2014a, table: 32-10-0052-01 (formerly CANSIM 002-0009)," https://www150.statcan.gc.ca/t1/tbl1/en/tv.action?pid=3210005201&pickMembers%5B0%5D=1.1&cubeTimeFrame.startYear=1926&cubeTimeFrame.endYear=1933&referencePeriods=19260101%2C19330101.

3. Engels quoted in Henry Bernstein, "Is There an Agrarian Question in the 21st Century?," *Canadian Journal of Development Studies / Revue canadienne d'études du développement* 27, 4 (2006): 450. Engels, Karl Marx's collaborator, sought to understand how peasants (or farmers) as a social force, in rural areas and beyond, functioned to either usher in or inhibit capitalism. In other words, he wanted to understand how class struggle played out in the countryside and analyze what kind of implications this had for the wider society, state formations, and the like, placing the struggles of farmers at the centre of his analysis.

4. I am drawing here, thematically, from food-regime theory. As the key exponents of the original formulation, Harriet Friedmann and Philip McMichael argue that periods of relative global stability from 1870–1914 and 1947–73 can be traced to particular constellations of global political power. The concept links relatively politically and economically stable periods of world history with particular hegemonic arrangements of the production, circulation, and consumption of food. This global stability was fractured by the instability of the interwar years, but the groundwork for the particular brand of American postwar capitalism was laid partly through expanded agricultural production throughout World War II and years following. See Friedmann and McMichael, "Agriculture and the State System: The Rise and Decline of National Agricultures, 1870 to the Present," *Sociologia Ruralis* 29, 2 (1989): 93–117.

5. In some ways, this was a second wave of concerted agrarian politics, at least in Ontario. After winning a record forty-four seats in the 1919 provincial election, the United Farmers of Ontario formed a coalition government with the Labour Party. Internal

tensions within the party coupled with shifting political tides resulted in the United Farmers only electing seventeen members in the 1923 contest and never making a serious challenge for formal political power – that is, governing power – again. See Anthony Winson, *The Intimate Commodity: Food and the Agro-Industrial Complex in Canada* (Toronto: Garamond, 1992).

6. Ibid.

7. Ruth Sandwell, "'Read, Listen, Discuss, Act': Adult Education, Rural Citizenship and the Canadian National Farm Radio Forum, 1941–1965," *Historical Studies in Education / Revue d'histoire de l'éducation* 24 (2012): 170–94; S. Veeraraghavan, "The Role of Farm Organizations," in *Farming and the Rural Community in Ontario: An Introduction,* ed. Anthony M. Fuller, 121–42 (Toronto, ON: Foundation for Rural Living, 1985).

8. "Urges Small Farms to Aid Unemployed," *Toronto Daily Star,* February 26, 1935, 26.

9. Ibid.

10. A dissatisfied and struggling farmer complained: "We were brought in here by the government.... [W]e try to get along but nobody can get very far.... [W]hen we came to the marsh we knew we would have a couple of hard years ahead of us.... We will keep on trying and trying hard to make a success of the Dutch settlement, but... we can't get much done with encouragement like the council of King township gives us." Letter to the editor, *Toronto Daily Star,* May 12, 1937, 5.

11. The term "bioavailability" refers to the extent to which nutrients are available to plants within a given soil system. Bioavailability is governed by more than simply the nutrient load within the soil itself, although nutrient levels are a crucial determinate. See N.B. Comerford, "Soil Factors Affecting Nutrient Bioavailability," in *Nutrient Acquisition by Plants: An Ecological Perspective,* ed. Hormoz BassiriRad (Berlin: Springer, 2005): 1–14.

12. In an ironic twist, the commissioner of fruit and vegetables for the federal government purchased sixty-five carloads of produce from Marsh farmers in 1937 at prices 50 percent higher than they were getting in Toronto. The produce was shipped, by rail, to communities in western Canada as part of a federal drought response. See "Vegetable Purchase Confirmed by Ottawa," *Globe and Mail,* October 6, 1937, 1.

13. "Holland Marsh Crops Are Finest in Years, but Market Lacking," *Globe and Mail,* September 25, 1937, 17.

14. Ibid.

15. Stop & Shop ad, *Toronto Daily Star,* September 30, 1937, 17.

16. Sandwell, "'Read, Listen, Discuss, Act,'" 173.

17. Ibid.

18. David Mizener, "Furrows and Fairgrounds: Agriculture, Identity, and Authority in Twentieth-Century Rural Ontario" (PhD diss., York University, 2009), 5. For a compelling history of the role of women in agricultural organizations such as the Women's Institute and others, see Monda M. Halpern, *And on That Farm He Had a Wife: Ontario Farm Women and Feminism, 1900–1970* (Montreal and Kingston: McGill-Queen's University Press, 2001). For more on the history of the agrarian movement in Ontario, see

Brian Tennyson, "The Ontario Election of 1919," *Journal of Canadian Studies / Revue d'Études Canadiennes* 4, 1 (1969): 26–36.

19. Veeraraghavan, "Role of Farm Organizations." Another important contemporary farm organization, the Christian Farmers Federation of Ontario, had various permutations starting in the early 1950s, though not emerging as a permanent fixture until the early 1970s. See John Paterson, "Institutional Organization, Stewardship, and Religious Resistance to Modern Agricultural Trends: The Christian Farmers' Movement in the Netherlands and in Canada," *Agricultural History* 75, 3 (2001): 308–28.

20. Harry Zwerver, "Farmers Working for Farmers: A Brief History of the Ontario Federation of Agriculture," Gulelph, ON: Ontario Federation of Agriculture (1986): 11.

21. Hannam quoted in ibid., 16.

22. C.F. Bulmer, "The Farm Products Control Act, 1937 Scheme: For the Marketing of Vegetables in the Holland Marsh District," 1937, Archives of Ontario, #6 Holland Marsh Growers Mktg Scheme, Legal Services Records of the Ministry of Agriculture and Food, RG 16-37, B262565.

23. "Many Ontario Farmers Cannot Sell Huge Crops: Toronto Mart Held Solution for York Area," *Toronto Daily Star,* September 29, 1937, 5.

24. By this point, Marsh farmers had largely solved their marketing problems, though many began selling their produce through the terminal – many still do today. See "New Food Terminal to Be Built by the Ontario Government," *Toronto Daily Star,* August 22, 1952, 13.

25. Bulmer, "Farm Products Control Act."

26. John McMurchy, *A History of Agricultural Marketing Legislation in Ontario* (Toronto: Ontario Farm Products Marketing Commission, 1998), 3.

27. T.A. Crerar, personal letter to M.F. Hepburn, February 17, 1937, Archives of Ontario, #20 Holland Marsh, RG 3-10, B307973.

28. In the end, Crerar did recommend that the program continue but suggested that, to be eligible for the program, the Dutch immigrants should have to demonstrate that they had savings of at least one thousand dollars. The program was part of a much larger wave of Dutch immigration to Canada from the mid-1930s well into the postwar years.

29. Jefferson quoted in "Claim Low Prices Ruinous When Marsh 'Co-op' Fails," *Toronto Daily Star,* August 10, 1938, 6.

30. Neinhuis quoted in ibid.

31. "W. H. Day Passes Suddenly: Helped Reclaim Marshes," *Toronto Daily Star,* July 6, 1938, 6.

32. "Four Families in Danger of Losing Homes and Land," *Toronto Daily Star,* February 4, 1938, 6.

33. Valenteyn quoted in ibid.

34. Nolan quoted in ibid.

35. Farm Products Control Board, "To the Honorable Minister of Agriculture for Ontario," 1938, Archives of Ontario, #6 Holland Marsh Vegetable Growers Mktg Scheme, RG 16-37, B262565.

36. The HMGA, along with twenty-seven other organizations across the province – some based on geography, others on crop type – formed the Ontario Fruit and Vegetable Growers' Association. This association remains by far the largest advocacy organization in Ontario for growers of edible horticultural crops. See http://www.ofvga.org/.

37. Ian Mosby, *Food Will Win the War: The Politics, Culture, and Science of Food on Canada's Home Front* (Vancouver: UBC Press, 2014). Agrarians in Canada have organized politically since at least the late nineteenth century, when the Grange first emerged in Ontario. Later, the Co-operative Commonwealth Federation (forebear to the New Democratic Party) led to modest electoral success during its existence, from 1932 until 1961, though by the 1950s, the federation was waning as a political force. Alan Whitehorn, *Canadian Socialism: Essays on the CCF/NDP* (Toronto: Oxford University Press, 1994); Leo Zakuta, *A Protest Movement Becalmed: A Study of Change in the CCF* (Toronto: University of Toronto Press, 1964).

38. "Figures Crop Loss Is $20,000 per Day," *Toronto Daily Star,* September 7, 1943, 5.

39. Davis quoted in ibid.

40. "Ontario's Farm Blitz Must Be Started Now Need for Help Urgent," *Toronto Daily Star,* June 8, 1943, 12.

41. "Onion Pickers Needed," *Toronto Daily Star,* September 18, 1941, 33.

42. "Holland Marsh Settlers Boost Victory Loan Campaign," *Toronto Daily Star,* February 26, 1942, 8.

43. James Murton, *Creating a Modern Countryside: Liberalism and Land Resettlement in British Columbia* (Vancouver: UBC Press, 2007).

44. E. Reaman, *A History of Agriculture in Ontario,* vol. 2 (Aylesbury, UK: Hazell Watson and Vieny, 1970).

45. All farmers in Ontario who net over seven thousand dollars annually must still belong to, and pay members' dues to, either the OFA or the Christian Farmers Federation.

46. "Spread Is too Big: Holland Marsh Vegetable Growers Form Union in Effort to Get More of Buyers' Money," *Globe and Mail,* August 19, 1948, 7.

47. Although National Farm Radio Forum ended in Canada in 1965, the model was very successfully exported around the world. By the early twenty-first century, similar forums had an estimated monthly global audience of 150 million listeners across seventy stations throughout 110 countries. See Sandwell, "'Read, Listen, Discuss, Act,'" 172.

48. See, for example, Friedberg, *Fresh;* and Gabriella Petrick, "Like Ribbons of Green and Gold: Industrializing Lettuce and the Quest for Quality in the Salinas Valley, 1920–1965," *Agricultural History* 80, 3 (2006): 269–95.

49. Fred Egan, "New Facilities Widen Holland Marsh Markets," *Globe and Mail,* November 5, 1946, 8.

50. "Holland Marsh Farmers Plan for $100,000 Co-operative Plant," *Toronto Daily Star,* January 8, 1945, 8.

51. Egan, "New Facilities Widen Holland Marsh Markets," 8.

52. Bradford West Gwillimbury Local History Association, *Governor Simcoe Slept Here* (Altona, MA: Friesens, 2005), 303.

53. "Express Road to Northland Bridges Holland Marsh," *Globe and Mail,* November 22, 1936, 3.

54. "Holland Marsh Growers Plow Under Two-Cent Lettuce as Housewives Pay 10 Cents a Head," *Toronto Daily Star,* August 20, 1948, 23.

55. A.W. Willford, "A Presentation to a Great Industry," *Trade and Transportation* (August 1949): 1, Bradford West Gwillimbury Public Library, Joe Saint Fonds, Holland Marsh, vol. 1, pt. 310, JSC-VI-310-15.

56. Louis St. Laurent, "To the People of an Important Canadian Industry," *Trade and Transportation* (August 1949): 3, ibid.

57. Ibid.

58. M.W. Campbell, "The Biggest Kitchen Garden in the Country," *Maclean's Magazine,* September 15, 1953, Simcoe County Archives, 10984 975-45 R4A S4 Sh2.

Chapter 4: The Production of Instability, 1954–80

1. James C. Scott, *Seeing like a State: How Certain Schemes to Improve the Human Condition Have Failed* (New Haven, CT: Yale University Press, 1998), 262.

2. The emergence of a fully global agriculture was facilitated by a number of developments, including the creation of more durable crops and the emergence of faster, more reliable storage and shipping technologies. There was also a more structural impetus at play, as national regulations regarding international trade, especially, were altered to accommodate the increasingly corporatized agricultural sector. See, for example, Harriet Friedmann and Philip McMichael, "Agriculture and the State System: The Rise and Decline of National Agricultures, 1870 to the Present," *Sociologia Ruralis* 29, 2 (1989). For more on the historical contours of global agriculture, see Sydney Mintz, *Sweetness and Power: The Place of Sugar in Modern History* (New York: Penguin Books, 1986); John Soluri, *Banana Cultures: Agriculture, Consumption, and Environmental Change in Honduras and the United States* (Austin: University of Texas Press, 2005).

3. Lake Simcoe Conservation Club quoted in "Extinction of Grounds for Nesting, Spawning Feared if Farms Grow," *Globe and Mail,* November 4, 1953, 15.

4. Bentley quoted in "Draining of Marsh Depletes Bird Life," *Toronto Daily Star,* October 11, 1926, 2.

5. Bride Broder, "Woman's Point of View: Theft from the Future," *Globe and Mail,* September 28, 1937, 13.

6. "Help for Homeland: Holland Marsh Planning $100,000 for Flood Aid," *Globe and Mail,* February 13, 1953, 4.

7. E. Stonehouse, "Holland Marsh on Display: Visiting Farmers Tour Famed Potato Acres," *Globe and Mail,* August 13, 1954, 5.

8. "Hope Process to End Day of Limp Lettuce," *Globe and Mail,* June 23, 1954, 8.

9. For more on the impact and history of the storm, see http://www.hurricanehazel.ca/.

10. T.R. Hilliard, "Recommended Basis of Payment for Farm Rehabilitation, Holland Marsh, Bradford," 1954, Archives of Ontario, #4 Hurricane Relief Holland Marsh, RG 16-9, B355358, 2.

11. J. Smith, personal interview, September 3, 2013.

12. "Hopes of 3,000 Are Killed as Holland Marsh Flooded," *Toronto Daily Star,* December 20, 1954, 1–2.

13. R. Blackmore, "Motionless Dirty Water Lies on Holland Marsh," *Globe and Mail,* October 18, 1954, 11.

14. Ibid.

15. "Prosperous Market Gardeners Penniless Refugees," *Toronto Daily Star,* October 18, 1954, 7.

16. This was initially a form of triage. Fearing that the entire Marsh could not be drained by the time winter arrived and the water froze, the decision was made to focus on saving the larger section east of Highway 400. In the end, winter arrived later than expected, and the drainage was speedier than anticipated, so the entire Marsh was drained.

17. Ken MacTaggart, "Borrow Pumps for Draining: Marsh Folk Gamble to Reclaim Land," *Globe and Mail,* October 19, 1954, 1–2.

18. Harold Hilliard, "Too Odorous for Man. Machines Will Clear Marsh of Vegetables," *Toronto Daily Star,* October 26, 1954, 25.

19. R. Blackmore, "Motionless Dirty Water Lies on Holland Marsh," 11.

20. J.T. Phair, "Letter to C.D. Graham, Deputy Minister of Agriculture," 1954, Archives of Ontario, #4 Hurricane Relief Holland Marsh, RG 16-9, B355358.

21. J.B. Carswell and D.B. Shaw, *Commission to Inquire into the Nature and Extent of the Damage Caused by the Flood in and Adjoining the Humber River Valley in Ontario* (Toronto: Canadian Federal Royal Commission Reports, 1954).

22. Interestingly, the Ontario Conservation and Reforestation Association was formed by Watson Porter, the editor of *Farmer's Advocate,* an agricultural trade journal.

23. Danielle Robinson and Ken Cruikshank, "Hurricane Hazel: Disaster Relief, Politics and Society in Canada, 1954–55," *Journal of Canadian Studies* 40, 1 (2007): 37–64.

24. Harold Hilliard, "Lake Huron Waste Area Seen as Holland Marsh Rival: New Canadians Earn $10,000 Average Wage Plan $1,000,000 Crop," *Toronto Daily Star,* November 5, 1955, 1; "North Ontario Seen as Future Breadbasket for Industrial South," *Globe and Mail,* March 25, 1955, 8.

25. Herbert quoted in "North Ontario Seen as Future Breadbasket for Industrial South," 8.

26. Hilliard, "Lake Huron Waste Area Seen as Holland Marsh Rival," 1.

27. "Bradford: The Heart of Canada's Vegetable Industry," *Toronto Daily Star,* November 15, 1958, 10.

28. Carey McWilliams, *Factories in the Field: The Story of Migratory Farm Labor in California* (1939; repr., Berkeley: University of California Press, 2000).

29. Don Mitchell, *The Politics of Food* (Toronto: James Lorimer, 1975), 1

30. Anthony Winson, *The Intimate Commodity: Food and the Agro-Industrial Complex in Canada* (Toronto: Garamond, 1992), 90.

31. Scott, *Seeing like a State*, 267.

32. For more on the history and implications of the transition away from postwar industrial lettuce to contemporary mixed greens, see Julie Guthman, *Agrarian Dreams: The Paradox of Organic Farming in California* (Berkeley: University of California Press, 2004).

33. Agriculture and Agri-Food Canada, *Crop Profile for Greenhouse Lettuce in Canada, 2011* (Ottawa: Agriculture and Agri-Food Canada, 2013), www.agr.gc.ca/pmc-cropprofiles.

34. J. Bake, personal interview, August 27, 2013.

35. P. Irvine, personal interview, September 25, 2013.

36. B. Lewis, personal interview, January 16, 2014.

37. Steven Stoll, *The Fruits of Natural Advantage* (Berkeley: University of California Press, 1998).

38. For a brief history of the Muck Crops Research Station, see http://www.uoguelph.ca/muckcrop/historystation.html.

39. The relationship between institutions, the state, farmers, land, agricultural production, and in situ agricultural research stations in the Canadian context is another area ripe for future study. Agricultural extensions, formalized through the land-grant system in the American context, has been well studied, yet relatively little similar work has been conducted on the dynamics of agricultural extension within the Canadian context.

40. The station, while small, has a reach beyond the Holland Marsh. It often collaborates on research projects with the University of California, testing various aspects of carrot cultivation for the California market, which produces several degrees of magnitude more carrots than all of Canada.

41. Jack Ralph Kloppenburg Jr., *First the Seed: The Political Economy of Plant Biotechnology* (Madison: University of Wisconsin Press, 2005).

42. The station similarly conducts trials on other farm inputs, including chemical fertilizers, pesticides, and fungicides. The results of all of the trials are communicated to the farmers through a variety of evolving means. Since it does not endorse any particular product or cultivar over any other, and in this respect, the station remains neutral.

43. P. Wilson, personal interview, January 20, 2014.

44. Mary Ruth McDonald, Shawn Janse, Kevin Vander Kooi, L. Riches, and Michael Tesfaendrias, "Muck Vegetable Cultivar Trial and Research Report," University of Guelph, 2013, 163.

45. Dominion ad, *Toronto Daily Star*, July 22, 1959, 21.

46. "Super-Mechanization Makes Muck Bloom," *Toronto Daily Star*, July 13, 1960, 10.

47. Paul Chisholm, "Collar and Tie Farming," *Monetary Times*, March 1962, n.p., Simcoe County Archives, Federal Farms Limited Fonds, 2008-56 E5 B1 R4B S5 Sh1.

48. Morris Latchman, "Remarks of Morris Latchman Concerning Federal Farms Limited and the Dale Estate Limited Made before a Financial Analyst Group New York City," November 29, 1962, 9, Simcoe County Archives, Federal Farms Limited Fonds, 2008-56 E5 B1 R4B S5 Sh1.

49. "Super-Mechanization Makes Muck Bloom," 10.

50. Latchman, "Remarks of Morris Latchman," 3.

51. "Money Markets," *Toronto Daily Star,* August 9, 1963, 6.

52. "Super-Mechanization Makes Muck Bloom," 10.

53. Latchman, "Remarks of Morris Latchman," 6.

54. Ibid., 7.

55. Ibid., 8.

56. Latchman quoted in Chisholm, "Collar and Tie Farming," n.p.

57. Ontario Labour Relations Board, "International Brotherhood of Teamsters, Chauffeurs, Warehousemen and Helpers, Local 419 and Federal Farms Limited, Commentary 16, 292," 1963, Ontario Workplace Tribunals Library; Ontario Labour Relations Board. "International Brotherhood of Teamsters, Chauffeurs, Warehousemen and Helpers, Local 419 and Holland River Gardens Limited, Commentary 16, 304," 1964, ibid. See also "Teamsters Organize in Holland Marsh," *Toronto Daily Star,* October 29, 1963, 26.

58. Ontario Labour Relations Board, "International Brotherhood of Teamsters," 1963, 5.

59. See, for example, CBC News, "Highbury CanCo Can Process Tomatoes in Leamington Heinz Plant," April 11, 2014, http://www.cbc.ca/news/canada/windsor/highbury-canco-can-process-tomatoes-in-leamington-heinz-plant-1.2606570; Armina Ligaya, "Heinz to Close Ontario Plant, Leaving 740 out of Work," *Financial Post,* November 14, 2014.

60. C. Mirza and Ross Irwin, "Determination of Subsidence of an Organic Soil in Southern Ontario," *Canadian Journal of Soil Science* 44, 2 (1964): 248.

61. It is worth pointing out that Mirza and Irwin published their results over fifty years ago. There is still muck soil in the middle of the Marsh, where it has always been deepest, but there is far less on its edges. Indeed, on its perimeter, some farmers have begun trialling mineral-soil produce, while others have built greenhouses to grow flowers and other horticultural crops.

62. Ralph Gregg, "Report of 'Special Committee' on Drainage and Related Problems of Holland Marsh," 1967, Archives of Ontario, #3 ARDA – Holland Marsh, Correspondence of the Minister of Agriculture and Food, 1967–70, RG 16-1, B388426, 2.

63. M. Bolton, "Pesticide Poisoning on Increase in Fish," *Toronto Daily Star,* May 17, 1969, 22; T. Claridge, "City Growth Called No Threat to Farms," ibid, January 26, 1977, 48; D. Dilschneider, "Pesticide Prober Says Ottawa Won't Help in Soil Study," *Toronto Daily Star,* April 15, 1970, 10.

64. J. Smith, personal interview, September 3, 2013.

65. As Ryan O'Connor has pointed out, the first wave of substantive environmentalism was rapidly emerging in 1970 in and around the Toronto area. Within this context, the Marsh, which already had a high profile, was something of an easy target. See O'Connor, *The First Green Wave: Pollution Probe and the Origins of Environmental Activism in Ontario* (Vancouver: UBC Press, 2015).

66. "Bradford South," *Toronto Star,* January 11, 1974, D3.

67. "Homegrown Charm of Other Yonge St.," *Toronto Star,* August 8, 1979, A03.

68. J.C. Olsen, "Dismayed over Billboards Defacing Holland Marsh," *Toronto Star,* February 14, 1972, 7.

69. At the same time, the development industry, through the Urban Development Institute, was already beginning to wage a counterattack to what they perceived as limits on their capacity to continue building outward. Indeed, they conducted their own study, concluding, somewhat dubiously, that urban expansion posed no risk at all for peri-urban agriculture. See Claridge, "City Growth Called No Threat to Farms," 48.

70. William Boyd, Scott Prudham, and Rachel A. Schurman, "Industrial Dynamics and the Problem of Nature," *Society and Natural Resources* 14, 7 (2001): 564.

Chapter 5: A Legacy of Contradictions

1. Harriet Friedmann, "Distance and Durability: Shaky Foundations of the World Food Economy," *Third World Quarterly* 13, 2 (1992): 371–83.

2. Laura Raynolds, David Myhre, Philip McMichael, Viviana Carro-Figueroa, and Frederick H. Buttel, "The 'New' Internationalization of Agriculture: A Reformulation," *World Development* 21, 7 (1993): 1101–21.

3. Harriet Friedmann, "Changes in the International Division of Labor: Agri-food Complexes and Export Agriculture," in *Towards a New Political Economy of Agriculture,* ed. William Friedland, Lawrence Busch, Frederick H. Buttel, and Alan Rudy (Boulder, CO: Westview, 1991), 65–93.

4. Michael Keating, "Holland Marsh Widely Polluted, Report Says," *Globe and Mail,* December 8, 1982, 4; John Power, "Simcoe's Fishing Future Gloomy," *Toronto Star,* February 2, 1983, D08; Joe Hall and Bob Graham, "Birth Defects High in Holland Marsh," ibid., June 18, 1981, A07; "Probe Rural Birth Defects," ibid., June 20, 1981, B02.

5. James Williams, Marion Todd, Marion Powell, Eric Holowaty, and David Korn, "On Assessing the Risks of Congenital Anomalies in the Holland Marsh and Surrounding Areas," Health Care Research Unit, Faculty of Medicine, University of Toronto, 1981, Archives of Ontario, #21 Lakes and Rivers – Holland Marsh, RG 12-45, B214163, 1.

6. J. Miles and C. Harris, "Insecticide Residues in Water, Sediment and Fish of the Drainage System of the Holland Marsh, Ontario, Canada, 1982–75," *Journal of Economic Entomology* 71, 1 (1978): 125–31; J. Miles, C. Harris, and P. Moy, "Insecticide Residues in Organic Soil of the Holland Marsh, Ontario, Canada 1972–57," *Journal of Economic Entomology* 71, 1 (1978): 97–101.

7. Nancy Beasley, an employee at the *Bradford Witness,* contacted the provincial Ministry of the Environment to find out the results of the water samples taken by the ministry in the summer of 1981. Beasley's inquiry was noted in a three-page memo sent to George Taylor, the Member of Provincial Parliament in the area, from N.L. Embree, a District Officer with the Ontario Ministry of the Environment. The memo, with "report not published" handwritten on the top of its first page, suggests that the request caused some concern among ministry officials. See N.L. Embree, "Holland Marsh Area

– Pesticides in Groundwater. Ontario Ministry of the Environment," 1981, Archives of Ontario, #21 Lakes and Rivers – Holland Marsh, RG 12-45, B214163. The three-page memo describes the results of recent water testing in the Holland River, which found high levels of DDT and organophosphorus compounds, in some cases in accumulations over ten times the "desirable levels" set out by the province.

8. The authors reported 28.3 incidents of congenital abnormalities per 1,000 births in the Holland Marsh over the study period compared with 9.5 incidents per 1,000 births in Aurora, Newmarket, and King City. Williams et al., "On Assessing the Risks of Congenital Anomalies," 2.

9. Joe Hall and Bob Graham, "Birth Defects High in Holland Marsh," *Toronto Star,* June 18, 1981, A07.

10. "Lake Simcoe Cleanup Ignored, Smith Claims," *Toronto Star,* June 9, 1981, D16.

11. See, for example, Renato Assunção, "Commentary: Statistical Assessment of Cancer Cluster Evidence – In Search of a Middle Ground," *International Journal of Epidemiology* 42, 2 (2013): 453–55; and Michael Coory and Susan Jordan, "Assessment of Chance Should Be Removed from Protocols for Investigating Cancer Clusters," *International Journal of Epidemiology* 42, 2 (2013): 440–47.

12. Williams et al., "On Assessing the Risks of Congenital Anomalies," i.

13. On July 6, 1981, Dr. Williams, the lead author of the feasibility study, met with three local medical officers of health, and representatives from the ministries of environment and health. Minutes from that meeting suggest that ministry officials pushed to qualify the findings. Indeed, the minutes note that Dr. Williams made changes to the document based on earlier feedback, including "rewriting the recommendations." The meeting notes also note that the public message of the report should include, "no need for alarm at this time, the situation continues to be monitored." The final feasibility report was published nine days later, on July 15, 1981. ("2nd meeting" July 6, 1981, Archives of Ontario, #21 Lakes and Rivers – Holland Marsh, RG 16-9, B214163.)

14. See, for example, Ministry of Health, "Investigating Clusters of Non-communicable Disease: Guidelines for Public Health Units," Wellington, New Zealand: Ministry of Health, 2015.

15. Williams et al., "On Assessing the Risks of Congenital Anomalies," 30.

16. W.B. Drowley, executive director of resource management, advised W. Bidell, assistant deputy minister of regional operations: "Please note the commitment by MOE [Ministry of the Environment] to monitor water and soil samples. . . . In view of the fact that this matter may well become active in the future I would recommend that the involved branches formalize the sampling and analytical program." Drowley, "Memorandum. Ministry of the Environment," 1981, Archives of Ontario, #21 Lakes and Rivers – Holland Marsh, RG 12-45, B214163, 1.

17. S. Nicholls, "Complex Probe of an Ailing Lake," *Globe and Mail,* January 24, 1981, 10.

18. Dennis Draper, Dale Henry, Fritz Engler, Sam Singer, John Antoszek, Steve Batten, and Mike Walters, "Phosphorus Modeling and Control Options," Lake Simcoe Environmental Management Strategy, 1985, https://atrium.lib.uoguelph.ca/xmlui/

handle/10214/13973; J.H. Neil and G.W. Robinson, "*Dichotomosiphon Tuberosus*: A Benthic Algal Species Wide-Spread in Lake Simcoe," Lake Simcoe Environmental Management Strategy, 1985, http://agrienvarchive.ca/download/L-Simcoe_D-tuberosus_B2-85.pdf (accessed July 17, 2013); R.L. Thomas and G. Sevean, "Leaching of Phosphorus from the Organic Soils of the Holland Marsh," *Ministry of Environment,* 1985, https://atrium.lib.uoguelph.ca/xmlui/bitstream/handle/10214/15729/OME_P_leaching_holland_marsh85.pdf?sequence=1&isAllowed=y (accessed July 15, 2013).

19. "Lake Simcoe Cleanup Plan Faces Delay," *Globe and Mail,* June 10, 1981, 10.

20. David Evans, Kenneth H. Nicholls, Yvonne C. Allen, and Michael J. McMurtry, "Historical Land Use, Phosphorus Loading, and Loss of Fish Habitat in Lake Simcoe, Canada," *Canadian Journal of Fisheries and Aquatic Sciences* 53, S1 (1996): 194–218.

21. S. Nicholls, "Complex Probe of an Ailing Lake," *Globe and Mail,* January 24, 1981, 10.

22. The Lake Simcoe Environmental Management Strategy was the centrepiece of the LSRCA's growing influence in the area and consisted of a multiyear research project meant to rehabilitate the water quality in lake.

23. Dennis Draper et al., "Phosphorus Modeling"; Rupke and Associates, "Calibration Study of the Holland Marsh Polder Drainage Pumps," Lake Simcoe Environmental Management Strategy, 1985, https://atrium.lib.uoguelph.ca/xmlui/handle/10214/13973.

24. Thomas and Sevean, "Leaching of Phosphorus from the Organic Soils of the Holland Marsh," 9.

25. Ibid., 12.

26. Jennifer Winter, Catherine Eimers, Peter J. Dillon, Lem D. Scott, Wolfgang A. Scheider, and Campbell C. Willox, "Phosphorus Inputs to Lake Simcoe from 1990 to 2003: Declines in Tributary Loads and Observations on Lake Water Quality," *Journal of Great Lakes Research* 33, 2 (2007): 381–96.

27. Karl Polanyi, *The Great Transformation* (1944; reprint, Boston: Beacon, 2001).

28. Reaume quoted in Ontario Standing Committee on Finance and Economic Affairs, "Pre-budget Consultations," 2014, n.p., http://www.ontla.on.ca/web/committee-proceedings/committee_transcripts_details.do?locale=en&BillID=&ParlCommID=8957&Date=2014-01-13&Business=Pre-budget%20consultations&DocumentID=27610 (accessed October 29, 2014).

29. A. Zylway, personal interview, January 20, 2014.

30. P. Irvine, personal interview, September 25, 2014.

31. I spoke with staff from the Lake Simcoe Region Conservation Authority at the Muck Vegetable Growers Conference. The LSRCA typically has an information booth set up as part of the trade show at the conference. In informal discussions, I learned that farmers are fairly reluctant to engage in or take advantage of any of the programs and services the LSCRA offer. An interview with another LSRCA employee, David McMichael, confirmed this, though he felt that tensions were lessening and farmers were becoming more amenable to a riparian planting program as a result of increased outreach and consultation. As he put it: "So over the years we've had limited uptake from farmers, by and large, along the river and the drainage canals, to plant buffers.

What we've been experiencing recently, and I'll say five years or so, has been a greater participation in planting buffers. D. McMichael, personal interview, April 3, 2014. Nevertheless, the general friction between conservation authorities and farmers has not gone unnoticed, apparently leading some in the LSCRA to consider dropping "authority" from their title.

32. Lake Simcoe Region Conservation Authority, "West Holland River Subwatershed Management Plan," 2010, 2, www.lsrca.on.ca/pdf/reports/west_holland_subwatershed_2010.pdf (accessed November 17, 2014).

33. According to the Ministry of the Environment, 4 percent of the phosphorus in Lake Simcoe originates in the Holland Marsh, 56 percent is from watershed streams, 27 percent is atmospheric phosphorus, 7 percent is from effluent from local sewage treatment plants, and 6 percent is the result of surrounding septic systems. Ontario Ministry of the Environment, "Lake Simcoe Phosphorus Reduction Strategy," 2016, n.p., http://www.ontario.ca/environment-and-energy/phosphorus-reduction-strategy (accessed May 21, 2021).

34. Ibid.

35. Ibid.

36. Ontario Ministry of Municipal Affairs and Housing, "Greenbelt Plan," 2005, 13, http://www.mah.gov.on.ca/Page189.aspx (accessed November 15, 2014).

37. Ibid., 17. According to the Greenbelt Plan, secondary uses are defined as "uses secondary to the principal use of the property, including but not limited to, home occupations, home industries, and uses that produce value-added agricultural products from the farm operation on the property." Ibid., 53.

38. Ibid., 49 (italics added).

39. Ontario Ministry of Municipal Affairs and Housing, "Provincial Policy Statement, 2014," 28, http://www.mah.gov.on.ca/Page10679.aspx (accessed January 7, 2015).

40. David Pond, "Ontario's Greenbelt: Growth Management, Farmland Protection, and Regime Change in Southern Ontario," *Canadian Public Policy* 35, 4 (2009): 414.

41. Shelley Petrie, Brad Cundiff, Anne Bell, and Burkhard Mausberg, *Greenbelt Agriculture: A Breakdown of Agricultural Facts and Figures in the Greenbelt* (Friends of the Greenbelt Foundation, 2008), 11.

42. Jessica Bartram, Susan Lloyd Swail, and Burkhard Mausberg, *The Holland Marsh: Challenges and Opportunities in the Greenbelt* (Toronto: Friends of the Greenbelt Foundation, 2007), 17, https://d3n8a8pro7vhmx.cloudfront.net/greenbelt/pages/14663/attachments/original/1615839004/The_Holland_Marsh_Challenges_and_Opportunities_in_the_Greenbelt.pdf?1615839004 (accessed November 12, 2014).

43. Ministry of Municipal Affairs and Housing, "Provincial Policy Statement, 2014," 28.

44. P. Irvine, personal interview, September 25, 2013.

45. Plans to widen Highway 400 through King Township were announced in the winter and spring of 2015. The section from King Road/Highway 11 through to South Canal Bridge (where Highway 400 meets the Marsh from the south) will be widened from six lanes to an interim eight lanes, including grading for the intended eventual ten

lanes. A number of overpass bridges will be replaced, including the South Canal Bridge. There will almost certainly be conflict over this massive infrastructure project.

46. G. Thompson, personal interview, September 3, 2013.

47. Martin Beaulieu, *Demographic Changes in Canadian Agriculture*, Statistics Canada, 2014 (accessed May 21, 2021 https://www150.statcan.gc.ca/n1/pub/96-325-x/2014001/article/11905-eng.pdf); Pond, "Ontario's Greenbelt."

48. Lovering quoted in Paul Brennan, "The Bradford Bonus: Reasonable Prices," *Toronto Star,* November 1, 1997, K1.

49. Terry Marsden, "Rural Futures: The Consumption Countryside and Its Regulation," *Sociologia Ruralis* 39, 4 (1999): 506.

50. "New King Mayor Renews Peaker Plant Fight," *Aurora Banner,* November 8, 2010; "Citizen Group Files Peaker Plant Injunction," ibid., October 25, 2010.

51. Avia Eek, "You Can't Eat Energy: Peaker Plant in the Holland Marsh," *Ontario Agriculture* (blog), December 19, 2009, http://ontag.farms.com/profiles/blogs/you-cant-eat-energypeaker (accessed September 7, 2014).

52. Ibid.

53. N. Southwort, "Farmers Feel under Siege as Cities Close In," *Globe and Mail,* November 25, 1999, A23.

54. David Lewis Stein, "Spare a Thought for 'Urban' Farmers," *Toronto Star,* April 20, 200, A27.

55. J. Bake, personal interview, August 27, 2013.

56. P. Irvine, personal interview, September 25, 2014.

57. B. Lewis, personal interview, January 16, 2014.

58. Ibid.

59. The conference was held in the Bradford and District Community Centre on April 9 and 10, 2014.

60. George Lazarovits, "The New Era of Diagnostics and Control," paper presented at Muck Vegetable Growers Conference, April 9, 2014.

61. J. Vo, "The Facts on Fence Row Farming," *Norfolk News,* August 1, 2014.

62. Lazarovits, "New Era of Diagnostics and Control."

63. David McNear, "The Rhizosphere-Roots, Soil and Everything in Between," *Nature Education Knowledge* 4, 3 (2013): 1.

64. Jack Ralph Kloppenburg Jr., *First the Seed: The Political Economy of Plant Biotechnology* (Madison: University of Wisconsin Press, 2005), 6.

65. Lazarovits quoted in Randy Telford, "Fence Row Farming: Uncovering the Secrets in the Soil," *Ontario Grain Farmer Magazine,* February 2013.

66. Lazarovits quoted in Blair Andrews, "How Does No-Till System Achieve 300 bu/ac Corn Yields? Beneficial Soil Bacteria?," *Country Guide* (May/June 2013): 35.

67. P. Irvine, personal interview, September 25, 2014.

68. H. De Jong, personal interview, January 20, 2014.

69. A. Zylawy, personal interview, January 20, 2014.

70. C. Roesch, personal interview, September 12, 2013.

Conclusion

1. Avia Eek (@eekfarms), "Bill & I did some grocery shopping tonight," Twitter, January 23, 2015, https://twitter.com/eekfarms/status/558785514414039041.

2. "Produce Markets," *Toronto Daily Star,* March 18, 1958, 18.

3. Michael Classens (@michaelclassens), "@eekfarms, Toronto Star," Twitter, January 23, 2015, https://twitter.com/eekfarms/status/558785514414039041.

4. Gunter Gijsbrecht, "Russian Embargo Costing Onion Sector Millions," *Fresh Plaza,* January 9, 2015, http://www.freshplaza.com/article/133416/Russian-embargo-costing-onion-sector-millions (accessed July 3, 2015).

5. Karen Davidson, "Onion Prices Barely Cover Cost of Production," *The Grower,* March 2015, 7, http://issuu.com/thegrower/docs/thegrower_march2015/7?e=2032842/11589712 (accessed July 3, 2015).

6. Particularly helpful community-produced works on the Marsh are Dorothy Cilipka, *The Holland Marsh: The Heart of Canada's Vegetable Industry* (Beeton, ON: Simcoe York, 2004); George Jackson, *The Big Scheme: The Draining of the Holland Marsh* (Bradford, ON: George Jackson, 1998); and Albert VanderMey, *And the Swamp Flourished* (Surrey, BC: Vanderheide, 1994).

7. Rod MacRae, "Do Trade Agreements Substantially Limit Development of Local / Sustainable Food Systems in Canada?," *Canadian Food Studies* 1, 1 (2014): 103–25.

8. Within this general direction, a more specific focus on the environmental history of agricultural labour in this country would be especially useful. My own work has fallen down in this respect, though not without making an effort. I ultimately decided that the story of farm labour in the Holland Marsh was a project unto itself, and rather than include a tokenistic overture, I chose to leave it largely unexamined. No doubt there are fruitful explorations to be made at the intersection of labour and agricultural history within the Canadian context. Holding farm labour as an analytic category of concern would likely be especially useful in identifying and isolating systemic injustice in the history of Canadian agriculture. Comparative studies between eras of distinctly capitalist farming of the contemporary period and the mercantilist and the seigneurial systems of Upper and Lower Canada, respectively, could be particularly illuminating.

9. Galt quoted in Harry Vander Kooij, "Holland Marsh," *Origins* 24, 2: 16.

10. Watson quoted in Ross Irwin, C.C. Filman, and R.G. Gregg, "Report of the Committee Appointed for a Drainage Engineering Study of the Holland Marsh Area, 1968," p. 2, Archives of Ontario, #3 ARDA –Holland Marsh, Correspondence of the Minister of Agriculture and Food, 1967–1970, RG 16-1, B388426.

11. Pierre Berton, "My Own History of the Next Half Century," *Toronto Star,* November 2, 1961, 31 (via ProQuest Historical Newspapers).

12. RE/MAX, "Market Trends Farm Edition," 2013, http://www.remax.ca/editorial/home/western/re/max-market-trends-farm-edition-2013 (page removed).

13. Farm Credit Canada, "2018 FCC Farmland Values Report", 2019, 16 accessed May 21, 2020, https://www.fcc-fac.ca/fcc/about-fcc/reports/2018-farmland-values-report-e.pdf.

14. RE/MAX, "Farm Report," 2014, 4, http://download.remax.ca/PR/FarmReport/FinalReport.pdf.

15. Alison Blay-Palmer, Roberta Sonnino, and Julien Custot, "A Food Politics of the Possible? Growing Sustainable Food Systems through Networks of Knowledge," *Agriculture and Human Values* 33 (2016): 27–43; E. Gunilla Olsson, Eva Kerselaers, Lone Søderkvist Kristensen, Jørgen Primdahl, Elke Rogge, and Anders Wästeflt, "Peri-urban Food Production and Its Relation to Urban Resilience," *Sustainability* 8 (2016): 1–21.

16. Terry Marsden, "Towards a Real Sustainable Agri-food Security and Food Policy: Beyond the Ecological Fallacies?," *Political Quarterly* 83, 1 (2012): 2.

17. Quoted in Alison Blay-Palmer, Guido Santini, Marielle Dubbeling, Hank Renting, Makiko Taguchi, and Thierry Giordano, "Validating the City Region Food System Approach: Enacting Inclusive, Transformational City Region Food Systems," *Sustainability* 10 (2018): 1679.

18. Government of Ontario, "A Place to Grow," 2019, https://www.ontario.ca/document/place-grow-growth-plan-greater-golden-horseshoe.

19. Peter Rosset and Miguel A. Altieri, *Agroecology: Science and Politics* (Blank Point, NS: Fernwood, 2017); Eric Holt-Giménez and Miguel A. Altieri, "Agroecology, Food Sovereignty, and the New Green Revolution," *Agroecology and Sustainable Food Systems* 37, 1 (2013): 90–102.

SELECTED BIBLIOGRAPHY

Archival Sources

Agriculture and Agri-Food Canada, Ottawa

Canada Land Inventory National Soil Database

Archives of Ontario, Toronto

#3 ARDA – Holland Marsh, Correspondence of the Minister of Agriculture and Food, 1967–1970, RG 16-1, B388426
#4 Hurricane Relief Holland Marsh, RG 16-9, B355358
#6 Holland Marsh Growers Mktg Scheme, Legal Services Records of the Ministry of Agriculture and Food, RG 16-37
#8 Return of Marsh Lands, RG 1-61, B24 1849
#9 Holland Marsh Multimedia Records, RG 16-276-8, B253134
#20 Holland Marsh, RG 3-10, B307973
#21 Lakes and Rivers – Holland Marsh, RG 12-45, B214163
#22 Holland Marsh Drainage Dyke – Township of West Gwillimbury (Simcoe), RG 19-122, B229599
Ontario Heritage Foundation – Holland Marsh

Bradford West Gwillimbury Library

Art Janse Fonds, Holland Marsh Scheme
Canal Improvement Project
Cleaning of the Canals and River
Council and Commission Minutes
Drainage Commission Correspondence
Issues between Marsh Townships
Reclamation of the Holland Marsh
Reports 1
Joe Saint Fonds, Holland Marsh, vol. 1 parts 310, 320, 330
Local History Collection

Online Archives

Biodiversity Heritage Library
Internet Archive
Commission of Conservation. "Improving Canadian Agriculture." 1912. https://archive.org/details/cihm_83706/page/n5
—. "Report of the First Annual Meeting." 1910. https://archive.org/details/commissionconser1910cana/page/n6
Ontario Department of Agriculture Bulletins
Our Stories. Innisfil Historical Society. Holland Marsh documents. http://www.ourstoriesinnisfil.ca/islandora/search/holland%20marsh%20?type=dismax

Ontario Workplace Tribunals Library

Ontario Labour Relations Board documents related to Teamsters Union, Federal Farms Ltd., Holland River Gardens, and United Farms Ltd.

Simcoe County Archives, Midhurst, ON

Art Janse Collection of the Holland Marsh Drainage Information, 38382, 38390, 38391, 38392, 38393
Federal Farms Limited Fonds, 16967
Holland Marsh, 10984
Rescue Work at the Holland Marsh, October 1954, 37972

Newspapers and Periodicals

Aurora Banner
CBC News Online
Country Guide
Financial Post
Fresh Plaza
Globe
Globe and Mail
Grower
Hamilton Spectator
Maclean's Magazine
Monetary Times
New Market Today
Norfolk News
Ontario Grain Farmer Magazine
Toronto Daily Star
Toronto Star
Witness News

Interviews

Bake, Jill [pseud.]. Personal interview with author. Holland Marsh, ON, August 27, 2013.

De Jong, Hugh [pseud.]. Personal interview with author. Holland Marsh, ON, January 20, 2014.

Irvine, Paul [pseud.]. Personal interview with author. Holland Marsh, ON, September 25, 2013.

Lewis, Brian [pseud.]. Personal interview with author. Holland Marsh, ON, January 16, 2014.

McMichael, David [pseud.]. Personal interview with author. Holland Marsh, ON, April 3, 2014.

Roesch, Charlotte [pseud.]. Personal interview with author. Bradford, ON, September 12, 2013.

Smith, John [pseud.]. Personal interview with author. Holland Marsh, ON, September 3, 2013.

Thompson, Gerry [pseud.]. Personal interview with author. Bradford, ON, September 3, 2013.

Wilson, Paul [pseud.]. Personal interview with author. Holland Marsh, ON, January 20, 2014.

Zylawy, Alex [pseud.]. Personal interview with author. Holland Marsh, ON, January 20, 2014.

Articles and Books

Akram-Lodhi, A. Haroon. "Contemporary Pathogens and the Capitalist World Food System." *Canadian Journal of Development Studies / Revue Canadienne d'études du développement* 42, 1–2 (2021): 18–27, http://doi.org/10.1080/02255189.2020.1834361.

Akram-Lodhi, A. Haroon, and Cristobal Kay. "Surveying the Agrarian Question (Part 1): Unearthing Foundations, Exploring Diversity." *Journal of Peasant Studies* 37, 1 (2010): 177–202.

Anderson, Darwin W., and C.A. Scott Smith. "A History of Soil Classification and Soil Survey in Canada: Personal Perspectives." *Canadian Journal of Soil Science* 91, 5 (2011): 675–94.

Anderson, David. "Depression, Dust Bowl, Demography, and Drought: The Colonial State and Soil Conservation during the 1930s." *African Affairs* 83 (1984): 321–43.

Anstey, T. H. "One Hundred Harvests: Research Branch, Agriculture Canada, 1886–1986." *Historical Series, Research Branch, Agriculture Canada* 27 (1986): 143–44.

Bernstein, Henry. "Is There an Agrarian Question in the 21st Century?" *Canadian Journal of Development Studies / Revue canadienne d'études du développement* 27, 4 (2006): 449–60.

Blaikie, Piers. *The Political Economy of Soil Erosion in Developing Countries*. London and New York: Longman, 1985.

Blaikie, Piers, and Harold Brookfield. *Land Degradation and Society*. London and New York: Methuen, 1987.

Boyd, William, W. Scott Prudham, and Rachel A. Schurman. "Industrial Dynamics and the Problem of Nature." *Society and Natural Resources* 14, 7 (2001): 555–70.

Bradford West Gwillimbury Local History Association. *Governor Simcoe Slept Here*. Altona, MB: Friesens, 2005.

Braun, Bruce. "Producing Vertical Territory: Geology and Governmentality in Late Victorian Canada." *Ecemene* 7, 1 (2000): 7–46.

Brenner, Robert. "The Agrarian Roots of European Capitalism." *Past and Present* 97 (1982): 16–113.

Bunce, Michael. "Thirty Years of Farmland Preservation in North America: Discourses and Ideologies of a Movement." *Journal of Rural Studies* 14, 2 (1998): 233–47.

Castree, Noel, and Bruce Braun, eds, *Social Nature: Theory, Practice, Politics*. Malden, MA: Blackwell, 2001.

Cilipka, Dorothy. *The Holland Marsh: The Heart of Canada's Vegetable Industry*. Beeton, ON: Simcoe York, 2004.

Cooke, Nathalie, ed. *What's to Eat? Entrées in Canadian Food History*. Montreal and Kingston: McGill-Queen's University Press, 2009.

Cronon, William. *Nature's Metropolis: Chicago and Great West*. New York: W.W. Norton, 1991.

Duncan, Dorothy. *Canadians at Table: Food, Fellowship, and Folklore: A Culinary History of Canada*. Toronto: Dundurn, 2006.

Engel-Di Mauro, Salvatore. *Ecology, Soils, and the Left: An Ecosocial Approach*. New York: Palgrave Macmillan, 2014.

Fiege, Jeff. *Irrigated Eden: The Making of an Agricultural Landscape in the American West*. Seattle: University of Washington Press, 1999.

Foster, Janet. *Working for Wildlife: The Beginnings of Preservation in Canada*. 2nd ed. Toronto: University of Toronto Press, 1998.

Friedberg, Susanne. *Fresh: A Perishable History*. Cambridge, MA: Belknap Press of Harvard University Press, 2009.

Friedmann, Harriet. "Distance and Durability: Shaky Foundations of the World Food Economy." *Third World Quarterly* 13, 2 (1992): 371–83.

Friedmann, Harriet, and Philip McMichael. "Agriculture and the State System: The Rise and Decline of National Agricultures, 1870 to the Present." *Sociologia Ruralis* 29, 2 (1989): 93–117.

Gandy, Matthew. *Concrete and Clay: Reworking Nature in New York City*. Cambridge, MA: MIT Press, 2002.

Giblett, Rodney James. *Postmodern Wetlands: Culture, History, Ecology*. Edinburgh: Edinburgh University Press, 1996.

Godwin, George. *Town Swamps and Social Bridges*. New York: Routledge, Warnes, and Routledge, 1859.

Goodman, David, and Michael Watts. "Reconfiguring the Rural or Fording the Divide? Capitalist Restructuring and the Global Agro-food System." *Journal of Peasant Studies* 22, 1 (1994): 1–49.

Guthman, Julie. *Agrarian Dreams: The Paradox of Organic Farming in California.* Berkeley: University of California Press, 2004.

Hajer, Martin. *The Politics of Environmental Discourse: Ecological Modernization and the Policy Process.* New York: Oxford University Press, 1995.

Halpern, Monda M. *And on That Farm He Had a Wife: Ontario Farm Women and Feminism, 1900–1970.* Montreal and Kingston: McGill-Queen's University Press, 2001.

Harris, Cole. *The Reluctant Land: Society, Space, and Environment in Canada before Confederation.* Vancouver: UBC Press, 2008.

Harvey, David. "Ideology and Population Theory." *International Journal of Health Services* 4, 3 (1974): 515–37.

Heynen, Nikolas, Maria Kaika, and Erik Swyngedouw. "Urban Political Ecology: Politicizing the Production of Urban Natures." In *In the Nature of Cities: Urban Political Ecology and the Politics of Urban Metabolism*, edited by Nikolas Heynen, Maria Kaika, and Erik Swyngedouw. New York: Taylor and Francis, 2006, 1–20.

Jackson, George. *The Big Scheme: The Draining of the Holland Marsh.* Bradford, ON: George Jackson, 1998.

Jones, Robert Leslie. *History of Agriculture in Ontario, 1613–1880.* Toronto: University of Toronto Press, 1946.

Kaika, Maria. *City of Flows: Modernity, Nature, and the City.* New York: Routledge, 2005.

Kautsky, Karl. *The Agrarian Question.* London: Zwan, 1899.

Kloppenburg, Jack Ralph, Jr. *First the Seed: The Political Economy of Plant Biotechnology.* Madison: University of Wisconsin Press, 2005.

Leopold, Aldo. *A Sand County Almanac: With Essays on Conservation from Round the River.* 1949. Reprint, Toronto: Random House, 1966.

Mann, Susan A. *Agrarian Capitalism in Theory and Practice.* Chapel Hill: University of North Carolina Press, 1990.

Mann, Susan A., and James M. Dickinson. "Obstacles to the Development of a Capitalist Agriculture." *Journal of Peasant Studies* 5, 4 (1978): 466–81.

Marsden, Terry. "Rural Futures: The Consumption Countryside and Its Regulation." *Sociologia Ruralis* 39, 4 (1999): 501–26.

McKay, Ian. "The Liberal Order Framework: A Prospectus for a Reconnaissance of Canadian History." *Canadian Historical Review* 81, 4 (2000): 617–51.

McNeill, John R., and Verena Winiwarter, eds. *Soils and Societies: Perspectives from Environmental History.* Isle of Harris, UK: White Horse, 2006.

McDonald, Mary Ruth, and Jim Chaput. "Management of Organic Soils." Ministry of Agriculture, Food and Rural Affairs, 1998, http://www.omafra.gov.on.ca/english/crops/facts/93-053.htm.

McWilliams, Carey. *Factories in the Field: The Story of Migratory Farm Labor in California.* 1939. Reprint, Berkeley: University of California Press, 2000.

Mintz, Sydney. *Sweetness and Power: The Place of Sugar in Modern History.* New York: Penguin, 1986.

Mirza, Cameran, and Ross W. Irwin. "Determination of Subsidence of an Organic Soil in Southern Ontario." *Canadian Journal of Soil Science* 44, 2 (1964): 248–53.

Mitchell, Don. *The Politics of Food.* Toronto: James Lorimer, 1975.

Mosby, Ian. *Food Will Win the War: The Politics, Culture, and Science of Food on Canada's Home Front.* Vancouver: UBC Press, 2014.

Murton, James. *Creating a Modern Countryside: Liberalism and Land Resettlement in British Columbia.* Vancouver: UBC Press, 2007.

Nash, Linda. *Inescapable Ecologies: A History of Environment, Disease, and Knowledge.* Berkeley: University of California Press, 2007.

O'Connor, James. "Capitalism, Nature, Socialism a Theoretical Introduction." *Capitalism Nature Socialism* 1, 1 (1988): 11–38.

O'Connor, Martin. "On the Misadventures of Capitalist Nature." *Capitalism Nature Socialism* 4, 3 (1993): 7–40.

O'Connor, Ryan. *The First Green Wave: Pollution Probe and the Origins of Environmental Activism in Ontario.* Vancouver: UBC Press, 2015.

Petrick, Gabriella M. "'Like Ribbons of Green and Gold': Industrializing Lettuce and the Quest for Quality in the Salinas Valley, 1920–1965." *Agricultural History* 80, 3 (2006): 269–95.

Polanyi, Karl. *The Great Transformation.* 1944. Reprint, Boston: Beacon, 2001.

Pond, David. "Ontario's Greenbelt: Growth Management, Farmland Protection, and Regime Change in Southern Ontario." *Canadian Public Policy* 35, 4 (2009): 413–32.

Prudham, Scott W. *Knock on Wood: Nature as Commodity in Douglas-Fir Country.* New York: Routledge, 2005.

Reaman, E. *A History of Agriculture in Ontario.* Vol. 2. Aylesbury, UK: Hazell Watson and Vieny, 1970.

Redclift, Michael R. *Frontiers: Histories of Civil Society and Nature.* Cambridge, MA: MIT Press, 2006.

Riley, L. John. *The Once and Future Great Lakes Country.* Montreal and Kingston: McGill-Queen's University Press, 2014.

Russell, Peter. *How Agriculture Made Canada: Farming in the Nineteenth Century.* Vol. 1. Montreal and Kingston: McGill-Queen's University Press, 2012.

Sandberg, Anders L., Gerda R. Wekerle, and Liette Gilbert. *The Oak Ridges Moraine Battles: Development, Sprawl, and Nature Conservation in the Toronto Region.* Toronto: University of Toronto Press, 2004.

Sandos, John. "Nature's Nations: The Shared Conservation History of Canada and the USA." *International Journal of Environmental Studies* 70, 2 (2013): 358–71.

Scott, James C. *Seeing like a State: How Certain Schemes to Improve the Human Condition Have Failed.* New Haven, CT: Yale University Press, 1998.

Smith, Neil. *Uneven Development: Nature, Capital, and the Production of Space.* Athens: University of Georgia Press, 2010.

Soil Classification Working Group. *The Canadian System of Soil Classification*. 3rd ed. Ottawa: Research Branch, Agriculture and Agri-Food Canada, 1998.

Soluri, John. *Banana Cultures: Agriculture, Consumption, and Environmental Change in Honduras and the United States*. Austin: University of Texas Press, 2005.

Stoll, Steven. *The Fruits of Natural Advantage*. Berkeley: University of California Press, 1998.

Stunden Bower, Shannon. *Wet Prairie: People, Land, and Water in Agricultural Manitoba*. Vancouver: UBC Press, 2011.

Sweezy, Paul M., and Rodney Hilton. *The Transition from Feudalism to Capitalism*. London: Verso, 1967.

Swyngedouw, Erik. "Modernity and Hybridity: Nature, Regeneracionismo, and the Production of the Spanish Waterscape, 1890–1930." *Annals of the Association of American Geographers* 89, 3 (1999): 443–65.

—. "Power, Nature, and the City: The Conquest of Water and the Political Ecology of Urbanization in Guayaquil, Ecuador, 1880–1990." *Environment and Planning A* 29, 2 (1997): 311–32.

VanderMey, Albert. *And the Swamp Flourished*. Surrey, BC: Vanderheide, 1994.

Vileisis, Ann. *Discovering the Unknown Landscape: A History of America's Wetlands*. Washington, DC: Island, 1999.

Walker, Gerald. "How the Holland Marsh Community Developed." *Canadian Geographical Journal* 58, 1 (August/September 1977): 42–49.

Wallerstein, Immanuel. "Globalization or the Age of Transition? A Long-Term View of the Trajectory of the World-System." *International Sociology* 15, 2 (2000): 249–65.

—. *The Modern World-System*. Vol. 1, *Capitalist Agriculture and the Origins of the European World-Economy, 1730–1840s*. New York: Academic Press, 1974.

—. "The Modern World-System and Evolution." *Journal of World-Systems Research* 1, 1 (1995): 512–22.

Warecki, George. *Protecting Ontario's Wilderness: A History of Changing Ideas and Preservation Politics*. New York: Peter Lang, 2000.

West, Paige. *From Modern Production to Imagined Primitive: The Social World of Coffee from Papua New Guinea*. Durham, NC: Duke University Press, 2012.

Winson, Anthony. *The Industrial Diet: The Degradation of Food and the Struggle for Healthy Eating*. Vancouver: UBC Press, 2013.

—. *The Intimate Commodity: Food and the Agro-Industrial Complex in Canada*. Toronto, ON: Garamond, 1992.

Wood, David. *Making Ontario*. Montreal and Kingston: McGill-Queen's University Press, 2000.

Wood, Ellen Meiksins. *The Origin of Capitalism: A Longer View*. London: Verso, 2002.

Worster, Donald. *Rivers of Empire*. New York: Pantheon Books, 1985.

Zakuta, Leo. *A Protest Movement Becalmed: A Study of Change in the CCF*. Toronto, University of Toronto Press, 1964.

Zeller, Suzanne. *Inventing Canada: Early Victorian Science and the Idea of a Transcontinental Nation*. Montreal and Kingston: McGill-Queen's University Press, 2009.

Zwerver, Harry. "Farmers Working for Farmers: A Brief History of the Ontario Federation of Agriculture." Guelph, ON: Ontario Federation of Agriculture, 1986.

INDEX

Note: "(i)" after a page number indicates an illustration; "(m)" after a page number indicates a map. All Acts are Ontario statutes unless otherwise indicated.